Discovering
Moths

Nighttime Jewels in Your Own Backyard

John Himmelman

Photographs and Drawings
by the Author

Down East Books / Camden, Maine

For David Ostrander,
who took a while to find the moths,
but find them he did!

ISBN 0-89272-528-1
Library of Congress Control Number: 2002109173
Book design by Faith Hague

Printed in China

FCI   5   4   3   2   1

Down East Books / Camden, Maine
Book orders: (800) 766-1670

www.downeastbooks.com

Contents

Preface

WHEN someone becomes absorbed in a pastime to the point where it becomes all-consuming, that person often feels compelled to share the passion with others. I guess it's like seeing a good movie and wanting your friends to see it, too. You become its ambassador or PR person, feeding on the energy of shared enthusiasm. This is how it is with me and the moths. This book is a way for me to share what it is about moths that keeps me up at night. At the same time, I've attempted to show my readers a bit about what makes a moth a moth, with the hope that the more they learn about this oft misunderstood insect, the more they will want to learn. (One way to do that is to visit my web page at www.connecticutmoths.com.)

I am not a scientist. I am a naturalist and a writer, and that is how I approach my subject. Although my interest in nature extends beyond the moths, I thought it would be interesting to focus on this one aspect of our fauna, because it is a topic not widely covered in natural history literature. Naturally, I am most familiar with my own experiences in my journey to learn more about this group of insects, so for good or bad I'm the person you'll be mostly reading about. However, this book could not have been written without the help and contributions of many who know far more than I do. The following people are among those who have contributed to my knowledge. Many have also given me more than a few moments of their time while putting together profiles of themselves, their experiences, or the insects for which we share a passion: John Acorn, Annette Aiello, Gary Anweiler, David Chesmore, Charles Covell, Jr., Lawrence Gall, Carol Lemmon, Jean-Michel, Robert Muller, Dale Schweitzer, David Ostrander, David Wagner, Doug Yanega, and Jeff Young.

I am especially grateful to David Wagner for his knowledge of Connecticut moths and for keeping me honest over the years. On more than one occasion he has made me look twice at a moth species I *thought* I knew.

If Charles Covell, Jr., hadn't written his book *A Field Guide to the Moths of Eastern North America,* I'd be getting way too much sleep. His book has kept me up countless nights trying to find the creatures depicted in its plates. Most of the common names used throughout this book

RENIA FLAVIPUNCTALIS

come from his reference guide. Although it went out of print during the time I was working on this book, I am happy to say it will soon be resurrected by another publisher.

Special thanks go to Andrew Brand and Cindi Kobak for thinking to call me when a moth I was looking for showed up in their yards.

More thanks go to my wife, Betsy Himmelman, who has supported my habit through the years and has kept me supplied with light sheets, rearing sleeves, and tag-sale bug zappers. Not the least of her contributions has been her good nature on the many nights I've woken her to show her a good moth that came to the lights.

And thank you to my editors, Chris Cornell and Karin Womer, at Down East Books for taking on a topic that may be somewhat out of the ordinary.

Introduction

IT'S 2:15 A.M. and I've made my last round of the night—well, actually, morning now. I sit at my desk, studying a small, winged creature through my magnifying lamp. Flipping through the pages of my reference guides, I try to match the wing patterns of my captive with those in the plates of the books. The moth flutters within the confines of the clear plastic cassette case, but it rests often enough for me to see the markings. The wings are washed in ochre, and in the center of each is a small, dark green spot. That spot is diagnostic, and at last I have a match. It's a Bicolored Sallow. I haven't seen one in two years. I record the date and any other information I can glean about this restless creature, then I bring it back outside to take its picture. It sits long enough for one shot, then takes off. I wish it well.

This is typical of an evening of moth watching for me. Other people are doing this, too, but not many of them. Not yet. Word that this fascinating diversion is out there waiting for us is just beginning to get around.

When most people think of moths, they think of the little, pale gray insects flying around their porch light, or hordes of Gypsy Moth caterpillars sprinkling a rain of droppings (frass) on woodland paths. Some people cringe at the thought of large Tomato Hornworms, the caterpillar being the most encountered form, deleafing their tomato plants, or tiny flour moths flying out of their kitchen cabinets. However, these pesky examples are but a few of that order, just a tiny percentage of a very large and captivating group of insects.

I find it easy to justify my attraction to moths. The hours suit my

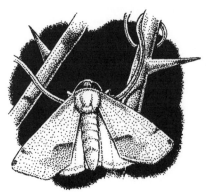

LEMON PLAGODIS

night-owl tendencies, and the quarry has all the elements to make for a fulfilling pastime. There are more than 2,300 species of moths in my home state of Connecticut, 11,000 in North America, and 110,000 species in the world. Many of them display colors and patterns that rival the most spectacular of butterflies. With so many moths out there, the chances of finding a new one on any night from early spring to late fall is very good. In fact, with so many moths, it's hard to remember them all, which allows one to rediscover them again and again.

Many people are afraid of moths. In a way, I can't blame them. Most of these insects are creatures of the night, and as with many animals that travel in darkness, they have a certain stigma. We tend to distrust what comes from places we cannot see. When I was taking a scuba diving course a few years ago, a large Cecropia Moth flew into the room. It circled, distressing most of the men and women in the class to the point of nearly clearing the building. At first, they thought it was a bat. Even when assured it was just a moth, they were no less alarmed. It took a bit of convincing to keep that moth from becoming a two-dimensional pattern on the wall.

But moths are about as harmless as a creature can be. They have no biting mouthparts; in some adults, such as the well-known Luna Moth, their "mouths" are essentially useless vestigial organs. They don't carry rabies, the bubonic plague, or any other diseases. They don't sting. They don't scratch, and they don't grow to disproportionate sizes and wreak havoc upon Japanese cities. Perhaps the worst that could happen is one could fly into your eye. That said, I should mention that in several species, such as the Limacodidae, or slug caterpillar moths, some of the larvae have stinging spines. The Flannel Moth caterpillar, looking like a furry "tribble" from an early *Star Trek* episode, seems to just beg to be stroked. But beneath those soft features are spines that break off into your skin. I've been told that the sting is worse than that of a large hornet, and I've chosen to accept that as fact without needing to find out for myself. I generally avoid touching any caterpillar that is covered with hair unless I know it is harmless.

So, what is a moth? Moths and butterflies, both in the order Lepidoptera, share many common traits. In fact, there are those who believe that butterflies evolved from moths many years ago to fill the lepidopteran day shift. Starting with the most obvious traits, butterflies and moths are insects, therefore consisting of three main body parts: head, thorax, and abdomen. Being insects, they have three pairs of legs, two antennae, and an exoskeleton. They have wings covered with tiny scales, which give them their color and pattern. This is the feature that sets them apart from other insects. The word *Lepidoptera*, the name of the order to which they both belong, means scaly winged.

Moths and butterflies go through four stages of metamorphosis, and as adults, they feed on liquids by uncurling a tube-shaped proboscis (although some adult moths don't feed at all). When making comparisons such as these, please keep in mind Talleyrand's Law: "All generalizations are wrong, including this one."

How do moths differ from butterflies? Moths have feathered or tapered antennae, designed for picking up the scent (pheromones) of a "calling" potential mate. The antennae on butterflies are either clubbed or hooked. Most adult moths fly at night, whereas butterflies are solar powered. Moths often have hairy bodies, the "hair" actually being modified scales. Butterflies, for the most part, have "clean" bodies. They also differ in their approach to a nectar source; moths usually flutter to a landing, whereas butterflies tend to settle in a precise or motionless manner.

I suppose I shouldn't leave out another very large difference between the two. Everybody loves butterflies. Gardens are planted to attract them. Organizations are formed to admire and preserve them. Books are written to identify them. They show up in paintings and logos and on T-shirts and are tattooed in interesting places on people's bodies. Moths have a long way to go in that department. But the growing interest in butterflies will carry moths part of the way. Butterfly watching today is where bird watching, the world's largest nonconsumptive outdoor pastime, was in the 1970s. And moth watching is now where butterfly watching was in the 1970s. We're getting there.

In this book I share with you a world that exists unknown to most of us in every yard, lot, forest, and field. It is a dark world, brightened by the existence of its winged denizens. We are strangers in this world, because we are for the most part diurnal creatures. When darkness sets in, we retreat to our well-lit homes to wait it out. It has been my experience that once a person discovers just a smattering of what can be found in that darkness, the setting sun becomes a prelude to an exciting part of the daily cycle. A prelude to discovery.

Welcome to the night.

❧ I ❧

On the Moth Trail

EARLY August. It's hot. It's dark. The air is thick with moisture, but there is no rain in the forecast. I don't particularly enjoy muggy nights, but I can find some good in them because the moths do. Tree crickets, stationed in branches throughout the area, collectively trill without pause. The song is so constant that the brain tunes it out, for a time. The sound has a way of easing itself in and out of your awareness. Field crickets chirp in the understory with equal vigor, becoming the euphonious pulse of the woods. In the distance, the dry, staccato tch-tch-tch . . . tch-tch-tch . . . *of True Katydids helps keep tempo.*

Fifteen people gather at the head of the trail. About half are adults, the other half children. Most of the children are boys. Most of the adults are women. All have flashlights, and the beams search the surrounding area in all directions. From a distance, I imagine, the group resembles a giant anemone, with waving tendrils of light. For some reason, things are far more fascinating when viewed under the light of a flashlight at night than they are during the day. Age has nothing to do with it, although I notice that most of the adults are looking toward the ground, while the children search the treetops. Could there be something profound in that? I can tell by the weakness of some of the beams that not everyone's flashlight will be shining by the time we made it to the end of the trail. I've brought a couple extras, just in case.

There is a very faint smell in the air that is not natural. It's sweet—

too sweet to be savored by most humans. It mingles with the familiar scents of mosquito repellent: citronella, DEET, Skin-So-Soft. These aren't really necessary tonight, but for some it would be unthinkable to enter a wooded trail on an August night without them.

That sweet smell is the product of the preparation that took place in the late afternoon, about five hours earlier. It's "stew" or "sugar"—or more appropriately, "bait"—that has been painted on the trees. It has long been known that several species of moths are attracted to sweet substances. It was probably first discovered at maple-sugaring operations, where leaking taps were found to be watering holes for certain scaly-winged patrons. Prior to human assistance, sapsuckers, woodpeckers, and broken branches were the exclusive providers of access to tree sap.

Many moths, like their butterfly cousins, have a curled proboscis designed for sipping nectar. Some moths, such as those in the sphinx and owlet families, seek out flowers that save the release of their sweet smelling lures for the "night sippers." I discovered this for myself several years ago while sitting with my wife, Betsy, on the front stoop of our house. Betsy's flower garden was laid out in front of us as we watched the setting sun play with the colors of the petals. When the sun disappeared behind the horizon, we immediately picked up a very strong, sweet smell coming from the garden. Some quick olfactory detective work led us to the patch of Asiatic lilies she had planted in the middle. Their scent was a bit strong for my liking. Although this was the real, natural stuff, it smelled like cheap perfume. It was Betsy who suggested that this was to attract moths. Wow, that made sense! At that moment I thought that was one of the greatest things in the world!

In the years to come, I would learn that there are many other flowers that play host to moths and that certain families prefer certain kinds of flowers. The sphinxes frequent the deeper, more tube-like flowers. The owlets, with their shorter proboscises, sip nectar from the shallower flowers, such as campions and buddleias. One of the most visited plants at night in my area is mountain laurel. I have counted up to eight species of moths on a single plant at one time. During the day, that same shrub is host to two territorial insects: the Hobomok Skipper (a small butterfly) and the Ebony Jewelwing (a damselfly). You can't walk by without getting "buzzed." Many plants work double shifts; they are visited day and night by a variety of insects, and the occasional hummingbird.

That moths have a "sweet tooth" has been known by lepidopterists for many years. They have long been taking advantage of this preference by painting trees with their concoctions in the hope of luring moths. Although the recipes are varied, and at times closely guarded secrets, certain ingredients are known to work well together. Brown sugar usually makes up the largest percentage of the mix. Add to this stale beer, fruit juice, maybe some old bananas or peaches, and maple syrup, and you've got yourself moth bait. Sometimes I'll add a little vanilla extract or a splash of liqueur. It's fun to experiment with different mixtures, although I have a tendency to forget what I put in the mix, making it difficult to repeat my greatest successes, or to avoid my inadvertent moth repellents. The most vital step in making moth bait is to allow it to ferment. The fermentation is what carries the smell through the forest on those still, warm nights—the smell that we were picking up, faintly, on this night.

Earlier, I had painted about forty trees along this half-mile trail through the woods. This was just a matter of dipping a brush in a jar full of the bait and slapping on the mixture, at eye level, in one-foot-square patches. Near each baited tree, I had tied a strip of orange boundary tape

The author baiting a tree

so I would know to check those trees for moths. The woods were part of the Platt Nature Center in my hometown of Killingworth, Connecticut. The nine acres of land—and the barn, which is the "Center" in Platt Nature Center—were bequeathed to the town land trust by Marion Platt in 1974. The local Boy Scouts cut a circuit trail through the woods shortly thereafter. It's easy to walk through, and covers several microhabitats: woods, field, and swamp. Perfect for finding a good cross section of moths.

The first baited tree is only twenty feet in front of us. We leave the field, and enter the woods. I always get a little nervous before bringing people out on these night forays. There is no guarantee that we will find anything. In fact, there have been many occasions when, on my own, I've come up practically empty. I warn the group that, at worst, it might be just a pleasant walk on a wooded trail on a hot, muggy night. I suggest that only one flashlight at a time—mine—be shone onto the trees. If you blast the moths in too much light, they will bolt. (The main purpose of their flashlights is to keep them from stumbling on the path.) Earlier, I had covered the lens of my flashlight with red cellophane. This seems to be less disturbing to the moths than bright white light. I issue one last warning: We have to keep our voices down as we approach the baited trees. Moths can hear, and some will flee a noisy approach. This elicits a few chuckles, but I assure them it's true. I still don't think they believe me, though.

The first few trees are vacant. No big deal; there are plenty left to go. I stop at tree number four, a white oak.

"There's something," I say. Two small moths rest on the silvery bark. They are mostly a dull black, with jagged white lines cutting horizontally through their wings. They are about the size of a postage stamp cut in half horizontally.

"Glossy Black Idias," I say. "I rarely see them come to lights, but they love the sugar." Everyone takes a turn looking at the idias. It reminds me of a reception line at a wedding, the idias playing the part of bride and groom. They are not the most exciting moths to look at, but most of the people seem genuinely pleased to see them. Part of the reason, I suspect, is the satisfaction of seeing that the bait really works. The idea of going out at night to look for moths along a baited trail has to be something that none of them ever imagined they would find themselves doing. Not too long ago, I would have included myself among them.

Some of the pressure has been lifted. At least we've seen something!

Distant moths are most easily found by sweeping the beam of a flashlight along the bark of the trees. When their eyes are hit by light, they glow. I learned this trick from Sheldon Driggs, a guide in Trinidad, West Indies. He showed us how—by holding our flashlights up to our temples and searching the trees and grass—we could see the eyes of the tarantulas, whip scorpions, harvesters, and other spiders. They glowed like tiny embers. I was amazed at how far away we could spot them. Twenty, thirty feet ahead of us, the tiny beacons gave away the insect's location. Sheldon didn't think twice about scooping up a wild tarantula with his bare hands. The tarantulas often rested inside the hollow railings along the path; before we moved on, Sheldon was sure to place them back inside the railing so a bird wouldn't eat them. I still have this picture in my head of Sheldon stuffing—STUFFING!—an unwilling tarantula back into its tight little shelter.

I discovered that Sheldon's light trick works well with moths, too. By having the beam of light originate from your temple, the light bouncing from the eyes of the moths reflects directly back to your own. Unless others were doing the same with their own light, you would be the only one to see the eye shine.

That night, back in Connecticut, we see the moths on the next tree about twenty feet before we approach it. There are several small sets of glowing eyes, but to my excitement, one set appears slightly larger.

"Okay. Everyone please keep your lights down," I say, speeding ahead to shine my light on what is the hoped-for quarry of the evening.

"Underwing!" I shout, elated. "Ilia Underwing. This is the big one!"

Everyone rushes to see it, but it is long gone before the first in line even gets close. I have forgotten my own admonition about keeping the noise down. "Damn!" I say to myself. "Darn!" I say aloud. There are kids with us.

I have a hard time containing my exhilaration at moments like these. That goes for birds, frogs, salamanders—everything. These moths are either going to teach me some control, or I will end up walking these trails alone.

Ah, but they can be a forgiving breed; there is another Ilia Underwing on the very next tree. It could be the same one.

"Okay," I whisper. "Here's another. Remember, no loud noises."

"You remember," says one of the kids. Kids—I love them.

•

Ilia Underwings are on the large end of the size scale within the genus *Catocala*. Many lepidopterists look forward to the emergence of the cato-cala, or underwing, moths during the mid- to late summer months. Most of these moths range in size from an inch to two and a half inches long; some, such as the Ilia, have a wingspan of up to three inches. They often sport a pair of drab, or "cryptically" colored, upper wings. This is to help them blend into tree bark, which they do with great success. But these moths hide a colorful secret: When they spread their upper wings, many reveal a bright, colorful set of hind wings. In some species, it is a blazing red or orange; in others, yellow or pink. Some are pure black, edged in white. It is believed that the coloration of the underwings serves a few purposes. One is as a display to aid in attracting a mate. Another is to startle a predator. A nuthatch ratcheting itself up a tree and coming upon a resting underwing would, in theory, be startled by the bright flash of the underwing—just long enough for the moth to get away. One hypothesis suggests that the black band that runs through the underwing, in con-junction with the color (or the white band against a black background in some cases), mimics the color and pattern of a wasp or hornet. A bird is likely to be more cautious in approaching a large, stinging insect, and he who hesitates . . . Once in the air, the underwings can be swift fliers. If the moth is forced to fly during the day, the bright flash of the hind wings may catch a bird's attention, but when the moth lands and closes its wings, the bird is left searching for the colors that originally attracted it. By then, the moth has melted into the bark of another tree.

The Ilia Underwing—or "The Wife," as it is sometimes called—is resting on the tree, its long proboscis uncurled and feeding on the bait. Its good size is enough to impress the group, but when it spreads its upper wings to reveal the deep red flags beneath them, the tree crickets' chorus is joined by oohs and aahs. That's when about half of the flashlights focus on the moth and scare it off. This is all right. Between the last two trees, we all have learned something about the sensitivity of moths. They are aware of us. They can be made to concede our existence by responding to our voices and irresponsible light flashing. We can shout ourselves hoarse at an ant, and it won't so much as miss a step. We can scream at a spider and it will most likely ignore us. Moths—the underwings, at least—have been given the ability to acknowledge our existence. They hear our voice as well as see us coming. So what if their acknowledgment is expressed by flying away? We don't begrudge that of the birds.

That moths can hear was a startling discovery for me. Moths just don't *look* as though they can hear. But some species can hear the sonar of bats and fly in an erratic escape pattern to elude them. Some species make sounds of their own to warn the bats of their unpalatability. There are even some that are said to "jam" the bats' sonar by producing sounds from their thorax. It's a war out there. Those with the best defenses live to tell the stories. A friend once told me that if you jingle your keys where a moth is resting, it will drop to the ground. Apparently, the high pitch of the keys hitting one another resembles the high-frequency calls of bats. You know I had to try this at the next opportunity. That night, I approached the moths gathered around the light in my yard. I gave my keys a shake and, sure enough, the moths scattered! They didn't go very far; they mostly fluttered around. But they reacted. They acknowledged me. Well, my keys, actually.

At this point, I relinquish the lead on the trail to the children. It just sort of happens. As soon as they realize that they can find the moths by the glowing eyes, the necessity for me being there diminishes. It becomes a contest among them to see who can find the next moth.

The children find the next baited tree with ease. It is host to four Glossy Black Idias and another new moth for the evening, a Copper Underwing. Although this moth is called an underwing, it is not a true catocala. It does share the same family, Noctuidae, with the catocala, but it is in a different subfamily, Amphipyrinae. The vulgar (or common) name refers to the coppery color of the underwings. I've found them to be common to abundant in my area, and on the wing, via several broods, from June to November. They spend the day under loose bark and leaves. Sometimes they find refuge beneath the shingles of houses. One summer day I lifted the cushion on an outdoor lounge in my yard and discovered twenty-five of them clustered together. As soon as they were exposed to sunlight, they scattered to the nearest trees and bushes.

We continue down the trail. Almost every tree has something feeding on the bait. Some trees are covered with carpenter ants, sluggish from their fermented feast. Millipedes wind their way through the crevices in the bark. Slugs make the journey up the trees to enjoy the ambrosial mix-

ture. *Seeing a yellow jacket on one of the trees reminds me that there was a nest nearby. (My kids found one of their nests the hard way the summer before.) I had noticed the entrance hole of this hornet while I was painting the trees and was careful to steer our route clear of it.*

The next catocala the children find is quite a bit smaller than the Ilia. Its upper wings are mottled in grays, blacks, and whites, but the hind wings, which it obligingly flashes at us, are an inky black bordered with white.

"Andromeda Underwing!" I whisper loudly. The moth gets hit with so many lights, it too flies off. We have the noise part down pat; the light discipline still needs work. Once again we find the same moth, or a different one of the same species, on another tree nearby. This time I ask one person to hold the light while I capture the moth in a clear plastic cassette case. As the Andromeda flutters within the confines of its temporary pen, it is passed around so everyone can get a look at the underwings. That is the goal of looking for catocalas: We seek out owls to hear them call; we seek out eagles to watch them soar; we seek out catocalas to see their underwings.

The other common name for Catocala andromeda *is the Gloomy Underwing. Perhaps this is in reference to its black hind wings. Or could it have reflected the mood of Achille Guenée when he named it back in 1852?*

The next catocala is an Ultronia—one of my favorites. It is resting upside down on a sugar maple. The upper wings of Ultronias are pale gray with lateral bands of chocolate brown. They are among the very few catocalas I find just as attractive with their wings closed, although it would be tough to out-do the White Underwing, Catocala relicta, *whose upper wings look like a triangular patch of birch bark. The Ultronia's hind wings are brilliant red, however, inspiring the nickname "Cherry-red Underwing." It is handsome both inside and out.*

With the glow of the moth eyes leading us from tree to tree, it becomes apparent that the orange boundary markers are no longer necessary. As we walk along the trail, I notice that our group has broken into two. The children lead, intent on finding the next tree; the adults, talking about everything under the moon, leisurely bring up the rear. At one point, as I push my way through a thick stand of bushes, I realize that the kids have led us off the trail. Now the adults lead as we backtrack to the path. Some quick shuffles, squeezes, and pushes, and the kids are back in front again.

The kids pass right by the next moth. It is resting on a white oak, about six feet up from the ground. The wingspan is only about three-quarters of an inch and the moth is jet black except for two large white spots on each upper wing and thin white stripes around the abdomen. If I were to squint, the oval white spots would be all I would see on that tree. The wings are thin and pointed and held at angles from the sides, giving the moth a rather unmothlike outline—more wasplike, actually.

I catch it in the cassette case so everyone can have a good look before we scare it off. I know this particular species of moth to be very skittish, especially under light. It flutters about at first, revealing its hind wings, which are jet black filled with white. Then it settles down. Although I am familiar with this moth, I was not aware that it would be attracted to bait. Not all moths are. This species is a frequent visitor to my lights, and I have often seen it flying during the day as well. I had recently watched a couple of them as they nectared at Betsy's impatiens.

"That's a moth?" asks one of the women.

"It's a Grape Leaffolder," I say.

The moth gets passed around while I explain that the caterpillars of this moth fold over the leaves of their host plant and use silk to hold them in place. They remain concealed from predators inside that cozy shelter, while they are feeding. A number of moths called leaffolders feed in this manner. There are also moths called leafrollers and leaftiers. It is easy to locate these caterpillars from spring to fall because their work is obvious. I find myself hard pressed to pass by one of those folded, rolled, or tied leaves without taking a peek at what is inside.

Most of the people find this Grape Leaffolder intriguing. Its scientific name, Desmia funeralis, is more interesting than the common name. It does appear to be dressed for a funeral. One person mentions that she had seen one of these moths before and thought it was a small wasp; she says now that she's sorry she killed it. Sometimes in the natural world, looking like a stinging insect is advantageous; sometimes it's not.

The last person takes a look and has the honor of releasing the moth. He opens up the case and it flies into the woods. All we can see before it disappears are the blurred white spots. It looks almost otherworldly.

We come across another Ilia, a few more Ultronias, and a good number of Copper Underwings and Glossy Black and Common Idias. Then, as we pass the huge pegmatite boulder (which I had also sugared, to no avail) that signifies we are about three-quarters of the way along the trail, we come upon a moth I had seen only once before: a Lunate Zale.

An entomologist friend, Carol Lemmon, taught me the proper pronunciation for this group of moths in the owlet family known as the Zales. Pronunciation can be a problem with these creatures, for me at least. Most often, my first acquaintance with a species is made when I am alone. Research in various books brings me to its name, but how to pronounce it can be a challenge. Fortunately, there is more than one way to enunciate some of these names, increasing my chances of getting it right. Carol told me that Zale is pronounced "Zah-lay." What a wonderful-sounding word! It just rolls off the tongue—Zaahh-lay. In one particular instance, however, that pleasant name has to stumble past a not-so-pleasant prefix; I've come across a moth called the Horrid Zale. ("Horrid" in this case comes from the Latin *horrida* and refers to the rough texture of the scales, not to the habits of the inoffensive insect.)

Our Lunate Zale is resting almost invisibly on the dark bark of a black oak. The moth's outline suggests a stealth bomber with scalloped edging on the wings. Various shades of deep brown and black with a wash of ochre help create the illusion that this is a chip of bark. Its species name, lunata, *comes from a small, moon-shaped black spot on the wing.*

The moth is sipping away at the sugar mixture, seemingly unaware of our presence. Another large dark moth flutters over our heads. "Whoa! What's that?" I shout, trying not to lose sight of it as it slips through the branches. It is roughly three inches across, very dark, and about the size of a large silk moth. But it is too late in the season for any in that group of moths to be out. This could be a good one!

LIGHT-FISHING FOR THE MYSTERY MOTH

I know of a species called the Black Witch, a rare migrant from South America. Dare I even hope this be she? I shine my light on it, trying to bring it in closer. It is a little like fishing. The flashlight is my rod and reel; the beam, my line. The moth dances within that beam, like a tiny marlin trying to snap the line. Sometimes it comes close enough to pluck it from the air before pulling out of reach. This goes on for about twenty seconds before it breaks free and disappears into the darkness. "What was that?" I ask aloud.

"I don't know," says one of the kids. "It was the size of a bat!" she says, holding her hands ten inches apart.

Yep, just like fishing.

This encounter reminded me of a story I heard about a couple of birders in Texas. They went out at night to find nightjars—birds in the whippoorwill family. When the birders discovered a large silk moth flying in the area, one of them shined a light on it. Then, from out of nowhere, a nightjar swooped in and snatched up the moth. That gave the birders an idea. Instead of seeking the more elusive nightjars, they would look for the silk moths. When they found one, they'd shine their light on it and bring in another bird! Had the moths been the quarry, it could have been frustrating, but because it was the birds they were after, they had a rewarding night.

We see the light from the nature center through the trees; we are nearing the end of the trail. There are only about five baited trees left, not counting the fallen log at the end of the trail where I had spilled the rest of the contents of my sugar jar. On nearly every tree there are a few Glossy Black Idias. We find a Davis' Tree Cricket sitting on a low-hanging leaf. It's a delicate pale green, the color of a young beech sprout. Most people do not get to see this very common insect that we all hear on warm late-summer nights.

Our last moth of the evening is a Cloaked Marvel—such a big name for a little moth. In fact, when I announce the name to our group and the word is passed down the line, excitement grows to see this moth with the name of an avenger for justice. A skulking hero of the night. A stealth wonder.

"Is that it?" asks one of the men.

"Afraid so," I say.

"Hmm," he responds politely, and moves on.

Sugaring for Moths

Here's what you will need for the bait:

* Beer (stale is best)
* Brown sugar

Optional items to add to the beer and sugar:

* Maple syrup
* Honey
* Sweet liqueur (peach schnapps, amaretto, et cetera)
* Orange soda (flat)
* Vanilla extract
* Mushy banana(s) or pear(s)
* Rotten watermelon

In a glass or plastic container, stir the ingredients until the mixture is syrupy. It should not be thin; you don't want the bait running down the tree. If the beer wasn't stale to begin with, let your concoction sit at room temperature for a couple of days. Do not cover it tightly or the accumulating gases may cause an explosion. A paper towel held over the opening with a rubber band works well.

The Cloaked Marvel is one of the smaller owlets, a tad smaller than a Cheeze-It cracker. Its upper wings are dark overall, with a kidney-shaped pool of white, called a reniform spot, toward the center of the wing. The male, which we are seeing, has a heavy lateral white dash on each of the wings. The moth is often found resting on oak trees, and has long been known to be attracted to bait. Actually, I am surprised we saw only one on this trip. They are usually better represented. Most people in the group are more impressed with the name than the moth itself. To its credit, though, it does earn a couple of "oohs."

The fallen tree on which I had spilled the rest of my bait was covered with ants. No moths. In fact, I notice that on trees where there are a lot of ants, the moths are absent. Not too hard to figure out why. When I am more careful with the painting and cause fewer drips, the ants are less likely to find the bait from the ground.

We break out of the woods and enter the field where we began. The search has taken us only about an hour. Two of the flashlights didn't

Using a clean paintbrush, apply this mixture in one-foot squares at eye level on the trees. This is best done at dusk. A moonless, cloudy, muggy night sets the best stage, but any night should bring in something. As you paint the trees, try not to let the mixture drip to the ground at the base; otherwise, carpenter ants will find it and take over the bait. Keep in mind that the bait may temporarily stain the bark of the tree. If this is a concern, you can soak a sponge in the bait and hang it from a branch at eye level.

The activity will peak between 10 P.M. and midnight. This is the time to be out there. Remember, too much noise or light will spook some of the moths. A piece of red cellophane held in place with a rubber band over the lens of the flashlight will make the light less disturbing to the feeding moths. Approach slowly, and you will be able to watch them drink up the sap with their long, unfurled proboscises.

Depending upon the weather and your mixture, the attracting quality of the bait usually lasts only a night or two.

Note: The best moth attractant I have ever come across was fermented watermelon. Cut it into small sections and smash it into the tree. Not only does it attract moths—the process is oddly fun!

---

make it all the way through, but all the people did. For some, this is the first time they have walked through the woods at night. For everyone, this is the first time they have actively gone out in search of moths. Moths! Those little insects that fly out of their kitchen cabinets or eat their clothes. What kind of person would give up an evening to seek them out? From the moment they stepped out of their cars, I respected their willingness to try something so out of the ordinary. I think most of them are genuinely surprised at how much they enjoyed themselves. If anything, I feel confident that now they will think twice before taking a swat at the next moth that accidentally finds its way into their house.

We say our good-byes and I watch the cars pull away. As the headlights fade into the distance, it is once again dark and quiet in the field. Quiet, save for the tree crickets in the branches, the field crickets in the grass, the katydids keeping rhythm. I turn and look toward the woods. I can't stop wondering what that big dark moth was that got away.

Oh, what the hell. I'll do one more round.

❧ 2 ❧

A Moth's Life

RIGHT outside my door, in a cage on my deck, are the eggs of a Polyphemus Moth. They were laid just last night by a female that my wife had found earlier in the afternoon. The moth looked freshly emerged, flawlessly crisp and clean. I had hoped that if I put her in a cage she would call in a male or two, enjoy a conjugal visit, get her eggs fertilized, and provide me with a brood to rear over the summer. The males never arrived, but she laid her eggs anyway, all over the place. There was a good chance that she had already mated the night before and had just recently broken free of the male before Betsy found her. The moths sometimes stay coupled into the next day. If this was the case, the eggs she had laid were fertile. I would know in two weeks, the time it takes for a Polyphemus Moth to hatch.

I brought in one of the eggs to have a closer look. It was oval and squat and looked like a tiny pillbox. It was just under three-sixteenths of an inch long, a bit over one-sixteenth of an inch wide, and one-sixteenth of an inch thick, about the size of a sesame seed. The top was pearly white washed with brown. It was edged with a deep brown band, and there was a white mark on it that resembled the side view of a spinning galaxy. The moth had glued this egg to a strip of paper I had put in the cage to give her something on which to oviposit. Unfortunately, she had stuck most of her eggs to the sides of the cage instead.

The egg I held in my hand was 100 percent potential. It was something wonderful waiting to happen. It was hard to imagine that this tiny bead could be housing what would be a moth to rival the great Cecropia in size. The Cecropia, which I was able to rear from egg to adult last year, is the largest moth in North America. Memories of the joy of watching this behemoth spread its wings and fly for the first time filled me with anticipation to experience the same with its cousin.

I measured the wingspan of the Polyphemus on my deck. Nearly six inches from tip to tip. If all goes well, what lies within the tiny egg on my desk will reach the same size.

But it has a long way to go.

It all starts with the egg. (Or does it start with the moth that lays the egg?) Moths and butterflies go through four life stages: egg, pupa, larva (caterpillar), and adult. They undergo what is referred to as complete metamorphosis, as compared to incomplete metamorphosis, which is the method by which insects such as grasshoppers grow, skipping the pupal stage and emerging from their eggs as miniature, though flightless, versions of the adult. The biological makeup of these nymphs, as they are called, is similar to that of the adult, barring the fact that they cannot call or reproduce. Not so with moths. A caterpillar is so unlike what it will turn into that it can seem like an entirely different creature. In a way, it is. And that caterpillar begins as an embryo within a tiny egg.

The eggs of moths come in a variety of sizes, shapes, and colors. They are laid singly or in clusters or wrapped around branches in bands. They may be attached to the future host plant under the leaves, in the leaves, on the bark, or in the buds, or they may be in the soil or broadcast over an area like seeds from a spreader. They can be found on the sides of houses, on cars, and—in my case—on a cage housing a female moth. Sometimes the eggs are covered with silk threads or plant material or are exposed to the elements. In the case of the Bagworm Moth, which commonly lives on the sides of houses, the eggs are laid on the outside of a small, tubular bundle of twigs sticking out from a shingle. The female moth, which is flightless, lives inside. When the larvae emerge, they feed on the twigs, literally eating themselves out of house and home.

The main purpose of the egg is to house and protect the growing embryo. This means it has to be tough enough to withstand the extremes of weather: drought, downpours, and the coldest of winters. In eggs that overwinter, there is an "antifreeze" present in the form of glycerol, or sometimes alcohol, to keep the fluid inside from freezing. But at the same time, this hardy egg must allow moisture and oxygen to penetrate the outer surface, and waste gases to exit. It also has to allow the caterpillar to escape when the time comes.

Upon emerging from its egg, the caterpillar usually eats the shell. This will be its last nonherbaceous meal. At this stage, the caterpillar is in its first instar. Instars are the caterpillar stages between molts. The caterpillar has most of the equipment it will need to eat, disperse, and survive. The head capsule, or simply the head, comprises the chewing mandibles, the sensory maxillae, a pair of reduced antennae, and two sets of six simple eyes, called stemmata. The eyesight of lepidopteran larvae is poor, and it's believed that the stemmata serve to sense light from dark. They can also recognize movement, which is important for prey avoidance, limited ability that it is. The antennae, located in front of the eyes, are sensory organs that along with the maxillae help the larvae figure out what they are eating. Many caterpillars are host specific, meaning they cannot eat just any plant and therefore need a way to determine if a plant is edible.

Depending upon the species, its body may be covered with hair, bristles, or knobs or may just be smooth and clean. The patterns also vary greatly and tend to be consistent within the species. A number of species feed communally. Some are loners. And some, as exhibited in a few of the Pyralidae, actually feed below the water surface. There is a caterpillar to fill every niche in the wild.

The larval body, however adorned, has thirteen ringlike segments. Located on the sides of the segments are nine pairs of spiracles, or openings through which the caterpillar breathes. The first three segments make up the thorax. The thorax bears three pairs of jointed thoracic legs, which are used for grabbing leaves and walking. The abdominal segments bear four pairs of barrel-shaped prolegs; the pair on the last segment is called the anal prolegs. (If the caterpillar has more than five pairs of prolegs, it's probably not a moth or butterfly but a sawfly, which is in the Hymenoptera family.) The prolegs are what the caterpillar uses to move and to hang onto a surface. The larvae in the Geometridae, or inchworm, family are missing the first couple of pairs of prolegs, forcing them to "inch" their way across the plants. At the bottom of the prolegs are pads covered with microscopic hooks, called crochets. If you have ever tried to detach a caterpillar from its perch, you may recall how difficult it was to get it to let go. It is important that caterpillars not fall. For one, they may never find their food source again. And they risk fatal injury or exposure to predators. To further ensure that they remain in place, lepidopteran caterpillars have the ability to spin silk. It comes from a pair of spinnerets located below the mandibles. Watch a caterpillar move across a branch; you may see the head go from side to side. The caterpillar is laying down a safety cord to catch it should it be knocked off the plant. The caterpillar can also use the silk to enclose itself within a leaf or cocoon and as an anchor when molting. In the early instars, some larvae feed the silk into the breeze and let it carry them away. This is called ballooning.

Once the caterpillar devours its egg, it begins to feed on its host plant. Because the caterpillar is so tiny, the most it can do is scrape away at the leaf's downy covering or eat through a single layer in the middle of the leaf. As the caterpillar grows, it becomes more capable and often moves to the edge of the leaf. A hole in the center of a leaf is more obvious to a predator than a nibbled edge, and the last thing a caterpillar wants to do is call attention to itself.

The caterpillar eats. The caterpillar grows. That caterpillars are eating machines has become a cliché. Acquiring nutrients and, in some cases, dispersal are the main reasons for its existence. Because its skin, or exoskeleton, is not very flexible, things get a bit snug as it grows. When the time is right, the caterpillar takes a break from eating and becomes inactive. The cells within the layer of skin beneath the outer layer multiply rapidly, beginning to separate the two. A thin layer of fluid builds in between. The caterpillar then creates a button of silk and attaches itself to the surface of its host plant by grabbing hold with its thoracic legs. Big gulps of air are taken in, causing the caterpillar to expand in size until the skin splits along the back. The caterpillar then pulls away from the shed exoskeleton, called an exuvia, and emerges as a soft, creased new instar. The exuvia is left behind, looking like a wrinkled pair of pants thrown on the bedroom floor. The whole process, from laying down a silk pad to molting, takes a day or two. The new skin is dangerously delicate. Even the mandibles are too soft to be used for chewing. In a few hours, the skin grows harder and the new instar resumes its routine. The caterpillar eats. The caterpillar grows.

In most caterpillars, molting takes place five times—in some species more, some fewer. But with each molt, the caterpillars grow larger and more proficient at taking in more food. A great number of species change appearance with each instar, some drastically. What might work to camouflage a larva that is only a quarter-inch in size may not work when that same larva is two inches long. Therefore, each change of appearance is meant to enhance the insect's ability to survive in its surroundings. If the caterpillar is palatable to birds, it will most likely take on cryptic coloration or disguise itself as something inedible, such as a bird dropping. If it is poisonous, it may advertise this with bold colors. Late-instar larvae suffer in not only being larger and therefore easier to find, but in being susceptible to parasitizing insects. These insects lay their eggs in or on the host. When they hatch, the parasitic larvae feed on the internal organs. A number of these insects locate their hosts by smell, so blending in with its background is of little help to the moth larva. Some caterpillars have evolved tendrils and bristles to help chase away the parasitic wasps and flies. Others will feed within curled-up leaves or behind a wall of silk. Some of the notodontid moth caterpillars rear up on their hind legs, making a more difficult target for the egg-laying Hymenoptera. Some shoot acid.

Then there are caterpillars, such as the carpenterworms, whose powerful mandibles allow them to bore into wood. They spend their entire larval cycle within a tree, somewhat dark and dismal surroundings, but caterpillars don't have the ability to appreciate the scenery or lack thereof. However, although the inside of a tree may seem like a safe place—if the caterpillars are not discovered by a woodpecker, whose barbed tongue can reach astonishing lengths—they may still have to contend with the long ovipositor of an ichneumon wasp.

Another problem faced by all caterpillars is the stinkbug. The Hemiptera, or true bugs, have piercing proboscises. They actively seek out lepidopteran larvae and suck them dry, leaving behind the empty, shriveled skins. I sometimes rear caterpillars outdoors within cloth bags wrapped around the branches that the larvae are feeding on. The Hemiptera will poke a nose through the bag and drain their mystery meal dry. It's kind of like a potluck dinner for stinkbugs.

At times we humans are the predators. In Africa, Australia, and South America, many caterpillars are eaten by people, either as a delicacy or as an important source of protein. In some areas, you can even buy canned caterpillars. I ate some moths once—their eggs, actually. I was on Cape Cod in Massachusetts looking for snakes with a group of people from the Wellfleet Audubon Sanctuary. Tom Tyning, the herpetologist who was showing us around, came across a cluster of Gypsy Moth eggs. "You can eat those, you know," he said. "You go first," I said. He brushed away the silk and hairs and popped a few eggs in his mouth. Okay, I thought, he's serious. I tried a few. Not bad. Tasted like walnuts.

It's tough being a caterpillar, and evolution has provided an ever-changing contest of adapt, fool, hide, catch on, readapt. The defenses we see are the result of this, and none is 100 percent effective. For every defense, there is an animal that has found a way to get around it. To ensure a continuous line of generations, the larvae may reproduce in large numbers, counting on their brethren to take the hit. They may make themselves invisible or undesirable as a meal. They may even cause pain. But some animals will decimate entire populations of the prolific species. The invisible will be found and the undesirable will be consumed by those with strong constitutions and an indiscriminate palate. Even the pain-givers will meet their match. This keeps the balance and makes sure that everyone, predator and prey, can at some point grab a meal.

The fortunate caterpillar that has survived this most difficult time gets to proceed to the next level—pupation.

Once the caterpillar has finished growing, it seeks out a protected site to undergo this next change. It has eaten its last nonliquid meal, and in some cases its last meal altogether. Many species signal the onset of this stage by turning darker. This may help them blend in better with their surroundings. They leave the host plant and "go walkabout." Some will find a leaf to enclose their developing pupae. The leaf may be rolled or folded around the caterpillar and held in place with silk. With silk moths, the pupae are either suspended from or attached to the side of a branch. Other moths spin a cocoon of silk and pass the time beneath the leaf litter, in the ground, or within a rolled leaf. Still others go into the ground, creating a cell in which they spend this period, tail down, as naked pupae. The latter method is employed by the sphinx moths and many of the owlets.

Only butterflies create what is called a chrysalis, which in essence is a naked pupa attached directly to a branch. However, in some circles the term is used for this stage in a moth's life, too. Although moth pupae may also hang from a branch or be plastered to its side, the pupa itself is attached either to a cocoon or within a leaf, which in turn is connected to the plant.

Once it has settled on its spot or created its shelter, the caterpillar molts one last time. Just prior to this, it doesn't look very healthy. In fact, it may appear dead, because the skin of the now inactive caterpillar shrivels up. During this molting, instead of the emergence of a new caterpillar with legs, eyes, and mandibles, the exoskeleton hardens and turns deep brown or rusty, like the skin of a beer nut. You can still make out the body parts because they are outlined in the pupa, but there are no protruding appendages (the few exceptions include the arched proboscis of a sphinx moth). At the end of the pupa is a bundle of hooks called the cremaster. In butterflies these little hooks are used to latch onto a plant while a chrysalis is forming. Moths use them to hold on to the inside of the cocoon.

Throughout the life of the caterpillar, it was secreting a juvenile hormone from a pair of glands called the corpora allota. This hormone prevents the growth centers, called imaginal buds, from triggering metamorphosis. In other words, the process of change is so compelling that it must be actively held in check. The caterpillar has now turned off this hormone, and the change begins to happen. The caterpillar body breaks down into a "soup," and all of its organs and appendages are absorbed, to be re-formed as the parts necessary to make an adult moth. The soup consists of the same chemicals that the caterpillar used to digest its food. This process is called histosis. The chewing mandibles must be replaced by a sipping proboscis. The very limited simple eyes become large and efficient compound eyes. The thoracic legs will be supplanted by long sensory limbs. Wing buds expand into thin, crumpled, branching extensions that, once filled with fluid, will carry the moth aloft. The abdominal prolegs are outta there.

This whole process can take just a few days, or it may last several months. Many pupae that overwinter go through a state of diapause, in which all this activity is put on hold. This allows the moth to emerge at a time when food will be available for itself, its offspring, or both. The signal that the time is right can come from several sources: warming temperatures, lengthening days, or increased moisture in the air. In tropical regions, where winters are not cold, the dry season fills that niche. When the rains come, they signal the end of diapause. Incidentally, overwintering eggs go through a similar state, releasing the caterpillars at the optimum time.

Like the caterpillars, moth cocoons and their pupae are subject to parasitism and predation. Mice are known to dig up pupae for a good source of protein. Beetles, spiders, and mites can pierce their surface to drink the yellow elixir within. I've observed downy woodpeckers and black-capped chickadees hammering away at Promethea Moth cocoons hanging from a branch. Then there are the ever-present ichneumon wasps, parasitizing the moths throughout every stage.

Most pupae are helpless during this period, but some have a limited means of defense. A number of them have the ability to move—not much, but enough to discourage a predator and send it searching for an easier target. If a pupa within a cocoon is being attacked by a parasitizing insect, it may have the ability to roll to the other side, away from the probing ovipositor. Some species that pass this stage as a naked pupa can clamp down on an insect's leg, proboscis, or ovipositor, trapping it within the sharp grooves of its abdomen.

But the best defense is to not be found at all. You can see for yourself how well this works by going into your yard and trying to find pupae. They don't exactly jump out at you. Yet look at all the leaves that have been eaten. Look at all the moths that come to your lights. The pupae must be everywhere. Of course you can unroll a leaf or lift a rock or a log and find naked pupae. Gardeners find them all the time while digging in the soil. But aside from those, which represent just a few of the many hundreds of species in your area, it takes some doing to turn them up.

When the time is right, the pupa darkens, signaling that the moth will soon emerge. This usually occurs during the day, which gives the moth time to prepare its wings for evening flight, but emergence time varies radically among the species. In fact, some species are prevented from interbreeding because they emerge at different times. This is the case with the Promethea and Tulip Tree Silk Moths. The Prometheas eclose—that is, emerge—from their cocoons in late afternoon. They begin mating shortly after. The Tulip Tree Silk Moths eclose later in the evening, thus will call later than their cousins. If two of them met up at a time when they were both raring to go, they could hybridize; however, this rarely happens.

If the moth is to emerge from a pupa within the ground, the skin splits enough for the moth to push out its head. It gulps air to expand its girth, splitting the encasing shell enough to free the body. It then has to plow its way to the surface. This is why the terrestrial pupae are situated near the surface, with the head up. If one somehow found itself head down and was not able to right itself, it would most likely never see the light of the moon.

If the pupa is within a cocoon, it can be more of a challenge to break free. Silk is a strong substance, and a moth that recently traded in its mandibles for a Crazy Straw cannot chew its way out. A few species are able to cut their way out using a sharp little ridge located on top of the head. Others prepare in advance. The caterpillar of the Cecropia Moth spins a one-way exit in the top of its cocoon. This allows the moth to squeeze out but nothing else to squeeze in. Some moths create a trapdoor that is easily exited by the adult. Still others may rely upon an enzyme called cocoonase, which is secreted from the head, to break down the interlocking connections of silk. This is followed by a thrusting of the wings to plow through the now-softened barrier.

In the case of a moth eclosing from a tight cocoon, it is essential that it squeeze out. I read an account in which a well-meaning human, in an attempt to help the moth, cut open the cocoon to make its exit easier, like helping a chick break out of its shell. However, the moth came out severely deformed. Squeezing out of a cocoon is part of the process it has evolved over the millennia. Perhaps it is necessary to push out excess fluids.

Once the now-adult moth is free, it needs to get its wings going. There is no room in a tight little pupa for a set of wings, so they grow crinkled up against the moth's upper thorax. The legs are working just fine, though, and the moth crawls to a nearby branch, where it begins to pump fluid, blood actually, from its body into the network of veins in the wings. Within an hour or so, the wings are filled to capacity and hang loosely from the moth's thorax. It will be another few hours before the wings harden enough for flight.

I have always thought that this point in a moth's, or butterfly's, life is wasted on a nonsentient creature. I would love to slip my brain into its head and experience the first time it flaps its wings and lifts into the air. Then I'd want my brain back again, because I couldn't deal with the stress of having everything out to eat me.

So now we have the adult moth. Although many folks see this form as the ultimate stage of this insect, others bestow that honor upon the caterpillar. For them, the adult is just a way for caterpillars to expand their range and make new caterpillars. I'm not one of those people. Although I do appreciate the many attributes, both physical and behavioral, of the caterpillar, it is the adult moth that inspires my obsession with the insect. Why? Probably because moths can fly.

When the caterpillar runs out of food and pupates early, the resulting moth is smaller than average. It is how this insect deals with a shortage of nutrients. Instead of dying of starvation or producing a weaker adult, it instead utilizes its resources to form a healthy but compact version of the species. If the caterpillar had an abundance of food, the adult moth is considerably larger. That is why there is such size variation among the adults of a species. The same occurs in butterflies. I particularly notice this in the Monarchs and Great Spangled Fritillaries, although this phenomenon occurs across the board.

I should explain just a little about the pieces that make up this animal. As with any insect, the moth has three body parts: the head, thorax, and abdomen. The head is unlike the head capsule formally borne by its auto-predecessor, because the components have taken on new purposes. The new compound eyes can see color beyond human range and into the ultraviolet spectrum. Moths still have a pair of simple eyes that are often hidden beneath the scales on the head. It's believed that, like the stemmata of the larvae, they help sense light and dark and may work in conjunction with the compound eyes.

The mouth is actually a tongue or, more correctly, a proboscis. It is made up of two separate laterally divided tubes that when "zipped" together form a straw. It is designed for probing and taking in liquid nourishment: nectar, water, and sometimes sap, mud, and animal droppings. When not in use, the proboscis is coiled and tucked into the palps, sensory organs located below the head.

The antennae are feathered, combed, or tapered. (If you come across a "moth" with clubbed antennae, you have a butterfly.) The antennae are loaded with sensory cells designed to pick up scents and register vibrations. The latter can be helpful when navigating on a windy night. The ability to sense air currents allows moths to adjust their flight accordingly.

The thorax is the muscle warehouse. Both the beating of the wings and movement of the legs are powered by the muscles in this area. This is the toughest part of a moth, hard shelled and sturdy, because it has to anchor these muscles. In many moths the thorax is covered with dense scales that have the appearance of fur. Real fur does not grow on Lepidoptera. No matter how much a moth's covering may resemble fur, it is formed of modified scales. A number of species of moths have hearing organs located on their thorax. The tiger and owlet moths are among them. (Other species, such as the inchworms and Pyralidae, have their hearing organs on their abdomen.) The ear of a moth is similar to that of a frog: It is simply a membrane, called a tympanum, stretched across an opening. Within that opening are sensors that relay sounds to the brain.

The wings of a moth lend the order its name of Lepidoptera, translated as "scaled (or scaly) wings." Four wings are present in most species, with the two on top called forewings and the lower set called hind wings.

Each of the four wings is made up of two very thin layers connected by braces and is held stiff by a network of veins. Air and a bit of blood are pumped into the veins, the arrangement of which is consistent within the families. Some female moths, however, are wingless. In this case, she lays all her eggs in one location, leaving the responsibility for dispersal to the larvae.

At the costal margin, or leading edge, of the hind wing is an apparatus unique to moths called the frenulum. It consists of little hooks—usually one in a male, two or more in a female—that catch the trailing edge, or inner margin, of the forewing. When a moth flies, all four wings are connected. Moths lacking a frenulum instead utilize a bulge, called a humeral angle, located on the hind wing's costal margin to keep the forewing from slipping behind it. Some of the more primitive moths have a little Florida-shaped projection, called a jugum, at the base of the inner margin of the forewing to hold the wings together.

The wings are the essence of the moth. These are what jump out at you, and their varying sizes, shapes, colors, and patterns sometimes make you forget that there is a moth attached. The colors and patterns are created by the arrangement of microscopic scales. The scales are powdery in texture and easily rubbed off. This may enable a moth to weasel out of a bird's beak or roll out of a spiderweb. The presence of white in the wings of moths and butterflies is actually a lack of pigment. The positioning of the scales determines how light is reflected, resulting in this hue. Some moths appear to have metallic scales, also the result of light reflection. Some groups of moths have no scales at all on their wings, causing the insect to resemble a bee, wasp, or fly. Most of these clearwing moths eclose with scales, but they are knocked loose in a powdery flurry upon the moth's first flight.

The wings of moths also aid them in warming. Whereas day-flying butterflies can bask in the sun, nocturnal insects don't have that option. Instead, they vibrate their wings rapidly, causing their whole body to shiver. This warms the flight muscles, a necessary preparation to becoming airborne. Contrary to popular belief, the blood of moths is not cold. Some moths maintain a body temperature of 100 degrees Fahrenheit while flying. Their scales help insulate the body, reducing heat loss. Most of the heat is generated in the thorax; that is why many moths have a "hairy" thorax. It keeps the powerhouse running.

Aside from housing the tympanum in some species, the abdomen is

A Cecropia Moth's Life Cycle

First instar larva hatching

Early instar larvae

Late instar larva

Cocoon

Cecropia Moth adult

Moth Caterpillars

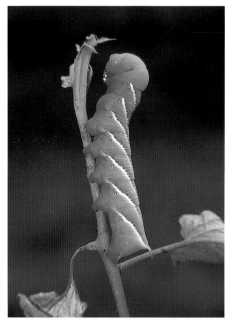

Tobacco Hornworm (Carolina Sphinx, *Manduca sexta*)

Salt Marsh Moth *(Estigmene acrea)*

Black-waved Flannel Moth *(Lagoa crispata)*

Spotted Apatelodes *(Apatelodes torrefacta)*

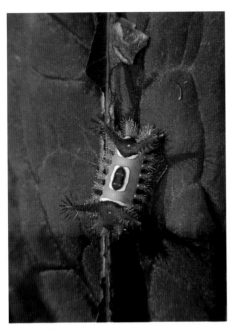

Saddleback Moth
(Sibine stimulea)

Morning-glory Prominent
(Schizura ipomoeae)

Brown-hooded Owlet
(Cucullia convexipennis)

Drexel's Datana
(Datana drexelii)

Sphinx or Hawk Moths *(Sphingidae)*

Laurel Sphinx
(Sphinx kalmiae)

Waved Sphinx
(Ceratomia undulosa)

hinx *(Paonias excaecatus)*

Silk Moths (*Saturniidae*)

Cynthia Moth *(Samia cynthia)*

Polyphemus Moth
(Antheraea polyphemus)

Promethea Moth
(Callosamia promethea)

Rosy Maple Moth
(Dryocampa rubicunda)

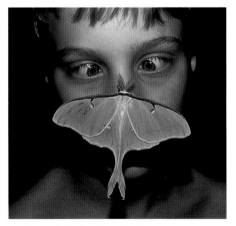

Luna Moth *(Actias luna)*
visiting author's son, Jeff

Imperial Moth *(Eacles imperialis)*

Tiger and Lichen Moths *(Arctiidae)*

Clymene Moths *(Hapola clymene)*

Nais Tiger Moth
(Apantesis nais)

Banded Tussock Moth
(Halysidota tessellaris)

Virgin Tiger Moth
(Grammia virgo)

Painted Lichen Moth *(Hypopepia fucosa)* on house

Giant Leopard Moth *(Ecpantheria scribonia)*

Lappet and Tent Caterpillar Moths (*Lasiocampidae*)

Lappet Moth
(Phyllodesma americana)

Large Tolype *(Tolype velleda)*

Forest Tent Caterpillar Moth *(Malacosoma disstria)*, left, and Eastern Tent Caterpillar Moth *(Malacosoma americanum)*

also where the genitalia are located. In males, there is a pair of anal claspers at the very tip, often concealed beneath the scales. These claspers are used to hold onto the female's abdomen during mating. From her abdomen the female also releases pheromones—microscopic chemical attractors that are sent aloft to float in the breeze. They can travel for miles. Cruising males pick up the scent with their large antennae and attempt to follow it upwind. When the male closes in on the female, he releases a small amount of his own pheromones. This allows her to recognize him as the same species. Many males often arrive, but the first one to lock on with those anal claspers becomes the sire of the next generation.

The female lays her eggs shortly after fertilization. She usually mates only once, whereas the males attempt as many times as possible to increase the ranks of their progeny. The males who are most successful will pass on the genes that gave them their edge. Maybe they're a little faster or hardier. Perhaps they're better able to pick up a wafting pheromone and zero in on it. The ability to be Johnny-on-the-spot increases the chances of that species continuing yet another generation. It's for the good of the family.

Adult moths are generally short-lived; once the mating and egg laying are over, so is their purpose in nature. I wonder how many of the moths that I come across are just biding their time after mating, sipping nectar from a flower here and there, having a snooze in the shade on a warm afternoon. The wings look worn and ragged. The thorax gleams with a shiny, chitinous bald spot. Will the moth end up as a meal for a lucky animal? Or will it just fall from a tree, dead, to be carried away by a procession of ants?

Some moths live for only a few days, some for a few months—the latter are often species that overwinter as adults. The average lifespan of a moth or butterfly is about two weeks. During this period the moths exhibit a number of behaviors and answer to a number of their compulsions involving feeding, migration, courtship, and mating. Throughout this time, a moth is in great peril from a huge variety of predators, disease, deadly fungi, foul weather, and human disturbance in the form of lights, cars, pesticides, habitat loss, cats (a threat I attribute to humans), nets, and big clomping feet. Any moth that dies of old age is just plain lucky.

A majority of moths feed at night and rest during the day. They have most likely been doing so since their emergence back in Jurassic times, about 150 million years ago. Moths have probably been around longer than that, perhaps by another 100 million years or so; it's believed that they share a common ancestor with caddisflies. The two insects are similar in many ways. Caddisflies always accompany moths at my light sheet. In fact, more than once I've mistaken a Holomelina tiger moth for a caddisfly.

Living a nocturnal life has its advantages. There are fewer predators than during the day. A large number of caterpillars utilize this time to feed. However, as we know, some predators specialize in darkness: predators that love to eat moths. Bats, mice, raccoons, skunks, frogs, salamanders, lizards, wasps, spiders, nightjars, and owls have been known to enjoy a moth or two. And a moth resting during the day can be found by an even wider variety of insectivores and omnivores. Their cryptic patterns, shapes, and coloration, bluffing eyespots, warning calls, and toxic insides are evidence of their attempt to thwart these perils. But, as with caterpillars, no camouflage is perfect, and moths get eaten night and day.

Yet enough of them survive to help pollinate our plants. If they did not, we'd be living in a bleak world, as they are responsible for a majority of plant pollination. They migrate to new areas, giving rise to new populations where the prey has not yet caught on to them. As a group of more than 110,000 species, they see to it that nary a woodlot, meadow, rainforest, or tundra is free from the pruning mandibles of their larvae.

The eggs of the next generation hatch, turning loose a cadre of hungry orphans. The moth that fertilized the eggs and the moth that laid them have become food for any of a great number of insectivores and scavengers. These are the same creatures that the caterpillars must evade in their attempt to make it far enough to add their genes to the pool. Many will not even get close. Some may survive the journey only to be snapped up by a hungry bird seconds before they mate.

I released the Polyphemus Moth from her cage this morning. She sailed across my yard and disappeared into the leaves of the surrounding woodlands. In another week or so, she will be dead, of natural causes or an unfortunate run-in with the wrong animal. She is through laying eggs, and I will look after them.

That one egg is still sitting here beside my keyboard. So much potential and so far to go.

Postscript: All the eggs hatched. Caterpillars doing fine.

~ 3 ~
Moth Families

THE best way to learn about something, anything, is to break it down into big chunks of generalizations. Familiarize yourself with those chunks and allow yourself, for the time being, to be satisfied in taking it only that far. Then, once you are comfortable with that general knowledge, you can move on to breaking the chunks down further. The chunks in this case will be the families of moths. I have selected fifteen of the most often encountered families and described what puts them together in their respective groups. Often, this is as far as even an experienced moth-er can take a species. If you just want to get a sense of the diversity in your own yard, that should be enough. If you want to take it further, you will need to consult some field guides (see Bibliography for more information).

Sphinx Moths or Hawk Moths
(Family Sphingidae)

Sphinx moths are one of the easiest species to recognize, both as adults and as larvae. The adults have robust, cigar-shaped bodies with long, tapered wings. Their wings often form boomerangs attached at the apex to their thorax. The moths are generally medium to large, with the largest in New England—the Carolina Sphinx—attaining a wingspan of up to four inches. When I was in South America a few years back, I came across the largest sphinx moth in the world, the Giant Sphinx. This monster has a

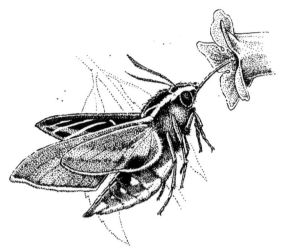

WHITE-LINED SPHINX MOTH *(HYLES LINEATA)*

wingspan of up to seven inches. Imagine having something that large buzzing at you from the darkness of the rain forest. Gets your attention.

Sphinx moths can be very fast fliers and often hover at flowers, sipping nectar through their long proboscis. In the air, in both speed and agility, they remind me of hummingbirds. It has been suggested that one of their common names, hawk moth, comes from their swooping flight. However, I wonder if it could have more to do with their feeding on the wing, which in the bird world is called hawking.

Their other name, sphinx moth, comes from a description of the caterpillar. While clasping a branch with its prolegs, the naked larva often lifts its head and thorax into the air, striking a pose reminiscent of the Sphinx in Egypt. The sphinx larvae are generally medium to large, and many have a horn protruding from the last segment. This feature gives the caterpillars of some species yet another name, hornworm.

The pupae are naked and develop in the soil. One interesting characteristic of a number of the sphinx pupae is the formation of a sheath to encase the developing proboscis. Sometimes it is separate from the body, forming a little handle.

Most sphinx moths are active at night, although some are active at dusk and a few are day fliers. The latter often resemble in appearance and sound such other day-flying creatures as bees and hummingbirds. These can be found nectaring on flowers among the insects and birds after which they are disguised.

Although some sphinx moths have proboscises longer than their body, other species do not feed at all. They rely on energy stored from food eaten as caterpillars to power their flight.

Moths in this family readily come to lights. Those remaining in the area the next morning are "tame" and easily coaxed onto your fingertip.

Silk Moths
(Family Saturniidae)

This family comprises medium to large moths that are burly in body and covered with very furry scales. Many of these moths sport a variety of eyespot patterns on their wings; in some species, such as the Polyphemus, the spots are in the form of clear windows. The larger species, because of their heavy bodies and broad wings, may resemble a small bat in flight. They get a lot of lift with each flap. There are forty-plus species of Saturniidae in North America, and this family includes the largest moth on the continent, the Cecropia. This giant can have a wingspan of up to half a foot.

A few in this family, such as the buck moths, fly by day. Some, including the Promethea Moth, are on the wing at twilight. Most, however, are nocturnal. Many species of silk moths have underdeveloped mouthparts and therefore do not feed as adults. Their lifespan is short, less than two weeks, because they rely solely on energy stored from their caterpillar stage. Once they emerge, they seek to hook up with the opposite sex. The female sends her signals (pheromones) into the air. The males use their "satellite dish" antennae to scoop up the pheromones and follow them back to the calling female. The males generally have wider antennae than the females, because it is their job to do the searching. The females usually mate and lay eggs within the first forty-eight

IO MOTH (AUTOMERIS IO)

hours of eclosure, leaving them with little to do for the rest of their nights.

The caterpillars of the silk moths, like the adults, are heavy bodied. They often have spines, hairs, or tubercles growing out of their segments. In some species, such as the Io Moth, these spines can sting.

The silk moths are named for their pupal stage, which is spent within a silken cocoon. Many species use this silk to enclose their cocoons within a leaf. Sometimes the leaf remains suspended from a branch through the winter. This is the best time to seek them out. When the leaves have fallen off the trees, the cocoons are more obvious. Once you find your first one or two, the rest become easier to spot. If you keep at it long enough, you begin to find them when you're not even looking.

The True Silkmoth *(Bombyx mori)* is a domesticated moth from China. It is not a Saturniid but is in the family Bombycidae. This is the moth that has been used in sericulture, or silk production, for thousands of years. The adult, larvae, and cocoon are white, as are many domesticated species of animals (turkeys, ducks, and chickens) in which color is unnecessary. As with other domesticated species, in which flight would make rearing more difficult, the adults of this species rarely fly.

Silk moths are readily attracted to lights. Bait is useless for most of them, because they don't eat. When handled, many species drop stiff-winged to the ground, mimicking a falling leaf.

Tent Caterpillars, Eggars, and Lappet Moths
(Family Lasiocampidae)

The Lasiocampidae family includes the species with the negative distinction of being the easiest of any caterpillar to locate; the Eastern Tent Caterpillar. The larvae of this moth reside with their many brethren in silken nests resembling sloppy white cotton candy spun by drunken carnies.

The adults are less recognized, but by early summer they are as common as can be expected, judging from all their tents. These are not our only Lasiocampids, however. There are about thirty different North American species in this family and roughly 1,500 worldwide.

In general, the adults are medium to large moths with dull-colored wings held tentlike over the body. Many have two or three bands across the forewings, the bands being a lighter or darker shade of the base color. The moth's shaggy body is stout, and the abdomen often extends past the relatively short, rounded wings. In the lappet moths, the hind wings of some species droop below the forewings and are flattened at the surface. The exposed hind wing edge is jagged, which enhances the dead-leaf disguise. These moths are named for the caterpillars, which have fleshy, flaplike structures called lappets running down their hairy bodies.

The eggs of the lappet moths are usually laid in large numbers. In the case of the Eastern Tent Caterpillar, the egg mass looks like an oblong shellacked wooden ball wrapped around a branch at the base of a fork in its host plant. The larvae emerge

LEFT: EASTERN TENT CATERPILLAR MOTH *(MALACOSOMA AMERICANUM)*; RIGHT: FOREST TENT CATERPILLAR MOTH *(MALACOSOMA DISSTRIA)*

in spring and spin a tent around this egg mass. The tent grows larger as more larvae emerge to help. Sometimes, though, the female moth didn't pick the best location for the egg mass, so the colony migrates to a nearby fork on the tree to set up shop there. The Forest Tent Caterpillar Moth—the adult of which looks like the photo negative of the adult Eastern Tent Caterpillar Moth—starts out the same way; however, although the two species feed together, the former does not make a tent.

The larvae of the tent caterpillars are furry and in some species brightly colored with bold and interesting patterns. This is not the case with the lappet moth caterpillars, which are more cryptically colored. They are very hairy on the sides and stay pressed tightly to the bark of trees, making them virtually invisible.

The Eastern Tent Caterpillars make forays from the tent to feed, then return to ride out bad weather and hot days. When it is time to pupate, they "go walkabout" to find a place to change within their tidy, egg-shaped cocoons. The lappet moth cocoons, on the other hand, are spun tightly against a branch, where, like the larvae, they become one with the surface.

The adult Lasiocampids have no working mouthparts, so they do not feed. They come to lights and are very tame, sometimes remaining in the area for days.

Tiger Moths, Tussock Moths, Wasp Moths, and Lichen Moths
(Family Arctiidae)

New England has three subfamilies of Arctiidae. This group includes some of the more ornately colored and patterned moths. Many people lump them all together as tiger moths, but only one group, in the subfamily Arctiinae, are true tigers. Their common name comes from the bold, striped patterns that a number of them show on their forewings.

It is difficult to generalize the appearance of the typical Arctiid. The most obvious common characteristics come into play at the larval stage. Most Arctiid caterpillars are densely hairy and overwinter at that stage beneath the leaf litter (although a good number overwinter as pupae). Their pupae develop within the shed hairs from the larval stage. New England's most famous Arctiid caterpillar is a true tiger moth that goes by the name of Woolly Bear. This orange and black larva is said to be able to forecast the severity of winter by the ratio of black to orange on its body. Of course, this has nothing to do with the weather. The variations just reflect the different instars, or stages, of the individual caterpillar. The adult is called the Isabella Moth, but in fame she takes a backseat to her caterpillar.

Within the Lepidoptera, there are two kinds of tussock moths—real ones in the family Lymantriid, covered later in this chapter, and a small group that shares with the tiger moths the subfamily of Arctiinae. What sets them apart from the other tigers are their parchmentlike wings, often translucent and marked in earth tones.

There are also two

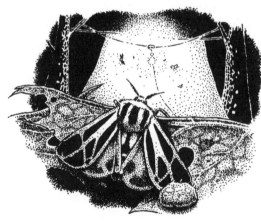

BANDED TIGER MOTH
(APANTESIS VITTATA)

kinds of wasp moths. One, including moths in the Sesiidae family, is covered later in this chapter; the other is a subfamily of the Arctiidae called Ctenuchinae. The latter includes many of the day-flying Arctiidae. Moths taking advantage of sunlight are open to predation. Wasps are often left alone by predators, as are moths that look like them. Some of the moths in this group resemble beetles.

The lichen moths, in the Arctiid subfamily Lithosiinae, are small and slender and often simply patterned with pale yellows or pinks. As their name suggests, their larvae feed upon lichen.

The Arctiids have two traits that help keep them from getting eaten. Many are highly distasteful, and their bright colors serve as warning flags to predators. They *want* to be seen, because it would do them no good to have a bird discover their undesirability *after* they had been accidentally eaten.

A number of the Arctiids can also produce sound. It can be used to attract a mate or, upon detecting a bat's sonar, warn the bat of its unpalatibility. I've heard recordings of this sound, which reminds me of a clicking Geiger counter.

Arctiids are easily attracted to lights. The day-flying species also can be found on flower heads.

Owlet Moths, or Cutworm Moths
(Family Noctuidae)

The owlets comprise the largest family within the Lepidoptera, with nearly three thousand species represented in North America. The adults are mostly nocturnal, a characteristic that has contributed to their common name of owlet, which suggests a tiny owl. The moths range greatly in size; one among their ranks, Giant Agrippa, a South American species with a wingspan of nearly twelve inches, is the largest in the world. Within this family is another notable species called the Vampire Moth. This creature of India and Malaysia uses a barbed tongue to pierce the hide of mammals and suck their blood.

The typical owlet silhouette is triangular. Their wings are usually held tentlike over the abdomen. They are generally medium sized with furry scales and stout bodies. The thorax is often prominent and from the side can resemble the hump on a buffalo's back. The large thorax houses the muscles for flight. Owlets fly very well, and many are adept

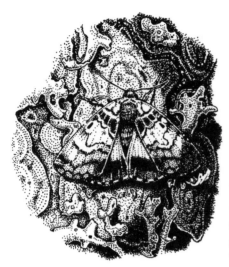

FALSE UNDERWING
(*ALLOTRIA ELONYMPHA*)

at outmaneuvering bats. The moths' flight pattern is not fluttery but direct, bringing to mind the flight of a duck—which suggests they have places to go and things to do.

Noticeable features in many of the owlets are two markings that often appear on the upper forewings. One, called the orbicular spot, is circular and can be hollow, solid, or partially solid. The other spot, always found below the orbicular spot, is the reniform spot. This is kidney shaped, hence the "reni" prefix, which refers to kidneys. As with the orbicular spot, it can be hollow, solid, or partially solid.

The caterpillars—often called cutworms because many of them cut plants down to the ground—are sometimes naked, sometimes hairy, or at times partially hairy. They are often stout but are occasionally slender. In other words, they are highly diverse in appearance. They are also diverse in food preference. For nearly everything that grows, there is a cutworm that eats it.

When it comes time to pupate, most owlets go into the ground and pass this stage as a naked pupa, although some species spin a cocoon.

The owlets come to lights and bait. In many areas they are the first moths to appear in the season; they have evolved to seek out running sap in late winter. They have very well developed proboscises and are active feeders.

Prominents
(*Family Notodontidae*)

The Prominents are a group of long-winged, long-bodied moths with a densely furry thorax and abdomen. In many individuals, the furry scales appear almost velvety, and the color of the head and thorax can be strongly contrasted. In some, a tall, crested tuft of scales sticks up behind the head like an unruly Mohawk haircut.

The Prominents are said to be named for a small scaly projection located *prominently* on the hind margin of each forewing. Another explanation is that the name refers to serrated humps that stand out *prominently* on the back of many caterpillars. Individuals in this family either hold their wings tentlike, similar to an owlet, or roll their wings to appear like a twig. In the latter case, the moth grasps a twig and thrusts out its body to look like a fork in the branch. The adults, colored in a variety of browns, tans, and grays, blend in with the woody parts of plants. Some species, such as the Black-rimmed Prominent, forgo the twig disguise to mimic a bird dropping. It is one of the more attractive bird droppings I have come across.

Of the number of genera (plural of genus) that make up this group, one of my favorites is the datanas. These robust moths remind me of snuffed-out cigar butts, being somewhat cylindrical and golden brown, with a head hidden within an anteriorly flattened brown-black thorax. Another favorite is the Chocolate Prominent, whose wings are patterned in rich, chocolatey browns.

The caterpillars are works of art. If they don't look like some kind of a lepidopteran stegosaurus, they may be sporting a long, tentacle-like tail, forked at the end, that waves in the air when they move. This waving is the result of their missing a pair of anal claspers, the anchors that most other caterpillars have to keep them "grounded." Actually, the tails are the anal claspers, but they no longer serve that function. When threatened, the caterpillars arch their back, lifting both their head and tail into the air. The perpetrator of the threat can feel fortunate that it didn't come across one of the several species in this group that shoots a spray of burning acid from its thorax.

This family of moths appears in midspring and is on the wing into October. The moths overwinter as larvae, so the caterpillars can also be found late in the season. Be-

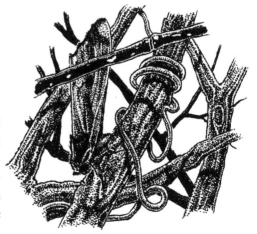

BLACK-BLOTCHED SCHIZURA
(*SCHIZURA LEPTINOIDES*)

fore the weather gets too cold, they go into the ground to ride out the winter within a loosely formed cocoon or just curled up.

The prominents come to both light and bait, but light seems to bring in more species. The moths can be very tame and easily handled.

Tussock Moths
(Family Lymantriidae)

Most families of moths have one particular species that represents them in a favorable or an unfavorable way. Unfortunately for this group, its best-known member is the Gypsy Moth. The White-marked Tussock is another that is not very well thought of because of its taste for the leaves of favorite shade trees. That's what moths in this family eat: trees and shrubs.

North America has roughly thirty species of tussock moths, with fewer than half of them occurring in New England. Because many look so similar, observers have the opportunity to get acquainted with the same handful every year.

The tussocks are generally medium-sized, dull-colored, fuzzy insects. Their wings are varying shades of grays and browns with jagged black lines running from the leading to trailing edges. There is a powdery aspect to the wing surface. In some species, the females are flightless, with their wings being greatly reduced or just useless.

When at rest, a tussock's scaly legs are spread out flat, with the front two legs often stretched straight out from the head. Some, such as the female Brown-tailed Moth, have poisonous tufts of scales on the abdomen to protect her eggs. Contact with these scales can cause a stinging rash. Like the Gypsy Moth, the Brown-

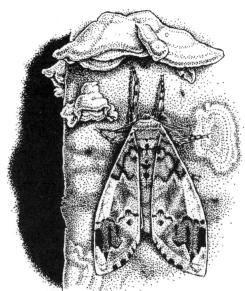

VARIABLE TUSSOCK MOTH
(DASYCHIRA VAGANS)

tail is an introduced species; although it has caused some damage to trees in the Northeast, its population seems to be shrinking. The only place I have found them is in Cape Cod, which seems to be their stronghold.

The name tussock is derived from a description of the caterpillars. It is very easy to distinguish this group from the others. The caterpillars are very hairy, which in itself is not unique to this family, but it is the arrangement of the hairs that sets this group apart. Two tufts of very long hairs protrude from the anterior and posterior ends of the caterpillar. Running along part of the back is a row of flat-cropped bristles growing in dense clumps, reminiscent of clumps of tussock grass that fill red maple swamps. The clumps of bristles have been compared to the bristles of a toothbrush.

Although the hairs can be irritating to the skin, these caterpillars also have another defense going for them. Growing from their abdominal segments are poison glands. In some species, these glands are brightly colored and give warning to predators.

When it is time to pupate, the larvae create a cocoon from their own hair. That hair is woven together in a mat that is attached flat against the surface of the tree. In the case of species whose females are flightless, upon emergence she merely pumps her scent glands to call a male. The males are able to pick up this signal from a great distance and fly in to fertilize her eggs. She then lays her eggs right on her old cocoon, where they will overwinter.

Because most tussock moths have no working mouthparts, they are not attracted to bait. However, they are easily drawn to lights.

Inchworm Moths, Loopers, Geometers, and Measuring Worms
(Family Geometridae)

Here is another family named for the caterpillar. We have all come across "bungee worms," caterpillars hanging upside down from a long thread of silk. Many of us have watched other caterpillars looping their way across a branch as if measuring the length with their body. This method of locomotion, unique to this family, is caused by the absence of two or three pairs of prolegs. This allows a number of the geometers to extend their bodies out from a branch to look like part of it. Many of them have an uncanny resemblance to twigs and other plant parts. You

WHITE SPRING MOTH
(*LOMOGRAPHA VESTALIATA*)

could be staring right at one for a long time without realizing it. As a result of the missing prolegs, their movement is jerky. There are brief moments when the caterpillar is still, which may make it more difficult to spot than the typical caterpillar undulating along with a more fluid movement.

North America is home to about a thousand different species of "geos," as they are sometimes called, with a worldwide species total of about fifteen thousand. They are the second-largest group in the order Lepidoptera.

The adults range from small to medium in size and are clean bodied and large winged. Their proportions are similar to those of a butterfly; therefore, so is their flight. Geometers flutter. At rest, the wings can either be folded over the back like those of a butterfly or held flat on the surface. Remember, however, when dealing with general descriptions of any family of animal, there are exceptions. Some Geometridae, such as the Pepper and Salt Geometer, are very "owlety" in appearance, both in body and wing. And some females have no wings at all.

Although the caterpillars can mimic twigs, many of the adults look like leaves. Some look like the bark of the trees where most of their days are spent. As far as shape goes, pick one. It depends upon what best makes them blend in with their background.

The same goes for color. Caterpillars are most often shades of brown, pale white, and gray. Because most of these moths are edible, they depend upon camouflage to live long enough to make new inchworms. There are some real beauties, though. The emeralds, for example, come in a variety of greens. The Lemon Plagodis is a mix of rich yellows and pink. The Jeweled Satyr Moth has markings painted in what appears to be liquid gold. (I came across this tropical species in South America a few years ago and brought it into my room to hold onto until morning to photograph. I could not sleep, thinking about it. What if it died overnight? I had to photograph it then. I shot a whole roll at 3 A.M. and finally went to sleep. In the morning, it was dead.)

The pupal stage of the Geometridae is spent within a cocoon that can appear to have not been worth the effort to create. The pupae overwinter at various stages and are attracted to lights throughout the year. Sugar bait also brings in a number of them.

Plume Moths
(Family Pterophoridae)

Frank E. Lutz, in his 1918 *Field Book of Insects,* wrote of this family, "If I should ever take up Lepidoptera as a hobby, I might be tempted to specialize on these delicate Plume Moths." *Delicate* describes them well. Their bodies are thin and powdery and held high on long, graceful legs. Protruding at oblique angles from the legs are pairs of long, pliable spurs,

the purpose of which I cannot guess. The thin, rolled wings are lobed (two lobes on the forewings, three on the hind wings) and fringed with long bristles. The hind-wing lobes, which are held out from the body horizontally, are deeply cut, resembling plumes, hence the common name. This gives the overall moth the appearance of the letter T. The skinny wings are not ideal for flying, as evidenced by the moths' poor aptitude in this area. Therefore, plume moths generally

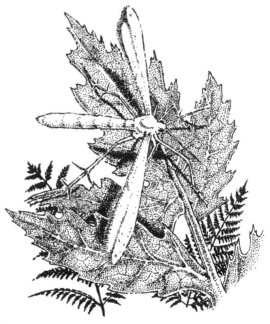

OPOSTEGA QUADRISTRIGELLA

remain close to their host plant. In flight, they bring to mind wispy heli-copters fighting an updraft.

The eggs are laid singly on the host plant. The caterpillars in this group have long, slender legs, or prolegs; their bodies are tapered at both ends. They're quite hairy and slow moving. A number of them roll the leaves of the plants and hold them closed with silk. Some of them chew their way into flower heads. I once watched one slowly work its way into a geranium bud, its head pushing deeper and deeper into the flower until the entire larva disappeared inside. That was the end of that geranium, or at least the best part of it.

A while back I discovered what appeared to be a miniature swallow-tail chrysalis hanging beneath the railing on my deck. It obviously wasn't a butterfly chrysalis; it was shorter than the circumference of the penny put next to it when I photographed it. It was pale ochre, angular, and covered with bumps, and it hung upside down by a cremaster. It had so much detail for such a tiny package. I brought it inside and checked it daily. When it emerged as a beautiful plume moth, I could not have been more happy, or surprised.

Many of the Pterophoridae fly in early evening and can be found near flowers. They also come to lights. Some overwinter, because adults are found fairly early in the season.

Grass Moths and Lawnmower Moths
(Pyralidae)

Those little white moths fleeing in advance of your approaching lawnmower are most likely representatives of this third-largest family of moths. When they land, closer inspection reveals an overall pale moth with rolled wings not much longer than three-quarters of an inch. Per-haps you have a Vagabond Crambus, with wing tips adorned in a drop of shiny gold. Or a Sod Webworm, looking similar but without the gold.

The Pyralids are another diverse group of moths that make it diffi-cult to offer generalizations. They are usually small—sometimes tiny—with wings either rolled or flat. Most are gray; all are somewhat delicate. Their bodies are clean and similar to the Geometridae, but their wings differ from this family in that they are smaller in proportion to the body. The wings are often long and thin.

The caterpillars are also diverse. They bore into stems, munch on moss, breathe underwater, chew on beeswax, and roll up leaves. A family so diverse in habit is bound to cross paths with humans, and this group contains some of our best-known pests. Corn farmers curse the European Corn-borer, which arrived from Europe in the early 1900s. Every kitchen has most likely been visited by the Indian Meal Moth and/or the Mediterranean Flour Moth. There's an individual of the latter species resting on the wall in my kitchen as I type this. Both of these moths arrived in

GRAPE LEAFFOLDER *(DESMIA FUNERALIS)*

the United States in the nineteenth century and have been raiding our stores ever since. Beekeepers shake their fists at the Lesser Bee Moths, which eat the wax in honeycombs while the bees are asleep. This is another introduced species (but so are honeybees). The thread common to all these pests is their introduction from another part of the world. What may not be a pest in one area can become one in another.

That said, these moths, and others that are considered pests, are still but a tiny fraction within the family. Most go about their lives without having any negative effect on the things people care about. One of my favorite moths, although it may be considered a mild pest by grape farmers, is more than welcome to feed on the wild grapes in my area, where the vines threaten to overtake the habitats they grow in. The Grape Leaffolder caterpillar turns into an attractive moth that I have found flying day and night. Its black wings have clean white spots that form pale arcs when the moth is in flight. Another, *Herpetogramma thestialis,* is a violet-brown moth whose wings are mottled with translucent windows.

Many of the Pyralids are attracted to lights and some to bait, but if you really want to see one, mow your lawn.

Moth Family Silhouettes

The moth silhouettes represent a certain individual typical of each family. Bear in mind that the shapes and sizes not only vary widely within families but often overlap among families. These samples are just clues to lead you in a particular direction.

SPHINX

OWLET

SILK MOTH

LASIOCAMPIDAE
(TOLYPE)

TUSSOCK MOTH
(LYMANANTRID)

TIGER MOTH

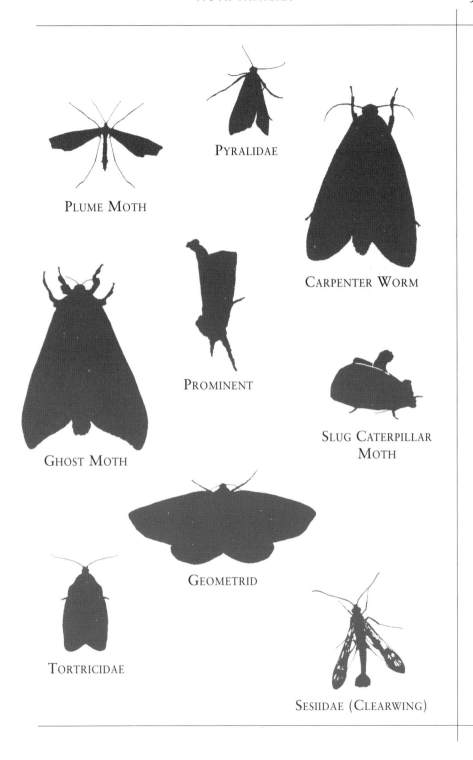

PYRALIDAE

PLUME MOTH

CARPENTER WORM

PROMINENT

GHOST MOTH

SLUG CATERPILLAR MOTH

GEOMETRID

TORTRICIDAE

SESIIDAE (CLEARWING)

Slug Caterpillar Moths
(Family Limacodidae)

What a name. What a moth. There is a genus of slugs in North America called Limax. The "Lima" in Limacodidae draws a comparison between the caterpillars in this group and those slugs. These moth caterpillars have no legs. They move by sliding across the leaf surface, usually the underside, attached by a suckerlike foot.

The adults are fairly small and fuzzy and may resemble miniature owlet moths in shape and form. Most of them have tan to brown wings, with few or no patterns, that are held tentlike over the body. Some individuals have striking grass green markings on the wings. In fact, any adult Limacodids that aren't some shade of brown seem to be green. One species, the Spiny Oak-slug Moth, has a pool of green on its upper wings. In some forms of this same species, the "pool" is broken up into small green puddles. A species in my area, the Smaller Parasa, has in addition to its green-marked wings a thorax completely covered in green fur. Although this is not true fur but modified scales, I am hard pressed to name another creature with a furlike covering that is green. A friend once suggested a sloth, but that's cheating, because its green comes from algae.

SKIFF MOTH AND LARVA
(PROLIMACODES BADIA)

There are about fifty different species of Limacodids in North America and more than ten times that number worldwide. A large percentage of them are in South America. In my area of Connecticut, there are fewer than twenty species, with thirteen of them present in my little town of Killingworth. The adults begin to appear at the lights in June. By late summer to early fall, their larvae are well developed and are feeding on the leaves of the cherries, hickories, oaks, and other broad-leaved trees. This is "leaf-flipping season" for the select group of people who set out to find the larvae. Why would anyone want to find them? Because they are bizarre and beautiful. These little "beads" are washed in a variety of reds, yellows, oranges, and greens. Some have ferocious-looking spines projecting from horns on their bodies, spines that can cause a painful sting if brushed against. The big prize of this group is the Monkey Slug, which resembles the shed exoskeleton of a tarantula. The "hairs" of this fake spider sting like the dickens.

By fall, the mature larvae create a cocoon in which they pass the winter. The larvae belonging to one of the species with stinging hairs somehow attach the hairs to the outside of the cocoon, creating, in effect, an electric fence to ward off predators. The cocoon is spherical and has a hinged top. In spring the caterpillar pupates; when it is ready to emerge as an adult moth, it pops open the top and squeezes out.

Slug caterpillar moths have poorly developed mouthparts and do not feed as adults. Because of this, they are not attracted to bait. Fortunately—for us, not them—they are easily lured to lights.

Leafrollers, Leaffolders, Fruit Moths, and Bell Moths
(Family Tortricidae)

This family of small moths includes two of our most famous species. One has for many years brought smiles to the faces of children; the other, a look of disgust. If you have ever bitten into an apple to discover a "worm" (hopefully not half a worm), you have met the larva of the Codling Moth, obviously not the smile inducer. This moth was accidentally introduced from Europe. The other, *Cydia deshaisiana,* is better known as the caterpillar in the Mexican jumping bean. I write more about this species in Chapter Six.

Adult Tortricids are generally rectangular in shape; some are bell shaped. On average they don't get much larger than an inch. The "tort" in Tortricid is most likely meant as a comparison between the shape of this moth and that of a tortoise. The moths hold their wings flat over the body with the leading edges tight against the surface on which they are resting. This and their cryptic colors and markings help them blend into trees and leaves. Most of the moths are shades of brown, tan, and gray. Their markings are often darker hues of their base color.

Like most moths, this group is named for its caterpillars. The tiny

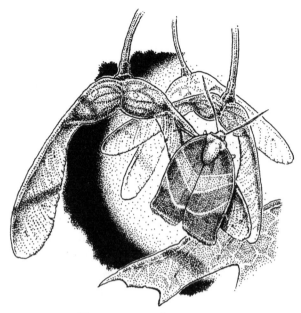

THREE-LINED LEAFROLLER
(*PANDEMIS LIMITATA*)

larvae of the leafrollers are among the more industrious of the Lepi-doptera and are known to roll leaves into tubes to feed within and pupate. The tubes are held closed with silk. These "nests" are easy to find in any deciduous forest.

The leaffolders do just that. Some cut out a section of leaf, fold it over, and enclose themselves within a little packet. When the leaves drop in autumn, the caterpillars remain inside this shelter, dry and safe, while they pupate.

This family also includes the skeletonizers. They feed on leaf tissue between the veins, leaving a crumpled skeleton behind. Each moth takes its own leaf and shelters itself within a tube made from its own frass (droppings) and held together with silk.

Then there are the borers, which tunnel into buds and fruit. Feeding birds get a little protein with their vegetables. The Baltimore oriole arrives in New England early to take advantage of the Tortricids living within the apple tree buds.

Tortricids usually overwinter in the pupal stage and can be on the wing into late fall. They are attracted to lights, but I have not found many coming to bait.

Carpenterworm Moths, Leopard Moths, and Goat Moths
(Family Cossidae)

At first glance, the moths in this family may resemble sphinx moths. They are medium to large and have long wings and heavy bodies with the abdomen protruding past the wings. As with ghost moths, which also resemble moths in this family, the venation of the wings is simple and primitive. There is not much color to them, either; the wings are various shades of brown, gray, and white. There is often dark brown mottling or webbing across the surface, giving the moth the appearance of a decaying leaf. When flying, their bodies seem a bit heavy for them. Their flight is not one that inspires envy.

One species in this family, *Zeuzera pyrina,* is called the Leopard Moth (not to be confused with the Great Leopard Moth, which is an Arctiidae). The wings of the Leopard Moth are translucently white with black spots. It is found all over the world and was introduced to North America from Europe in the mid-1800s. Like many moths in this family of nearly five hundred species, the male is much smaller than the female, often nearly half the size.

The best-known carpenterworm in North America is a species that most of us have only seen dead. Some people have even boasted about eating it. The species name is *Hipopta agavis,* best known as the "worm" in the bottom of a bottle of mescal, a Mexican liquor. Its common name is Agave Worm. This Cossidae, which feeds on the agave plant, apparently adds a certain flavor to this Mexican drink. The addition of the worm to this drink began as a test. The live worm was dropped into the mescal. If it was still wriggling by the time it reached the bottom, the spirits were safe to drink. The worm was, in effect, a canary in a coal mine.

LEOPARD MOTH *(ZEUZERA PYRINA)*

Incidentally, you will not find this larva in the bottom of an authentic bottle of tequila, which is produced only in the Mexican town of Tequila. This similar but different drink is often confused with mescal.

A common species native to the United States is the Carpenterworm Moth. This large insect has translucent brown wings that are webbed with darker brown markings. The female has a wingspan of more than three inches. The larvae are what lend this group their name of carpenterworm. The caterpillars, which can grow up to two and a half inches long, bore into the wood of living deciduous trees. Because the wood they eat is not high in nutrients, many of the species take an extra couple of years to develop. The larvae don't smell very good; at some point in their history with humans, their aroma has been likened to that of a goat, hence their other common name of goat moth. I don't know what a goat smells like, but the next time I come across a carpenterworm, I will sniff it and find out.

When they are ready to pupate, the larvae work themselves to the entrance of the hole they bored into the tree. The pupae can be found protruding from the holes in summer.

Sugaring for the adults is futile, because their mouthparts are useless. They do, however, come to lights.

Clear-winged Moths and Wasp Moths
(Family Sesiidae)

Wasp moths are mostly day-flying species that look nothing like a typical moth. They are small to medium sized and have thin, clear wings like those of the Hymenoptera (wasps, bees, et cetera), pinched "waists," and legs that dangle in flight. They look so much like wasps that I wonder if they scare each other. I remember one August afternoon when, while flipping leaves in search of slug caterpillar moth larvae, I came across what I thought was a thread-waisted Polistes wasp. It rested on a leaf that I was about to grab. I pulled my hand away and looked at the insect more closely. Something about it led me to believe it wasn't a wasp. Then I noticed the scales on the edges of the wings, the long, unsegmented antennae, and, most notably, the absence of chewing mandibles. It was a Banded Ash Clearwing Moth. Once I was positive it was a moth, I coaxed it to crawl onto my finger. Despite the fact that I knew I was holding a harmless Lepidoptera, the knot in my stomach revealed that I

believed otherwise.
Something deep in-
side me was still
being duped in the
same way that other
predators which
evolved alongside
stinging insects
would be.

These moths not
only look very much
like wasps, they buzz
like wasps, move
like wasps, and fly
like wasps. When

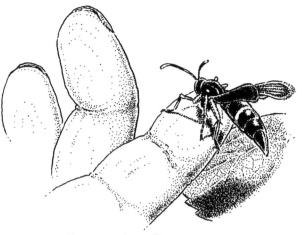

BANDED ASH CLEARWING
(PODOSESIA AUREOCINCTA)

threatened, some will move their abdomen into a stinging position. Fortunately, for anyone who encounters one of these insects, the most it
could do is "frass ya."

Most of the larvae in this family bore into the wood and roots of
trees. Some are considered pests. Many gardeners are familiar with the
Squash Vine Borer, which invades the stems of pumpkins, squash, and
the like, cutting off the nutrients to the fruit. The adult is a beautiful creature with a fiery red abdomen and bushy red legs. My wife grows squash
every year, but they're free of these moths. I secretly hope for a couple of
them and would be more than happy to replace any lost vegetables with
a trip to the grocery store.

Their pupae are naked and able to move through the tunnel made by
the caterpillar, an adaptation shared with the Hepialidae.

The best way to find clear-winged and wasp moths is by searching
flowers in the afternoon. They are active nectar sippers and can be distinguished from real wasps and bees by their use of a proboscis, which is not
present in the Hymenoptera. Pheromones are available commercially to attract a number of these species. Although this method is generally used to
remove the moths from an area where they are causing harm to a particular crop, you can also use the pheromones to call the moths to your yard.

The only Sesiidae I know of that comes to lights is the Maple Callus
Borer. This attractive little flylike moth with a bushy red tail appears in
early summer.

Ghost Moths and Swifts
(Family Hepialidae)

This family comprises the most primitive of the Lepidoptera. Most written accounts describing Hepialidae begin with the adjective "unusual" or "peculiar." In W. J. Holland's *The Moth Book*, first published in 1903, he wrote, "Some go even so far as to deny that they are lepidoptera at all. This is, however, an untenable position."

What's so unusual about these moths? For one thing, something called a jugum is present on the trailing edge of the forewing. This is a little fingerlike projection that helps hold the wings together in flight. It is not found in most moths, which instead have evolved a frenulum (which works like Velcro) for this purpose. Also, the venation of the fore- and hind wings is simple, a primitive characteristic. The arrangement of veins and the shape of the fore- and hind wings are similar, whereas in most moths, the fore- and hind wings are very different.

The Hepialidae range from medium to large in size and are often washed in shades of brown with silver, white, or black markings on the forewings. In the tropics they are found in a variety of pastel colors. They have very short antennae, a long, cigarlike abdomen, and long, narrow wings. The adults hold their wings tentlike over the abdomen. When at rest, the moths hang from their front two tarsi (foot segments), an unusual (there's that word again) position for a moth.

There are about five hundred species of ghost moths in the world. The common

SILVER-SPOTTED GHOST MOTH
(STHENOPSIS ARGENTEOMACULATUS)

name is possibly based on the European species *Hepialus humuli.* The male is silvery white and, like most ghost moths, it hovers, creating a ghostly appearance. In Europe, these moths are also called swifts in reference to their fast, swooping flight.

The females broadcast their eggs while in flight, sometimes by the many thousands, over grass and shrubs. In some species, the early instars consume fungus before molting into the tunneling root feeders that nearly all of the larvae become. In China, a species of ghost moth often has the misfortune of feeding on a fungus called *Cordyceps sinensis,* which thrives in the caterpillar's body and eventually kills it. The Chinese have made use of this parasitic relationship; Chinese caterpillar fungus is a popular herbal remedy for a number of ailments. The caterpillar is dried and sold along with its embedded fungus. The flavor has been described as sweet.

Ghost moths pupate within the tunnels made in the host plants during the larval stage. The pupae, covered with spines and serrated ridges, remain mobile. This allows them to work their way to the surface when they are ready to eclose.

Because their mouthparts are merely vestigial, the moths are not attracted to bait. They don't seem to respond to lights very often in my region, either, although single individuals have come to my lights on two occasions.

❧ 4 ❧

A Light in the Window

MY neighbor called me on the phone. "A friend of mine stopped by yesterday," she said. "She told me that she saw the man next door to me lurking behind a big glowing sheet on his lawn at one o'clock in the morning. She wanted to know if I was aware of this, and if there was something wrong with him."

There was no question who that man was. "What did you tell her?" I asked. She paused a moment. "I wasn't sure what to say," she answered. "I told her that I was pretty sure that nothing was wrong with you and I thought your being out there had something to do with bugs."

It occurred to me then that the purpose of the call was to satisfy my neighbor's curiosity, not her friend's. When I explained to her that she was right and that my "lurking behind a big glowing sheet" did have something to do with bugs—moths, actually—her response sounded polite yet somewhat concerned. I couldn't blame her. It *is* a curious sight. How do you tell the average person that this is what you do at night? You are supposed to be inside watching TV—or better yet, sleeping—when the hands of the clock swing around to that northeast grouping of numbers. But there are a few of us who are too restless to sit inside while the real show is happening outside our doors. We marvel at what the rest of the world is missing as the creatures of the night gather at our glowing invitation.

It has long been known that moths are attracted to light. We're all familiar with the expression "like a moth to a flame." How often do such acute biological observations get worked into our language? "Busy as a bee," "busy as a beaver," "lazy as a sloth." Sayings such as these suggest a familiarity with the animal with which one is being compared. "Dumb as an ox" tells me something about oxen: They probably don't do well at crossword puzzles. The fact that the moth made it to this list suggests that, at least subconsciously, we are paying attention to them. When we say "like a moth to a flame," we are describing an uncontrollable compulsion to fling ourselves into something that is not good for us. With regard to that particular behavior in many moths—and a great number of other insects, actually—the implication is right on the money.

In an old poem entitled "Cupid's Candle," Felix Carmen compared the moth's attraction to light to a man's attraction to love:

> Round her flaming heart they hover,
> Lured by loveliness they go
> Moth-like, every man a lover,
> Captive to its gleam and glow...

The poem goes on to compare a moth's fate when it reaches the flame to a man's when he succumbs to love. Whereas a man usually survives this encounter, for moths it is the ultimate fatal attraction.

Prehistoric men and women were most likely the first to observe a moth's penchant for flame. They were the first moth watchers. Of course, instead of comparing their fatalistic flight to primitive love, or admiring their unique beauty as they circled over their cook fire, these early humans probably just appreciated their crunchiness. Could this have been the dawn of the midnight snack?

Before electricity, entomologists set out candles to bring in their quarry. Or they wandered the dark woods with lanterns, nets, and traps. This worked, but to a lesser degree than do modern techniques. However, these researchers were not hampered by ambient light as we are.

The typical incandescent lightbulb brings in moths with some success. Just look up at the lifeless silhouettes in the globes of your ceiling lights or porch lights. The porch light is an ideal place to begin one's journey into the world of moths. On a summer night, a variety of species will circle or rest around the light. I sometimes get so wrapped up in looking at the moths in these places that I've been discovered lurking outside someone's front door before I got around to ringing the bell. The funny thing is that people usually come out to see what I was looking at before I go in. Many of them can't believe that they had been walking right past this display of creatures their whole life. Others just say, "Get inside. You're letting the bugs in."

The best way to attract moths is to use a black light or, even better, a mercury vapor light. Black lights, also known as ultraviolet lights, emit a greater spectrum of light, increasing the variety of "receivers," or moths. Remember high-school science and the acronym "ROY G. BIV," which lists the seven colors of the light spectrum? The light thrown off by a UV bulb begins after violet, at the end of "BIV," a place where our own visual capabilities end. Moths see lights that we do not. So do butterflies and who knows how many other creatures. There are colors in flowers we never see, which are seen by insects. By concentrating some of those colors at night, one can create an inescapable trap for moths. During the day, or in areas of ambient light, the lure is weakened. There's too much competition. Shine a flashlight in a lighted room and observe how that beam is washed out by the surrounding light.

Black light setup using a bug zapper with disabled electrifying grid

Mercury vapor light is produced by an electric arc within vaporized mercury trapped in a glass container. It has a different spectrum than black light, and it burns much brighter than any other available light. (Many streetlights use mercury vapor bulbs for that reason.) They can be expensive, though, and a single drop of rain can shatter the bulb.

There has been a lot of discussion on why moths are attracted to light. The consensus seems to hold that moths are not so much *attracted* to lights as they are *trapped* by them. The light becomes a sensory overload that disorients the insects and sends them into a holding pattern. A hypothesis called the Mach band theory suggests that moths see a dark area around a light source and head for it to escape the light. Another theory suggests that moths perceive the light emanating from a source as a diffuse halo with a dark spot in the center. The moths, attempting to escape the light, fly toward that imagined "portal," bringing them closer to the source. As they approach the light, their reference point changes and they circle the light in a hopeless spiral trying to reach the portal. Everyone is familiar with moths circling their porch lights. Their flight appears to have no purpose, but they are, it is believed, trying to *escape* the pull of the light.

Add to these theories the oldest of all—that moths use the light of stars and the moon to orient themselves when they are traveling. Moths migrate for a variety of reasons, and their eyes are very sensitive to light. Bear in mind that even where the moon is not visible, it is still out there. Although no moth that I know of has been able to reach the moon, moths do in effect accomplish this when they reach our lights. The lights are so bright that this accomplishment may actually be closer to that of reaching the sun. Moths have not evolved to deal with this; the advent of artificial illumination is relatively recent. But let's say a moth has accomplished the equivalent of reaching the sun. What do moths do in the bright light of the day? They come to rest, which is what is witnessed when we see them at our porch lights.

Perhaps all of these theories come into play at different times, or in combination, or perhaps they're all wrong. But whatever the reason, lights bring moths. For my light unit, I prefer using a bug zapper that has had the "zap" part of it disabled. This is just a matter of taking off the top of the *unplugged* unit, then snipping and closing off the transformer wires. It's a simple task, because the light and the electrified grid are usually on separate circuits. The idea of doing this came from Bob Muller, who has been watching moths for more than my lifetime. While camping in Florida, he had set up a mercury vapor light to see what moths were around. A raccoon knocked over the bulb, breaking it. So Bob set out to find a new one. Having no luck, he bought a bug zapper. He later came up with the idea of disconnecting the electrocuting grid to make it non-lethal. These units are built to be hung outdoors and can withstand wind and rain. The lights are ultraviolet; depending upon their size, they can cover an area up to a mile in diameter. Because most folks seem to find the zappers useless as mosquito killers, they can often be found at tag sales for a couple of bucks. (My wife, who usually comes across them, has stopped telling the tag-sale hosts why she buys the zappers. Some people just can't imagine why someone would want to attract bugs without the intention of killing them. Bugs are bad. They are the enemy.)

At the start of every mothing season, usually around March in the Northeast, I hang a light over a branch where the lawn meets the woods.

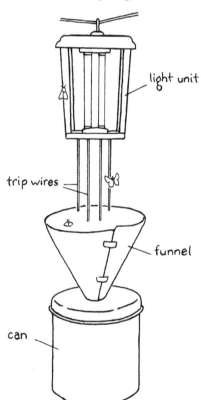

trip wires

light unit

funnel

can

HOMEMADE FUNNEL TRAP SETUP

Edges and trails are the best spots for bringing in moths, because they allow the light to travel unimpeded by too many trees while still drawing from the woods, where many of the moths are. Some larger moths actually follow trails, which is why you can easily find silk moth cocoons along roads and field edges.

Directly underneath the hanging light I place a bucket with a funnel poking through the lid. Inside the bucket are cardboard egg cartons for the moths to rest on. Without them, the moths would fly around and batter their wings. The last step is to hang some straight wires—in my case, straightened wire coat hangers clipped to about a foot in length—from the bottom of the light. I plug in the light when it gets dark. Here's what happens. The moths are drawn to the light. The sensory overload from the light causes them to circle the light frantically, trying to escape. The wires hanging from the bottom of the light "trip up" their wings. The moths fall into the funnel and into the bucket, where they find a safe place to rest within the egg cartons. The next morning, the well-rested moth watcher opens the lid to reveal a variety of captives. The moth watcher then revels in his cleverness, has a look at his quarry, and releases them.

You can buy commercial traps that do the same thing. Robinson Traps use a mercury vapor light protruding from the top of a metal bucket. They work beautifully. But I like to make my own for the same reason that some people prefer to build their own bluebird boxes or brew their own beer. Being more connected to the process makes the results so much sweeter.

One of the problems with this trap technique, however, is that it is indiscriminate. In my area, I have to stop using the funnel traps by mid-May because they attract June beetles as well as moths. It is quite disconcerting to open the bucket in the morning to find it half filled with a writhing mass of beetles. The moths are crushed from the sheer mass of beetles crawling all over one another. It is at this point that I put aside the funnel bucket to rely on my favorite method of bringing the moths to me: the infamous glowing sheet.

It always looks like laundry day in my yard. Betsy, God bless her, allows me to string up big white bedsheets on our property from March through December (sometimes all year). She knows that sometimes it's easier to placate an obsessed man than to fight him. But she enjoys what the sheets bring in, too . . . sometimes.

The hanging of the sheet is a ritual for me, the anticipation of which builds through the coldest winter months. It entails simply stringing a line about six feet off the ground between two trees, attaching the sheet with safety pins, and weighting down the bottom. I hang my light from a second line so it is resting in the upper middle area of the sheet. I plug in the light and wait for nightfall. The sheet has two advantages over the trap method. One, the light is bounced off the white surface of the sheet, which concentrates it in a big, square, glowing mass. Two, the sheet creates a landing pad for the moths. They are stirred up by the light, then settle on the sheet and often stay there until daybreak, or sometimes for days at a time. I try to avoid letting this happen, though. They have a life to live and shouldn't be wasting it sitting around on a big white sheet.

Indiscriminate Killers in Your Yard!

With the onset of summer, a host of fauna are spurred back into action. Although most are welcome, some are not, and one species in particular is downright dreaded: the mosquito. Our dislike for this insect is evident in all of those glowing blue lights we see hanging in our neighbors' yards. Bug zappers. You know it's summer when our yards are glowing and the sounds of the night are punctuated by the explosive sizzling of electrocuted insects.

But we have been duped. Although these devices are sold to rid our yards of these pests, they do nothing of the kind. Mosquitoes are not strongly attracted to light—ultraviolet, incandescent, mercury vapor, refrigerator light—none of it. They are attracted to body heat and to carbon dioxide exhaled by animals. What may be confusing us is that piled up at the bottom of these devices are insects that appear similar to mosquitoes. Nonbiting midges, which *are* lured to lights, are major victims of this attraction. A close look will reveal that these midges are missing the piercing proboscis of mosquitoes. I discovered this for myself many years ago when I had fallen prey to the hype. Going out to see how well the zapper had done its job through the night, I found in the bottom tray a pile of thousands of what I first thought were mosquitoes. It wasn't until I looked more closely that I realized there wasn't a mosquito in the bunch. They were all midges and a variety of other insects, including moths.

Once I've had a look at the night's quarry, I grab the end of the sheet and give it a good shake. The moths scatter in a silent cloud of powdery wings and come to rest on the surrounding vegetation. This presents many good opportunities for photography, because the moths are posing in a natural position upon living props.

Their lingering can cause a problem, however. It doesn't take long for the local birds to discover the ready meals waiting for them. Blue jays, tufted titmice, black-capped chickadees, and eastern wood-peewees arrive at first light, snapping up the moths. One year, an eastern phoebe built a nest fifteen feet from the sheet to shorten the distance of her morning sorties. Yellow jackets are an even bigger problem. Once they find the easy pickin's, they don't let up until all the smaller moths are gone. They hover in front of the sheet, shopping for just the right moth, then they land on it, sting it, and carry it off to their underground nest.

In one study, cited in an article by Erik Blom, only 31 of almost 14,000 insects killed by bug zappers were female mosquitoes (males don't bite). In another study, of 10,000 insects killed, 8 were mosquitoes. What bug zappers *do* attract are many insects that prey upon mosquitoes. In yet another study, nearly 2,000 of the dead insects were species that preyed upon mosquitoes. For every mosquito that got zapped, 250 mosquito predators were taken out of action.

Think of this: Throughout our history of battle with the mosquito, in which entomologists have been called upon for a solution, have you ever seen "authorities" employing bug zappers?

In addition to killing off mosquito predators with these zappers, we are killing off members of a group of important flower and tree pollinators— the moths. Over the years that I have been photodocumenting the moths of Connecticut, I have attracted to my yard more than 700 of the more than 2,300 species of moths in my state. I use a bug zapper in which I've disabled the electrifying grid by clipping and closing off the wires connected to it. Had it been working as the manufacturer intended, it would have killed tens of thousands of pollinating moths over the years. And that's just one zapper in one yard.

If you have one of these zappers, I urge you to unplug it. Continuing to run it will gain you the gratitude of the skeeters.

Bald-faced hornets, an "atypical" kind of yellow jacket, have a different approach. They grab the moth, bring it to a branch, snip off the wings with their mandibles, and carry the body back to their aboveground nest. Sometimes they remove the wings while in flight. I was able to track down a nest of bald-faced hornets by following a trail of wings. The nest was underneath the eave of my studio, and I dispatched it later that night. Yes, I play favorites.

Periodically, I move the sheet to a different location. This usually buys me a few weeks before the birds and insects work it into their feeding pattern. I also keep the light off for a few nights a week. Not only does it break the pattern of the hunting predators, it allows the moths in the area to go about their business without being disturbed.

A typical July nightly ritual might go like this. Commercial on TV. I announce to the family, or the dogs if everyone else is asleep, that it's time to "check the lobster traps." I put on my headlamp, grab three or four empty clear cassette cases, and head out the door. Immediately the sounds of the night—crickets, katydids, frogs—slap the lazy TV malaise from my senses and I'm wide awake. In the distance I see the sheet, glowing like some strange otherworldly apparition. As I get closer, I can make out shapes on the sheet. I'm looking for big shapes mostly. They are easier to look up in my books.

Already I can see one I know well. It's about three inches across and deep magenta with two round eyespots staring out from yellow-edged wings. These Promethea moths have been visiting for about a month now. When I get to the light, I stop and slip a finger underneath the resting moth. It grabs hold with its clawed tarsi as I slowly bring it closer to my face for a better look. A midge buzzes in my ear and I try to knock it loose with a raised shoulder. The Promethea lets go of my finger and flies, stiff-winged and sloppily, into the grass a few feet away. The light really messes up the larger moths' ability to fly. I pick up the moth and put it back on the sheet, making a mental note to get up early in the morning to move it into the woods. The blue jays found the sheet last week.

As I shine my light over the assortment of moths, I estimate about thirty different species. A moderate catch. About a sixth of them are "micromoths," ranging from the size of the capital "A" in this sentence to the length of a fingernail. Most have been, and probably always will be, unidentifiable from my perspective. Some people specialize in micromoths, but that kind of dedication is beyond my scope and abilities. That doesn't mean I don't look at them. It is easy to marvel at some of the beauty and detail in the tiniest of creatures, and I am learning to swallow my frustration at not being able to put the correct name on everything I see. Sometimes I give the regular moths names of my own. Instead of Unidentified Micromoth #1 and #2, I mentally refer to them as the Tiny Woodchip and the Ragged Grass Clipping.

Tonight on the sheet a Blinded Sphinx has made its first appearance. Its hind wings are hidden beneath a scalloped set of forewings, and I know why. Beneath those wings are a secret weapon saved for emergencies: each hind wing is marked with a very noticeable eyespot. I gently lift the wing for a peek. There they are, blue irises surrounded by a heavy black circle set on a pale raspberry base. A threatened moth would flash those eyespots, parting its forewings like lifting eyelids to startle a would-be predator. Big, staring eyes are scary things in nature.

I wonder, with these big beautiful eyes, why it is called the Blinded Sphinx. Could the name refer to its status at rest, when, in a way, the "eyes" are "closed"? Ruminations of the wee hours.

Through the sheet I see a shadow of something from the other side. It's about two feet off the ground and too large to be a moth. I know what it is; it has been there every evening for the last four nights. I'll go around to greet it in a minute or so, when I'm done inventorying this side.

Tonight, Eastern Tent Caterpillar Moths make up the majority of Lepidoptera on the sheet. Recently, there had been a hatch of them. Their numbers aren't too bad this year, so I don't mind them. Actually, in years when there are a lot of Eastern Tent Caterpillars, the cuckoo population is healthy. They are one of the few species of birds that can digest the hairy larvae. The hairs irritate the lining of the stomach of most other birds. A couple of Forest Tent Caterpillar Moths are also on the sheet. The Eastern is dark brown with two ochre lateral lines, whereas the Forest is ochre with two dark brown lateral lines.

A fair number of Pale Beauties have touched down on the sheet. These are delicate, translucent, pale green geometers with a white stripe running laterally through their wings. The moths are about the size of a Cabbage White butterfly. The Pale Beauties are the tiny angels of the moth world, more suited to that title than the moth that actually goes by the name "The Angel," which is also on the sheet this night. The Angel does have somewhat of an ephemeral look—it's a pale, creamy color—and its puffy legs are held stiffly on the sheet. The wings are jagged at the end, supposedly to give it the appearance of a ragged leaf. It has two clear little "windows" forming mock holes in the wings, perhaps to add to the illusion. I leave these moths where they are sitting, because I've photographed them in the past, and move on to one I haven't seen before. This is always exciting. I can't get over the fact that within a week in my own backyard, I can usually discover, and eventually identify, creatures I have never even heard of.

There is one lone representative of this new moth. It's sitting quietly, head pointing up, toward the outside edge of the sheet. Although it's only about the size of nickel, its wedge-shaped profile and heavy thorax suggest something in the Noctuidae, or owlet, family. The base color of the wings is dark gray, but it looks as though someone dipped a paintbrush in silver and swirled a rounded pattern across the wings. In the light of my headlamp, I notice a faint patch of pink toward the body. These markings are unusual, and I am sure I've never seen this moth before.

Now comes the tricky part. I reach into my pocket, pull out an empty cassette case, and open it with my thumb and fingertips. I slowly move it toward the waiting moth, like a gaping snake approaching a cricket. Then with a quick snap, I close it around the moth. Got it! The moth flutters within the clear confines of the case, which I put into my pocket. The darkness usually settles down a frantic moth.

A quick scan over the rest of that side of the sheet turns up nothing else new, and I walk to the other side. The shadow I saw earlier belongs to an American toad that has discovered an easy source of food. It crawls partway up the sheet and waits for a moth to land within striking distance. A short lunge, a nab, a swallow. Except for a pulsing throat, it's sitting motionless once again.

The other night, a young green frog was stationed at the bottom of the sheet. I would never have found it if I hadn't heard the hiccuppy gulp it made when it snapped up a moth. I've also come across wood frogs, pickerel frogs, spring peepers, and red-backed salamanders taking advantage of the table I've set for them. Because of all the amphibian activity at the sheet, I have made it a point to (1) watch where I step when I head out at night, and (2) wear shoes should I forget to implement Step 1.

One night, as I was concentrating on a caddisfly that had made its way to the sheet, something brushed against my calf. I let out a holler and jumped back, smack into a tree. When I looked down, I saw my cat, Jupiter, who seemed unfazed by my embarrassing display. That's the thing about doing this at night. There are all sorts of things flying and buzzing and hopping and scurrying around you, and the only ones you can actually *see* are sitting on the sheet. It's kind of exciting. There is nothing like having a giant water bug, also known as the Eastern Toebiter, come out of the darkness, buzzing like a three-and-a-half-inch hornet, and slam into your back. Or a two-and-a-half-inch-long fishfly, probably one of the sloppiest fliers on the planet, getting noisily tangled in your hair. They can give you a pretty good nip. Little midges fly in your ears and up your nose. I once felt something crawling up my leg and looked down to see a spring peeper working its way up to a better vantage point. One year I heard the leaves rustling on the other side of the sheet and assumed that the cat had gotten out again. I finished up surveying the first side of the sheet and walked around to check the other side. "What are you doing out here, Jupiter?" I said. I froze when I saw a mother raccoon teaching her two young how to pluck moths off the sheet. They looked at me calmly and walked away. One of the young had the wings of an Ilia Underwing poking out the sides of its mouth.

I've learned to avoid wearing a white shirt when I go out so I don't become an extension of the sheet when I stand close to the light. I've gotten so I don't mind critters landing and crawling on me while I'm outside, but I like to avoid having them hitch a ride into the house. Many's the time I've been sitting on the couch after one of my forays only to have a bug fly out of my hair. If I don't catch it and let it out, I have to spend the rest of the night listening to the cats crashing into things around the house as they go after it.

Both sides of the sheet this night hold a number of the same moths; Eastern Tent Caterpillar Moths and Pale Beauties make up the majority. Two Painted Lichen Moths, looking like a pair of black and red glue-on fingernails, are mating in the corner of the other side of the sheet. They are attractive little moths and not too difficult to raise from eggs. If I were to put them in a brown paper bag, there's a good chance that one of them would lay tiny yellow eggs on the side. Their dark, spiky larvae feed on the lichen that grows on the trees from which the sheet is hanging.

Vagabond Crambuses are scattered here and there on both sides of the sheet. These Pyrallids hold their pale wings rolled over their body. They are about the size and shape of the rolled-up paper found in a fortune cookie. I call them Lawnmower Moths because they are among the little white moths that fly up from the grass when you mow your lawn. At first glance, there is nothing remarkable about them. But don't trust that first glance. Next time you see one of those little moths fly up from the grass, watch where it lands. Then drop to your knees and get very close to it. If it is the Vagabond Crambus, you will notice a gold band at the very end of its rolled wings. The moth looks as though it was dipped in pure molten gold that "beaded up" where it settled as it cooled.

Another moth catches my attention. A Beautiful Wood Nymph! These owlets are purple and yellow with a heavy white band running down the wing. The moths are supposed to resemble bird droppings. And they do, but they are the most beautiful scat I've ever laid eyes on. Perhaps they're disguised as droppings of birds that have fed on grapes, which is one of the plants the larvae of this species feed upon. The moths rest with their two front legs stretched out in front of them. The legs are covered with dense fur, giving them the appearance of long pantaloons.

But there is something a little off with this one. It's kind of small. Could it be the *Pearly* Wood Nymph? A friend had e-mailed me a week ago to tell me he had a Pearly Wood Nymph at his light station (a light station being the place where you set up your light). I was jealous, never having seen this moth before but familiar with it from photos. I snatched up the moth in my cassette case and head back to the house.

On the coffee table in front of my couch, I have stacked every moth book I own. The most-used book, *A Field Guide to the Moths of Eastern North America*, by Charles Covell, Jr., is so beat up that the catocala pages are falling out of it. This is the reference I go to first. I start with the easier of the two moths, the Wood Nymph-like one. I open up the plate that has both the Beautiful and Pearly Wood Nymphs on it and hold the cassette, in which the moth is calmly resting, over the pictures. I have a match. It *is* a Pearly Wood Nymph! "YES!" I shout. I take the cassette and run upstairs to show my wife. As I go past the clock on the wall, I notice it is 12:15 A.M. Betsy told me that I'm no longer allowed to wake her up to show her moths. But I'm busting! Oh well, it'll have to wait.

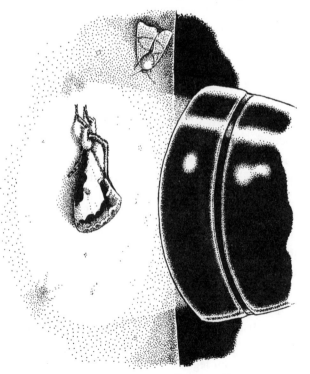

NEW MOTH FOR THE YARD LIST—PEARLY WOOD NYMPH

I've gotten into the habit of making a sketch next to my notation of the moth. This helps me later when I go through my slides. The act of drawing the moth helps commit it to memory. I sketch the Pearly Wood Nymph and put the moth in the refrigerator. This keeps it from fluttering around and exhausting itself. As far as I know, it doesn't harm the insect; the conditions are no different from that of a chilly night. I will photograph the moth later that night. I have to admit that sometimes I forget, or just get too lazy, to photograph it, so the moth remains in the refrigerator until morning. I have to smile at the thought that my kids think it's normal to find live moths next to the milk and eggs.

It's time to move on to the next moth. I study it closely in the cassette and flip through the pages of similar-looking moths. On plate thirty-one in Covell's guide I find something that resembles it. I hold the moth over the picture and, "YES!" Another match!

It's a *Paectes oculatrix,* or Eyed Paectes. Once I have an ID and have made my sketch, I like to learn as much as I can about a species. According to the Peterson guide, the Eyed Paectes feeds on poison ivy. That's a point in its favor. This is confirmed in the book *Arthropods of Florida.* Another book, *Cutworm Moths of Ontario,* calls it uncommon, as does Holland's *The Moth Book.* I find it also in *Papillons du Quebec,* a guide to butterflies and moths by Louis Handfield. Under *Paectes oculatrix* it says, "*Lieux secs et lieux rocheux ou sablonneux en general. . . .*" I must be getting tired, because none of this is making sense. Then it occurs to me that it's in French, and I don't speak French. Onward I move.

In a reverse search on poison ivy I find mention of Eyed Paectes in John Eastman's *Forest and Thicket* as a "dull brown moth whose caterpillar feeds on poison ivy," along with another owlet caterpillar, the *Marathyssa basalis,* or Light Marathyssa. I look for a picture of *Marathyssa basalis* in my Peterson guide. It's an interesting-looking moth with a distinct pattern; however, it is not as common as the *Dark* Marathyssa, which feeds on staghorn sumac. Because sumac doesn't grow in my area, the poison ivy eater is probably the moth I have. Now that I've somewhat familiarized myself with it, I may be able to pick it out in a lineup.

Tomorrow night, and perhaps the next, I will not run the light. I feel it is important to allow the insects in the area time to go about their business undisturbed. Within the course of a month, the light is probably burning about two weeks—sometimes more, sometimes less. I don't think I'm missing anything on those nights when it's off. I often go out with a flashlight to check what is nectaring at the flowers. Or I'll paint some trees, an act that not only is less disruptive to the moths' busy schedules but actually helps them out with an easy meal. And if a few species slip by me in the dark, who cares? This is supposed to be fun. If it becomes an obligation, I'm quitting.

These are the roads I travel at night. One moth leads to another, which leads to another. On some nights I share the experience with friends. We set up our lights, paint some trees, sit in lawn chairs, drink beer, hoot for owls, and talk about everything under the stars. Somehow beer and moth watching go together, an observation I have made both on my own and in being out with other lepidopterists. Every once in a while we check for a good moth. If something of interest shows up, we comment on its finer points, take turns photographing it, then return to the lawn chairs. In the first chapter, "On the Moth Trail," I used the analogy of "fishing" for moths with a flashlight. I can't help comparing the two. Half the fun of fishing, for a lot of people, is sitting in the boat and chewing the fat. Catching a fish is almost an inconvenience, but it's what got you out there, so you rebait the hook.

What makes mothing even more appealing is that I can do it anywhere I go. I have a rechargeable battery to run a portable black light that I bought from a biological supply company. I've hung a sheet in nearly every state I've visited—in the woods, on the beach, even outside my hotel room (after a bit of explaining first). Even without the battery, I can sample areas far from electricity, which is the best place to find moths. The black light can be plugged into the cigarette lighter outlet in any car. I can pull up to a patch of woods, drape a sheet over the window, and plug in my light. At times it brings in big mammals, namely Hominids. They give in to their curiosity to ask me what the hell I'm doing. I explain to them that I am trying to bring bugs closer to me and invite them to have a look. Most of the time they think it's pretty cool.

For me there are fewer joys more satisfying than pulling up to a patch of dark and setting out my beacon. The possibilities of what it can bring in are endless. It's ironic in that I abhor light pollution. But if there is a light on the side of the road or the side of a building, I'm drawn to it like the moths that have no choice. It appears I've begun to take on the trait for which they are so well known.

✺ 5 ✺

Seasons of the Moth

Spring sugaring's over;
The sallows are done;
The aspen's young leaves
Shimmer gold in the sun:
Sing hey, then, for ova;
Ichneumons forestall—
Camelina, palpina, dictaea and all!

The oaks in the forest
Are emerald hued;
The grass-stems at dawn are
With spangles bedewed:
Sing hey for the larvae
That on the tray fall—
Croceago, quercana, P. ridens and all!

High summer is tempered
With westerly breeze,
And sugar appears on
The trunks of the trees:
Sing hey for the moths that

Respond to its call—
Pyralina, ypsilon, promissa and all!

Now evenings are shorter;
The goatsucker's gone;
The leaves of the birches
Are yellow and wan:
Sing hey, then, for pupae,
Both great ones and small—
Carmelita, orion, T. munda and all!

— P. B. M. Allan, from Talking of Moths, *1943*

WE place a lot of importance on calendars. We rely upon them to compartmentalize our lives—lives that were meant to advance outside of the boxes that calendars put them into. But calendars carry our history and our future. They bring order and expectation. And they are solely a human thing. It is we who turned solar revolutions into years, lunar cycles into months, religious tradition into weeks, and the Earth's rotations into days. As far as the rest of nature is concerned, there are just four time periods, and they are divided into categories of cold and icy; wet and buggy; warm and lush; and cool and fruity. Between the peaks of those periods are times of transition, often used for moving between one and another.

It is anticipation of the next season that has rooted me in New England. I love the crisp, clean air of winter, the newness of spring, the lushness of summer, and the colors and smells of autumn. However, at the end of winter, I am tired of the snow and cold. At the end of spring, I am tired of the rain and blackflies. As summer draws to a close, I am ready for respite from the heat. And late autumn, once the leaves have fallen, can be a time of gray emptiness. These feelings make the upcoming seasons all the more welcome. Think back to how miserable you felt the last time you had the flu. Then recall how alive you felt the first day it lifted. Seasons allow us to experience this for weeks at a time four times a year, year after year, throughout our lives.

Naturalists mark the seasons in a number of ways. Each season holds a return of nature's fauna and flora that had been absent. Migrating birds pass through, flowers bloom, trees bear fruit. Fish migrate to different bodies of water, frogs trill, mushrooms sprout, woodchucks whistle, katydids chirp, and snow fleas leap. We have a general idea of when they will leave and a general idea of when they will return. And when they do, they are welcomed back as long-lost friends.

For me, the calendar begins in March. This can probably be attributed to my weariness with winter at this time. Of all the seasons, winter wears thin the quickest. This is coupled with the fact that spring brings about the most dramatic change—an explosion of nature and natural phenomenon in my area. On the first few warm, rainy nights of March, we can witness the migration of the spotted salamander as thousands of them travel to vernal pools, often before the snow has melted. Those who are there to see them become more than witnesses, as we too have migrated from our cozy, dry homes to these vernal pools, often helping the amphibians cross the roads where passing cars pose a threat. A daytime search of these pools may reveal the ephemeral fairy shrimp, which dance in the sunlight filtered through the surrounding trees. Spring peepers and wood frogs fill the damp nights with their calls, nights whose silence until then had been broken only by the occasional hooting of an owl or howling of coyotes.

The spring ephemerals, holdovers from the Ice Age, bloom in our forests while crocuses and snowdrops push up from the ground along the edges of our yards. Red-winged blackbirds, the earliest passerine migrants, are filling marshes with their harsh song, "conk-o-reee." Mourning Cloak butterflies float over the mostly barren ground, stopping to sip nutrients from the mud and, if available, the "leavings" of our dogs.

And the moths awaken. Finally! Enough of them to justify setting up my light sheet.

March is the month of the sallow. The Mustard, Straight-toothed, Morrison's, Chosen, Figure Eight, Grote's, and my favorite, the Fawn Sallow, are among the moths that kick off the season in my area. These are Noctuids, those heavy, fuzzy, buffalo-backed, triangular moths also known as owlets. The sallows are in the Noctuidae subfamily of Cuculliinae and derive their common name from the English moths known as sallows, whose caterpillars feed on willow. Sallow is a derivation of the Latin *salix*, meaning willow. Some of the sallows are straw colored, a hue that could be described as sallow, but I believe that is more of a coincidence. One trait they all share, besides their early awakening, is two pairs of "eyelashes," one set in front of the eyes and one set behind. This gives a number of them somewhat of a doe-eyed look.

Sallows are able to get a jump on the season because they overwinter as adults. They ride out the freezing weather in the crevices of trees, under bark, in woodpiles, and beneath shingles. They have a robust look, which I suppose is not surprising, since they are able to survive what winter throws at them. One may wonder what a moth may find to feed on at the onset of spring. Virtually nothing is blooming in the evening, when they are active; yet they have evolved working mouthparts, which must be good for something! The answer to that question has long been known by maple sugar farmers, who find these moths in and around their sugar buckets. The sap is flowing in the maples, beeches, and birches at this time of year, and nature, including humans, has provided a number of ways for a moth to get at it. Broken branches and, to some extent, woodpeckers leave exits for the sap, which the moths are able to home in on. Because the moths at this time of year are "sapsuckers," sugaring can be fruitful and can attract a number of species that may not be lured by lights.

I mentioned the Fawn Sallow as my favorite March moth. It truly is fawnlike in color and, in a way, texture. It is covered with soft orange-brown scales with white markings and has big, doelike lashes over its eyes. Whereas many late-winter moths are the color of wet tree bark, which makes sense considering their habitat at this time of year, the Fawn Sallow stands out as crisp and dry. Upon observing this moth, I am left with the feeling it is sending the message that winter is ending and it's safe to come out and show yourself. Although I am greeted by other sallows earlier in the month and am thrilled to be seeing them for the first time, I do not see the light at the end of winter's tunnel until I come across the Fawn Sallow.

Then comes April, a month in search of itself. One day you could be basking in eighty-degree weather, and the next you're digging your car out of a foot of snow. But whereas March held just a promise of spring, April is truly the end of winter. You cannot have winter and hear pine warblers trilling in the trees and phoebe beaks snapping midges from the air. You cannot have winter and hear American toads trilling in the woods and see plumes of blooming forsythia and beds of lemon-colored daffodils. Butterflies such as American Ladies, Red Admirals, and Eastern

Commas are growing in number, having overwintered as adults and migrated north. More notably, some butterflies have emerged from their chrysalids, a more risky endeavor because they don't have the hardy makeup of their overwintering cousins. Spring Azures—little blue flakes of sky—and the more solemn Juvenal's Duskywings have evolved to survive that risk and are on the wing.

The moths are growing both in number and variety. Whereas the month of March belonged to the sallows, April belongs to the quakers, pinions, woodgrains, The Scribbler, and the Lappet Moth. The quakers and woodgrains are in the subfamily Hadenininae. Like the sallows, they are Noctuids but are distinct in that hair covers their eyes. Two different woodgrains come to my lights, the Confused and the Bicolored. They both look like dark splinters of wood with the grain running along the length of their wings. They are more tapered than the triangular quakers and could easily be mistaken for a broken twig. In shape and color, the quakers look much like the sallows: compact, furry triangles, earthy in color. I've recorded seven species in my yard between February and October. Both the early and late appearance is evidence of their spending the winter as adults. The pinions, related to the sallows, are similar in appearance to the woodgrains but larger, and they're more streamlined than the sallows and quakers, with "woody" patterns and colors.

My two favorite moths at this time of year could not look any more different from each other: the Lappet Moth and The Scribbler. One is a sedate, rusty tuft of fur; the other is a lively, finely etched green, black, and white geometer. I call them Mutt and Jeff. They appear at the same time each year, almost to the day. That, and their shared food preference of alder, birch, and willow, is about all they have in common.

Lappet moths are Lasiocampids, in the same family as the Eastern Tent Caterpillar Moths, with which we are all familiar. Lappets remind me

LAPPET MOTH
(*PHYLLODESMA AMERICANA*)

of sleepy brown buffalo; I find them clinging to the sheet in the morning. They have an odd way of resting, with their scalloped hind wings drooping beneath their forewings. When approached, they drop to the ground, seemingly lifeless, and stay there a long time. Finally, they seem to sense that danger has past and they crawl into the leaf litter to await nightfall.

The Scribbler is more dashing in appearance, with butterfly proportions, a trait shared by most geometers. Marked with alternating pale olive, white, and black etchings, it probably evolved to blend in with the lichens, but it stands out in the crowd at the moth sheet. Unlike the Lappet Moth, it takes off in the air when approached, although I can occasionally get one to perch on my fingertip.

May is spring and everything we associate with that season. At long last, the trees are green with leaf and filled with neotropical bird migrants such as the warblers, vireos, and tanagers. May is the month of the highest bird density in Connecticut. The familiar "teecha-teecha-teecha" of ovenbirds greets me in the morning, and the ringing "ee-o-laaaayy" of wood thrushes ends the day.

Sulphur-winged locusts return to my meadow, taking buzzy flight in advance of my footsteps. Six-spotted tiger beetles, in their polished green armor, hunt for insects in the shadowy edges of my woods. Pools of water are filled with the tadpoles of wood frogs, spring peepers, and American toads. Green frogs are strumming their banjos along the edges. The spring field crickets are chirping again.

One long-awaited moth is expected to make its appearance any night now. Almost everyone knows the moth by sight. It is one whose arrival I am obligated to share with friends who would not otherwise get to see it because they live in areas where its numbers have been diminished.

But while I am waiting for this moth, others are arriving in droves. Some nights the light sheet is literally covered with insects. One of the more common groups is the eupithecias. These tiny, indistinct geometers have long wings that are held perpendicularly from their sides and flat against the surface, forming little brown Ts. The plagodis moths are also appearing. I get five different species of these wavy-winged geometers; the most attractive, the Lemon Plagodis, is also the most common. This moth is a crisp lemony yellow with a heavy wash of pink on the forewings. Sharing these rich colors are the first silk moths to arrive, the Rosy Maple Moths. These fuzzy-bodied insects are covered in yellow and raspberry pink. Even the legs are pink. Sometimes they cross their front legs at rest, giving them a regal feline look. I always thought they looked delicious and couldn't put my finger on why. Then one morning my daughter blurted out that they looked like sherbet. That was it! From then on, I called them Rosy Sherbet Moths.

The Rosy Sherbets have always been special to me, because I credit them with introducing me to the joys of watching moths. I remember seeing one on my screen door many years ago and being so taken by its appearance that I had to know what it was. I drove to the library that day and found it in a book on insects. It was the first moth I'd ever looked up. While flipping through the pages, I got a taste of what else could be found out there. I was hooked.

May is also when the Zales reappear. Six different species of these broad-winged Noctuids arrive, including the Colorful Zale, a scallop-winged chunk of bark with pumpkin orange patches flashing between washes of cream and brown.

During the day, you may be lucky enough to come across a Grape-vine Epimenis. These day-flying Noctuids resemble butterflies. Their upper wings show a flash of white on a dark background, and their hind wings are a stunning cherry red. I also see among the low flowers Common Spring Moths, little black moths with large white patches. Or are they little white moths with black borders? They gather in the sunlight along woodland trails.

Night after night, more species of moths make their appearance. Night after night, I make notes of what showed up and take pictures of those I may have missed the season before. But I am still waiting for the big one. The one that says of the season there is no turning back.

Then, often following a particularly warm spell, I see it. I can tell what it is from the moment the sheet comes into view. Its silhouette is unmistakable, a two-tailed manta ray dwarfing all the insects around it. The Lunas have awakened.

The Luna Moth does something to me. It hits me deep down in a place where I accept the existence of magical things. Its magic is evident in how it affects me and others who see it. Its beauty is ethereal and its nature ephemeral; it doesn't live much past a week or two. It emerges from its cocoon in the leaf litter, then mates and lays eggs within the first forty-eight hours. Then it has the rest of its nights with nothing to do. No purpose. It doesn't eat. It doesn't drink. All its energy comes from the

Luna Moth recognized
on opposite side of sheet

leaves it ate as a caterpillar. That energy is finite and cannot be replenished. It is like a toy airplane powered by a twisted rubber band. Once the rubber band unwinds, the propeller stops turning and the plane falls to the ground.

The Luna Moths continue to appear in my area through the month of June. June is like a seventeenth birthday, right in between two milestones. Turning sixteen is spring. Turning eighteen is summer. The black-flies have ceased their irritating swarming about our faces, and the mosquitoes are not yet in full force. The deerflies, however, occupy the niche of biting pests, allowing us to be grateful of the benefit of screens. At this time of year, the bird migration has ended, leaving behind those that chose to nest in the area. The wildflowers are rising in forest and meadow and filling up butterflies with their nectar. The folded-winged skippers, sparrows of the butterfly world, are skimming across the tops of the tall grass.

At the moth sheet, the sphinx moths rule. Also called hawk moths, these members of the Sphingidae family are the fastest fliers in the lepidopteran world. They also have representatives of their family in the air from morning to night. Hummingbird Moths and Snowberry Clearwings, resembling, respectively, hummingbirds and bumblebees, sip from flowers during the day. If you are a defenseless moth out in the sunlight, it would behoove you to look like anything but a moth, and they do. In the evening a number of the sphinxes are found hovering at the flowers, their long proboscises dipping into the stores of nectar. One of the larger moths I find is the Waved Sphinx. With a wingspan of nearly four inches, it is often mistaken for a small bat. It is one of the more common hawk moths wherever it occurs. Larger yet is the dusk-flying Carolina Sphinx, better known as the Tobacco Hornworm, whose caterpillar is notorious for eating tomato plants down to the ground. The Carolina Sphinx has a wingspan of up to four and a half inches. The big daddy is the Poplar Sphinx, with a wingspan of four and three-quarter inches. Like the Luna Moth, this silvery giant of the river bottomlands does not feed as an adult.

Luna Moths, although still present in small numbers into July, begin to peter out by the end of June. They are replaced by the Promethea, Polyphemus, and Cecropia Moths. The Prometheas emerge from their cocoons at dusk and, like most Saturniids, rely on stored energy gathered as caterpillars. They are the color of a stormy twilight sky, deep magenta with a bolt of white lightning crackling down the wings. I come across these moths with great regularity, because they favor sassafras, which grows in my region.

The Polyphemus Moths are rarer in my parts, but when I am fortunate enough to see them, it is at this time of year. From wing tip to wing tip, they can measure nearly six inches. They are unmistakable, with their four eye-shaped windows shining through their great tawny wings.

The Cecropia Moths, with their six-inch wingspan, are the largest Lepidoptera in North America. This distinction goes to the female of the species, which can be nearly twice the size of the male. The female calls in the wee hours of the morning, making it difficult for most people to witness these moths in flight, but I have seen it. With each downbeat of their powerful wings, their heavy body is lifted to the apex of its length, which then drops with the opposite stroke. The strokes are slow and deliberate for a moth due to the great surface area of the wings.

Although silk moths admittedly steal the show in June, the little emeralds hold their own. Members of this aptly named group of Geometrids aren't much wider than a guitar pick and range in color from lettuce green to pistachio. In fact, one of their group is called the Pistachio Emerald. It is among the smallest of the Geometrinae, the group comprising the emeralds, but that diminished size seems to have concentrated its color.

Then there are the Hypeninae, or Bomolochas. These brown-and-gray flying triangles are sometimes referred to as deltoids because of their shape. Blow one up in size and it would have fit neatly atop Ben Franklin's three-cornered hat. One of the characteristics that sets these moths apart from others is their overly long labial palps. These are sensory appendages that project from beneath the head and in this group are nearly twice the length of the head. I also just like saying the word

"Bomolocha." It's even more fun to say when you touch your fingers to your thumb and shake your hand in the air like a pizza man.

In my backyard I get the Flowing-line, Baltimore, Dimorphic, White-lined, Mottled, and Deceptive Bomolocha. I should say that I *think* I get the last one.

June also brings out the tussock moths, the furry kittens of the moth world. At rest, their hairy legs point in six directions. They remind me of winged wolf spiders. The tussock, or Lymantriid, moths have in their family a black sheep. The Gypsy Moth, introduced from Eurasia, has stirred up all sorts of trouble since its introduction to America. I go into more detail on this species in Chapter Six.

In the words of Gaylord Johnson in his 1926 book *Nature's Program*, "In July the year is full grown, lusty." Johnson takes us through each month with high-spirited prose describing what makes that time of year special to him. Of this midsummer month, he writes:

> In July, the true aim of all the spring outburst of greenery and blossoms becomes apparent. Look at the branches of the dogwood tree that was a mass of white in May, and you will find the little green seed vessels. Look among the leaves of last April's violet bed at the edge of the thicket, and you will find tiny pods filled with hard little seeds. Look at your trousers or golf stockings when you come home from your walks and you will have to pick out the burrs and the little barbed and hooked seeds, the "seed tramps" which have stolen a ride with you, hoping to be dropped again upon ground far from where they grew.

Although my golf stockings have been replaced with tube socks, I think he nailed it. July is, in essence, the apex.

It is also the season of highest insect density. The birdcalls have been replaced by the drone of mosquitoes, bees, wasps, flies, and all manner of buzzy-winged Diptera and Hymenoptera. The butterflies are peaking; because of this, July is the month chosen to census their populations. The crickets are going full tilt, the song of the spring field crickets having been joined by those of the Carolina and striped ground crickets.

As far as the moths go, July is a continuation of June. Many of those I saw the previous month are now regulars. Some are looking a bit dog-eared. Lepidopterists refer to them as "rags." Some are freshly emerged offspring of moths seen earlier in the season. A number of moths go through several broods every year and disappear and reappear from spring to fall.

One group of moths that thrives at this time of year is the Arctiidae. These include the tiger, lichen, tussock, and Ctenucha Moths. In my yard alone I have come across eighteen species of this colorful family in the month of July. Many species in this family are toxic as adults. The bold and bright coloration is a warning to predators to stay away. Some of the Arctiids take their advertising a bit further and emit high-frequency sounds to ward off bats. Those sounds identify the moths as the distasteful Arctiids, which bats learn to associate with insects best left alone. Some of the nontoxic moths mimic the sounds of their unpalatable cousins, putting one over on the bats.

However, that said, I have found tiger moth wings on the ground, suggesting they don't taste all that bad, at least to some birds. I've also read of a man who was hand-feeding them to a flycatcher that was lingering in his light trap area, as they often do. The bird kept coming back for more and didn't seem the worse for it.

Three of the most striking members of this family are the similar-looking Banded, Nais, and Virgin Tiger Moths. All three are tapered triangles, their black wings laced with heavy pale orange webbing. Their underwings range from deep salmon to ochre and are the clue to telling the difference among them. The Banded Tiger is by far the most common. I also see an explosion of the Clymene Moth at this time of year. That's another word I like to pronounce: "Clie-*meenie*." These tigers fly day and night. The first time I saw one was while leading a butterfly trip. There were two, actually, and they were resting on a hosta leaf. Each was about an inch long and had a creamy jack-in-the-pulpit-shaped pattern on the upper wing surrounded by a rich, chocolatey brown. The exposed underwings were a pale orange that extended onto the back. I got so excited I shot an entire roll of film of them, leaving myself with no way to photograph anything for the rest of the day. Later that night, they were all over my light sheet.

Within the family Arctiidae are the lichen moths. One of them, the Painted Lichen Moth, is very common. It is about the size of a long pinkie fingernail and is streaked with scarlet and black. I once was able to gather eggs from a pair. The eggs hatched into the tiniest, fuzzy black caterpillars I'd ever seen. Throughout the rest of the season, I fed them lichen growing from the trees in my yard. They ate, and ate, and ate . . . but never changed. November came around, and they were still caterpillars. What was going on? I mentioned this to a friend, who reminded me that these were Arctiids, and many larvae in this family overwinter as caterpillars. Of course! They were not due to pupate until spring.

Another Arctiid found this time of the month is the Isabella Moth, which is best known by the caterpillar, the Woolly Bear. It is often the case that the more interesting the caterpillar, the duller the adult, but the Isabella is an exception. The adult, with a wingspan of up to two and a half inches, is subtly attractive. The forewings are the color of parchment etched with soft brown lines. They cover underwings that are a wash of pink and yellow, reminders of the rewards of looking beyond (or beneath) the surface of things.

Now we enter the dog days of summer, August. The air is heavy and filled with the ceaseless ringing of cicadas. It is a sound so incessant that it becomes part of us. The nights, too, are charged with endless sound, although from different creatures entirely: the crickets, coneheads, and katydids. The crickets call from the ground with a variety of trills, chips, and "tinks." The coneheads, dunce-capped relatives of the diurnal grasshoppers, buzz loudly from the tall grass. They are surrounded by the arboreal katydids, which scratch, tick, and lisp from the trees and shrubs.

Late in the day, common nighthawks are booming high in the air. They have begun their southern migration. Young pickerel frogs streak through the grass, avoiding the roaring lawnmower. New England aster and joe-pye weed are well in bloom, acting as way stations for migrating butterflies such as the Monarchs, which will begin their long, southward journey at the end of the month.

We have, at last, entered catocala season. There is such a thing, at least among lepidopterists. Why do these moths get such attention? For one thing, their underwings have such bold and colorful patterns that they have become the moths' common name, "underwings." They also form one of the largest genera in the Lepidoptera world, giving scientists nearly endless material to work with, new discoveries to make, and puzzles to solve. Perhaps, though, it is the method of capture that lures admirers. There is great satisfaction in laying out sugar bait and watching these creatures come in for a drink. It gets you out in the woods at the cusp of the year, a time when nature is heavy and ripe. As you go from tree to baited tree, you are enveloped in the sounds and smells of the underwing world and you wonder why you don't spend more time among them. There is a tactile element, too. The leaves and branches are pushing into the narrow woodland trails, brushing against you as they do the wings of the catocala.

Although some of the underwings begin to appear in July, the month of August holds the greatest number and diversity of this group. In my town of Killingworth, I have recorded twenty-one species, fifteen of those in August. Only twice have I come across my favorite, *Catocala relicta*, or the White Underwing. If you were to peel off a wedge of bark from a white birch, you would have the twin of this moth. The White Underwing, also known as the Forsaken Underwing, is a northern species whose larvae feed on poplars and trembling aspen. It spends its day resting upon white birches and other light-colored trees, where it is virtually invisible. Its underwings are jet black with white bands.

It is this moth's scarceness, and its resemblance to my favorite tree, the birch, that make it so appealing to me. It is the rare white tiger in my parts, and yet common enough for me to have seen it twice. It has not spoiled me, as have many other creatures of the day and night that I sometimes take for granted. A sighting is always possible but happens too infrequently to be expected. And the unexpected keeps things interesting.

As far as birches go, I see them as symbols of the northern forests. A birch grove is an enchanted place, transporting me back to the days of my ancestors who lived among them. They are bright, crisp shards of light in a green and golden forest, and any creature that lives among them, that *is* them, carries a piece of that magic. That's what moths are to me. Yes, they are biological creatures subject to the laws of the universe, but

WHITE UNDERWING

if that's all they were, I wouldn't be so interested in them. The White Underwing epitomizes that sentiment as no other moth has been able to do.

Until September.

The ninth month awakens another moth that brings a smile to my face the first time it appears. Summer is near an end and I am glad. The hawks have begun migrating along the coast, heading south for the winter. They are concentrated at Lighthouse Point in New Haven, Connecticut; many people make pilgrimages there to watch them on their way. At this place, too, Monarch butterflies are on the move, beginning their three-thousand-mile journey down to Mexico. None will return, but their offspring's offspring will the following spring.

Among the late season blooms are the Cabbage Loopers, flapping madly from flower to flower. Often mistaken for skipper butterflies, the cabbage loopers have wings with little fish-shaped white "stigmas" that look painted on. At rest they look like battleships.

I'm seeing a lot of darts at the light sheet now; of the nineteen that come to my yard, thirteen are with me this month, five of them having just arrived. Darts are members of the fuzzy, buffalo-backed owlet family and are in the subfamily Noctuinae. They are generally unremarkable brownish moths with a variety of woody patterns. They are somewhat the shape of arrow fletching and hold their wings tentlike over their body. Some have names such as Old Man Dart and Venerable Dart, making me wonder whether their namers were attributing to them some kind of wisdom. Other names, such as the Flame-shouldered Dart and Fillet Dart, awaken memories of summer barbecues. Then there are the Smith and Norman Darts, named after a couple of long-gone entomologists.

The dart, regardless of the species, is a moth's moth. It ain't fancy. It ain't flashy. It is a robust, steady-flying insect that takes a beating and keeps at it. I have seen these moths worn well beyond recognition, to the point where I wondered how they got where they were, the moon glinting off their now-bald thoraxes, wings practically beaten to stubs. On the rainiest of nights I see them. In late winter under snow-covered boughs I see them. They are the Labrador retrievers of the moth world, dependable and seemingly unstoppable.

September is also the slug caterpillar moth caterpillar season. The larvae of the moths in this family, Limacodidae, are legless, colorful buttons often covered in a varying array of spines. They feed beneath the

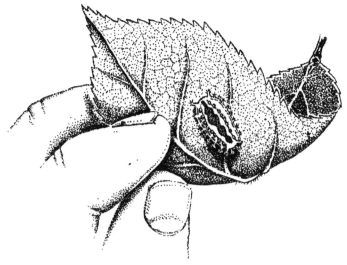

LEAF FLIPPIN' FOR SLUG CATERPILLAR MOTH CATERPILLARS
REVEALS AN *ADONETA SPINULOIDES*

leaves of deciduous trees, sliding along on a sluglike foot. They are the oddities of the caterpillar world, and every season several of us go out looking for them. Finding these creatures involves flipping over the leaves of hickories, cherries, maples, and oaks. It's a game of lepidopteran peek-aboo. Some years we've been able to find up to five different species in an outing, as well as a host of other caterpillars. What I like about this hunt is the pace. We don't cover a lot of ground, but we're out with our friends, the conversation is good, and we get to enjoy the confused looks of other people in the park.

Then it returns, the moth I have been eagerly awaiting. *Tolype vellada,* or the Large Tolype. If there could be just one moth on this planet and I had some say in choosing it, this shaggy sheepdog would be well up in the running. A relative of the Lappet Moth (remember "Mutt"?), the Large Tolype shares that same sleepy characteristic. It remains in place all day and well into the following night, resting, unmoving, apparently unaware of its surroundings. It is like a furry little white and gray stuffed animal that you can pick up, pass around, and put back again without it seeming to have noticed. (I have read that the hair tufts at the tip of the female's body cause a skin irritation but have not experienced that myself.) I am forced to alternate my lighting nights to give these moths a chance to go about their business. Otherwise, with their sedentary days and attraction to lights at night, they could well spend the rest of their adult existence on the light sheet. This would be a terrible waste of life. It's interesting that this moth shares the same coloration as my other favorite, the White Underwing. Like that underwing, the Large Tolype makes me think of cool northern forests of birches and aspens. However, that's just my own projection, and an inaccurate one, because the Large Tolype can be found as far south as Florida. It does have a little cousin, nearly identical except for the smaller size, called the Larch Tolype. This is a northern species that I encounter less frequently.

The Large Tolype is with me almost until the end of October. Its last vision of the world is the blazing colors of autumn.

If May is spring and July is summer, then October is autumn. The Monarch butterflies and hawks are still moving south and have been joined by the shorebirds along the coast. There is a quiet frenzy in the air as all forms of insects and animals prepare in their own way for the onset of winter. There is still time, but the days are getting shorter.

In general, the moth numbers are decreasing, but the darts are still going strong. So, too, are the autumn sallows. The sallows open and close the big moth show, arriving in March and disappearing in November, or December at the latest. In October I come across the Bicolored, Straight-toothed, Sloping, Dotted, and Footpath Sallows. Some of these first appeared in September; some are freshly emerged in this opal month. They are the color of the goldenrod that surrounds them at the edges of the wood, and of the yellow and brown leaves on the forest floor.

In a time of year when the maple leaves are yellow, ragged, and dotted with brown spots, there appears a moth that is yellow, ragged, and dotted with brown spots. It is the Maple Spanworm. If ever there were a moth that was meant to live within the season it emerges, it is the Maple Spanworm. An atypically heavy-bodied, owletlike Geometrid, this moth has tattered-looking wings that could have been fashioned from the leaves of the surrounding sugar maples. When I come across this moth, I am immediately struck by the fact that I am staring at the end result of natural selection. How could it evolve to look any more like its surroundings and still be a moth? When threatened, it even drops like an autumn leaf, floating to the ground on stiff, unflapping wings. Although there are other surprising mimics in the world of Lepidoptera, I can always find some room for improvement. Take the hairstreak butterflies. Most have little filaments resembling antennae on their hind wings that are meant to attract a predator's attention to the nonvital parts of its anatomy. In essence, it wants birds to take a bite out of the fake head instead of its actual head, which would be fatal. Many of these hairstreaks have evolved eyespots adjacent to these fake antennae to make the ruse even more convincing. Some even have a little dab of white on the eyespot, giving it a shiny, rounded look like a real eye. But I can usually see a way that the butterfly could look a little better. The eye could look more like an eye, the antennae more like antennae. Not so with the Maple Spanworm.

November is the month of the Mad Moon. It is the month, too, of thanks, both to our veterans of war and for our autumn harvest. The latter—Thanksgiving—is my favorite holiday. The air is brisk, the ground crunchy with leaves, and commercialization of this holiday has yet to spoil it for me. It is a celebration that has remained as down to earth as one can in this age.

To help the birds partake of the harvest, the feeders go up in my yard: sunflower seeds for the black-capped chickadees, tufted titmice, and white-breasted nuthatches; suet for the downy and hairy woodpeckers; cracked corn on the ground for the mourning doves, white-throated sparrows, and song sparrows. Other birds will appear as winter approaches. Sterile female yellow jackets are flying about aimlessly. They will not survive the season and are just riding out the last few days of their lives. Neither will the true katydids survive; they're still calling, but more slowly. As a friend put it, their "katy-did . . . katy-did-it" now sounds like "I'm-still-here . . . how-'bout-you?"

I'm down to about eighteen species of moths now that I can identify. Remember those little T-shaped eupithecias from April? They're still making an appearance, although these are the descendants of the earlier individuals. The sallows are still here; about four species are turning up. Some years it's more, some less.

Carpet moths consistently appear at this time of year. These include the Bent-line, Double-banded, and Labrador Carpet Moths and one simply called "The Gem." The eupithecias are technically carpet moths, in the family Larentiinae, but they are not what come to mind when I think of this group. Many of the adults look like washed-out bird droppings as they rest with their wings held flat against leaves and bark. Their scalloped patterns, in various shades of white and brown on broad, rounded wings, add to the "splat" effect. Another type of moth we call carpet moth has no relation to those in the Larentiinae family. The Tinead carpet moths are tiny creatures whose larvae feed on natural fibers such as wool and fur that are found in clothes and carpeting. They are among the clothes-eating pests that give moths a bad name. But the Larentiinae carpet moth larvae feed on herbaceous plants and have no desire to eat anything you care to lounge in or upon.

With the month of December, the New England moth season has dwindled from November's trickle to an occasional drip. Although my nights have been freed up, most of my available days are spent along the Connecticut River watching eagles, or in fields trying to locate an interesting sparrow. Waterfowl have come down from the northern waters and Maritime Provinces of Canada to ride out the winter in the open water of Long Island Sound. I spend many a cold winter morning squinting through my birding scope, trying to pin a name on some speck on the water a half a mile away.

Only one moth can actually be expected to come to my light at this time of year—the Bruce Spanworm. I should mention that by "light" I now mean porch or window light. By December, the equipment is down. I do welcome the break, and it makes that one moth, ol' Bruce, all the more appreciated.

The Bruce Spanworm emerges as an adult in late fall. The male is about as drab as a moth can be, with semitranslucent, pale gray-brown wings. He resembles an old, decaying leaf and is of the typical geometer shape with butterfly proportions. The female, however, is a different creature entirely. She is a small, scaly brown cigar with no wings. She doesn't need them; the male comes to her. Like the male, she has a high tolerance for cold, and she does her egg laying in late fall, sometimes early winter.

Occasionally, another moth appears in December. Like the Bruce Spanworm, its wings are a translucent gray-brown with faint brown markings. It is only about five-eighths of an inch long and half as wide. It's a little Tortricid with a big name, the Black-headed Birch Leaffolder. "Black-headed" refers to the caterpillar, not the adult. The moth doesn't really belong out this late in the year. But nature does that to her creatures. She tests them. She sends them to places where they don't belong. She has them appear in habitats that are not yet ready for them or are no longer suitable. Every species of animal is pushed to the limit. It's how populations expand and adapt. If the little Black-headed Birch Leaffolder were able to carve out a niche this late in the season, it would expand its opportunities, because it would virtually have the season to itself.

But I don't see that happening just yet. Most of these moths die by mid-November. I do have to respect them for trying. These aberrant late species are the Lewis and Clarks of their kind. Actually, they are probably more the George Mallorys, because they don't live to tell about it.

As for January, the only moth I come across is the occasional Indian Meal Moth, which has the uncanny ability to find its way into people's homes. It has no down season, because our furnaces and food keep its habitat just the way it likes it. This moth breeds year-round, much to the dismay of its hosts. It is the European starling of the moth world, an introduced species that we wish had never left home.

One can find wild moths at this time of year, though. When the leaves are off the trees, the cocoons of the silk moths become easier to spot. I always look for them in winter. The one I come across most frequently is the Promethea Moth. Its cocoons, the color of pale brown paper bags, are suspended from the branches of sassafras and cherry trees. They are about as wide as a finger and are attached to the branch by a thin strand of the leaf they are wrapped in. I enjoy spotting them, and every year I bring a few home to rear. I follow a self-imposed rule of taking only one for every five I find. Once the moth emerges, I try to return it to the spot where I found it. In some cases I take more of a population if the cocoons are along the edge of a road that I know will be mowed, trimmed, or cleared in early spring.

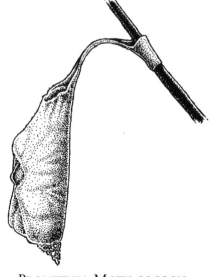

In February, the big ship of winter has begun to turn. It's still cold. Snow is on the ground and blizzards are in the forecast. The dogs are still spending just enough time outdoors to take care of busi-

PROMETHEA MOTH COCOON

ness before returning to their spot in front of the fireplace. The cats have long stopped trying to slip past us out the front door.

In some years, this is the month that pussy willows sprout cottony buds. This is also a month of great anticipation, not only for the warmer days of spring but for an answer to the question, Will the groundhog see his shadow? If on February second he emerges and does not see his shadow—well, good news, winter is soon to be over. And if he does? We're in it for another month and a half.

I have a different way of forecasting the end of winter. When *Phigalia strigataria*, the Small Phigalia Moth, emerges from the woods and sees its shadow in my porch light, winter is coming to an end. This indicator doesn't have quite the fanfare as Punxsutawney Phil, but I see a lot more Small Phigalias in February than I do groundhogs. In fact, I see about a half dozen different species of moths this time of year. Whereas on the other side of winter the trailblazers worked at extending their season from fall to winter, these moths are getting an early jump on the season. The Small Phigalia, and the other phigalias that appear in late winter, are pale gray geometers with wavy dark lines running through their wide wings. Their numbers will have greatly multiplied by March, but I can usually count on finding one or two clinging to the shingles on a February morning.

Grote's Pinion, Distinct Quaker, Bruce Spanworm, Black-headed Birch Leaffolder, and Straight-toothed Sallow have also been found pushing the season in February. These are all moths that I can say with certainty have seen snow. They have ventured out on relatively warm nights, seeking out other adventurous moths of their kind, only to be trapped by someone's porch light. I generally don't keep a light on at night for just that reason. But every once in a while I am compelled to sample the cold-season Lepidoptera, driven by a need for signs that winter is coming to an end.

And it always does. March is right around the corner, waiting to release her wild things into the night.

6

Of Moths and Men

TOKYO is in trouble. Godzilla is on the rampage, and there appears to be no way to stop him. All hope lies in convincing the diminutive Fairy Twins of Infant Island to sing that song. Oh, that magical song. It takes some doing, but eventually they are persuaded. They begin to sing: *"Mosura, ya! Mosura, Dongan kasakuyan, indo muu. Rusuto uiraadoa, Hanba hanbamuyan, Randa banunradan, Tonjukanraa, Kasaku aanmu..."*

A giant silk moth sails into the scene. Mothra. Length 130 meters, wingspan 250 meters. Weighing in at a formidable 15,000 tons, she is a force to be reckoned with. As if that were not enough to intimidate those earning her displeasure, she can whip up hurricanes and lightning bolts with a flap of her wings, broadcast a flurry of poisonous dust on those below, and shoot death rays from her antennae.

But Mothra is summarily killed by Godzilla, scorched by a blast of the reptile's flaming breath. I guess when it comes down to it, Mothra is still just a moth. However, moths, like all living things, reproduce. And fortunately for Tokyo, Mothra has left behind two offspring. Her eggs hatch, and the twin caterpillars return to avenge the death of their mother. With a call that can be compared to very large fingernails sliding down a chalkboard, they approach the great fire-breathing lizard and spray streams of silk with the velocity of a pair of colossal fire hoses.

GODZILLA VERSUS MOTHRA

Godzilla becomes encased in the sticky filament and falls helpless to the ground. Tokyo is saved . . . for now.

This was my introduction to moths. I was about five years old when I saw *Godzilla vs. Mothra*, and it made a strong impression on me. What stands out most in my memory is the image of the two caterpillars shooting silk at the big lizard. What a bizarre defense it seemed. Battle, as I understood it then, meant slapping, hitting, half nelsons, shooting, throwing things, and, yes, breathing fire. Where did this whole silk thing come in? This was pretty cool. But little did I know then that I had learned something. Caterpillars produce silk. Granted, at the time I thought they shot it out of their face to defend themselves from large bipedal reptiles, but it was one step in the direction toward learning about the Lepidoptera.

Owlets (Noctuidae)

Flame-shouldered Dart
(*Ochropleura plecta*)

Common Oak Moths
(*Phoberia atomaris*)

Beautiful Wood Nymph (*Eudryas grata*)

Owlets (*Noctuidae*)

Formosa Looper Moth
(*Chrysanympha formosa*)

Two-spotted Looper Moth
(*Autographa bimaculata*)

Oldwife Underwing
(*Catocala palaeogama*)

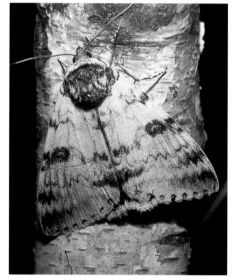

White Underwing,
"The Forsaken Underwing"
(*Catocala relicta*)

Lunate Zale
(*Zale lunata*)

Colorful Zale
(*Zale minerea*)

Brown Panopoda
(*Panopoda carneicosta*)

Yellow-banded Underwing
(*Catocala cerogama*)

Owlets *(Noctuidae)*

Spotted Grass Moth
(Rivula propinqualis)

Dark-spotted Palthis
(Palthis angulalis)

Prominents *(Notodontidae)*

Drexel's Datana
(Datana drexelii)

White-dotted Prominent
(Nadata gibbosa)

Thyatirid Moths
(Thyatiridae)

Hooktips
(Drepanidae)

Dogwood Thyatirid
(Euthyatira pudens)

Rose Hooktip
(Oreta rosea)

Inchworms and Geometers
(Geometridae)

Red-fronted Emerald
(Nemoria rubifrontaria)

Pepper and Salt Geometer
(Biston betularia cognataria)

Inchworms and Geometers
(Geometridae)

Showy Emerald
(Dichorda iridaria)

Large Lace-border
(Scopula limboundata)

Northern Selenia
(Selenia alciphearia)

Pale Beauty
(Campaea perlata)

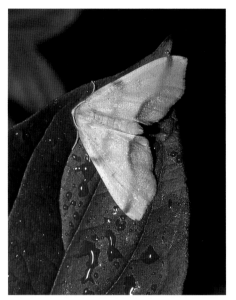

Lemon Plagodis
(Plagodis serinaria)

White Pine Angle
(Semiothisa pinistrobata)

False Crocus Geometer *(Xanthotype urticaria)*

Pyralidae

Eustixia pupula

Herpetogramma thestialis
(male and female)

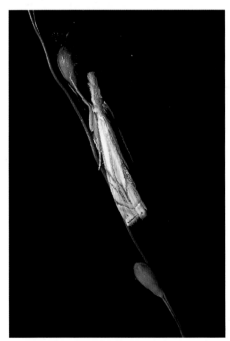

Crambus agitatellus

Indian Meal Moth
(Plodia interpunctella)

It wasn't until many years later that I wondered about those eyespots on Mothra's wings. In the world that exists beyond Infant Island, eyespots on moths and butterflies are used to deter or misdirect a potential predator, usually of the feathered variety. I'd hate to see the bird that this moth evolved to evade. Could it have been Rodan?

At about that same time, I saw another giant moth on the big screen. This one was far more docile and magnanimous; it carried Dr. Dolittle on its back. When I first saw this, Mothra popped into my head. I remember hoping that this great moth wouldn't be called into action while the good doctor was still mounted upon its thorax.

Speaking of moths on the screen, I can't help but think of the movie *Strange Brew,* which was released in the early 1980s. In a scene I will never forget, the two "hosers," Bob and Doug McKenzie (Dave Thomas and Rick Moranis), enter a movie theater, one carrying a big jar filled with moths he had collected the previous night. As soon as the movie begins, he unscrews the top of the jar and the moths, attracted to the light of the projector, exit the jar and cover the lens, making the movie impossible to see. What a wonderfully brilliant and devious act! I can only imagine how many times this was repeated in movie theaters throughout the country. Fortunately for the theater owners, the movie wasn't a huge hit, reducing the chances of copycat moth attacks.

Moths and humans have been clashing and coming together for all of recorded history and, I would assume, well before that. Moths have been the subject of contempt and reverence, destruction and art. In A.D.1258, a Persian poet named Muslihuddin Abu Muhammad Abdullah ibn Mushrif-uddin Sa'di (wisely, he later shortened it to "Sa'di") published a series of poems about his travels. They were collectively called *The Gulistan,* which translated means "The Rose Garden." In an excerpt from one of the poems, the knowledge of a moth's penchant for light, or fire, is revealed:

> *O bird of the morning, learn love from the moth*
> *Because it burnt, lost its life, and found no voice.*
> *These pretenders are ignorantly in search of Him,*
> *Because he who obtained knowledge has not returned.*

The moth becomes somewhat of a tragic figure, having gained wisdom that can never be used.

In fourth-century Greece, there is mention of moths, specifically their larvae, in a collection of animal descriptions called the *Physiologus*. The descriptions are not so much scientific as they are allegorical. The collection, from tales that date back even farther in human culture, are used to explain the beliefs of Christianity. We find mention of moth caterpillars under the category "Worms":

> The silk-worm is a leaf worm; from the threads it weaves, we make silk. It gets its name because it empties itself when it makes thread and only air is left inside its body. The caterpillar is a leaf worm, often found enveloped in a cabbage or a vine; it gets its name from *erodere*, "to eat away." Plautus recalls it in this way: "She imitates the wicked and worthless beast, wrapped in vine leaves." It folds itself up and does not fly about like the locust, which hurries from place to place, in all directions, leaving things half-eaten, but stays amid the fruit that is destined to be destroyed and, munching slowly, consumes everything.... The worm found in clothes is called *tinea* because it gnaws at fabrics, and burrows into them until they are eaten away. For this reason, it is called pertinacious, *pertinax*, because it works away all the time at the same thing....

I get the feeling from reading these descriptions that "worms" were not considered very good Christians. They are right down there with the snake.

We can go a little further back to 350 B.C., where in the *History of the Animals* Aristotle writes:

> Other animalcules besides these [worms] are generated ... some in wool or in articles made of wool, as the ses or clothes-moth. And these animalcules come in greater numbers if the woolen substances are dusty; and they come in especially large numbers if a spider be shut up in the cloth or wool, for the creature drinks up any moisture that may be there, and dries up the woolen substance. This grub is found also in men's clothes.

It only makes sense that the moths most closely associated with our daily lives are the ones that get noticed and mentioned in the literature. And the form with which we most often came in contact in our homes was the larva, or, in Aristotle's time, the "worm." The clothes moths have been around us since we have been wearing clothes. The Irish called them

"Hounds of Fur" be-
cause of their voracity
in eating their rai-
ment. The term *hound*
at the time was a de-
rogatory one. More
than two millenniums
after Aristotle, clothes
moths are still, in the
words of the late en-
tomologist Frank E.
Lutz, "corrupting our
treasures."

Clothes moths are
just unwitting mem-
bers of a small group
of moths that have set
the standard for judg-
ing all moths. They

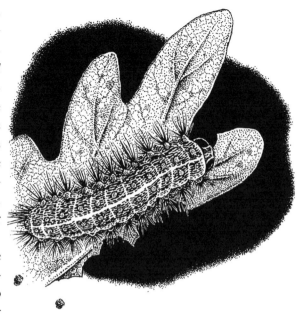

GYPSY MOTH CATERPILLAR

have always been thought of as pests within the general populace. When
I am doing a talk on moths, I am always asked the question, "Now, what
about those moths that eat your clothes?" or "How about those moths
that get in my cabinets?" More than one person has asked, "What good
are they?" To which I answer, "What good are we?"

Of the roughly eleven thousand species of moths in North America
fewer than one percent give us a hard time. Admittedly, some of them
can make themselves unwelcome. Many of these have been accidentally
introduced, such as the Eurasian Codling Moth, which infests apples,
and the Indian Meal Moth and Mediterranean Flour Moth, our un-
invited kitchen guests. And then there is that well-known and reviled
defoliator of trees, the Gypsy Moth, brought here intentionally as a potential silk producer but released by accident.

I first encountered Gypsy Moths in 1969. I was ten years old, on my
first camping trip in Saint James, New York. My father took my brother,
four friends, and me on an overnighter in a patch of woods that is probably no longer there. We had no tents, sleeping bags being judged as ad-
equate shelter for a clear summer night. We left late in the afternoon, and
it was growing dark by the time we arrived at our destination. Dad's plan

was to find a place away from the road to lay out the bags. The whole idea was to give us the experience of sleeping under the stars.

As we lay in our sleeping bags in the dark under the trees, we began to notice the sound of raindrops. It pattered on the leaves above and around us. "If it starts coming down harder, we'll leave," said my father. My great-grandfather's place, where we had set out from, wasn't too far away. But, strangely, we weren't getting wet, and one by one we drifted off to sleep.

The next morning I awoke dry and well rested, although the droplets still seemed to be falling. Then I noticed that my sleeping bag was covered with thousands of tiny brown granules. I looked around and saw that similar granules were bouncing on the leaves all around me. Then I heard a scream. One of the girls had rubbed her face and squashed a fuzzy caterpillar on her cheek. The remnants formed a yellow-brown semicircle of goo. The goo anchored a smattering of long grayish hairs. In the light of the morning, we discovered that those "droplets" we were hearing were actually droppings. We had spent the night being rained upon by caterpillar crap. This completely freaked out one of the girls (the one with the squashed caterpillar on her face), and we hightailed it out of there.

That was a memorable introduction to *Lymantria dispar,* better known as the Gypsy Moth. It was given its common name in 1742 by Englishman Benjamin Wilkes, a butterfly collector who had noted the wanderlust of this moth. However, we owed that night of raining frass to a French painter named Etienne Leopold Trouvelot, a portraitist who left France during the overthrow of the government in 1852 to move to Medford, Massachusetts. He had an interest in entomology, mostly silkmoths, and had immersed himself in finding a better way to produce silk. He was having some difficulty raising silkworms, because they often died of disease, and he wanted to find a more hardy species. In 1869, he returned from France with what he hoped would be the solution. He had procured the eggs of the Gypsy Moth, a native of Eurasia. The larvae of this species were said to produce an ample amount of silk. Perhaps, he thought, this silk could be used for sericulture.

Trouvelot experimented with the moths on his property at 27 Myrtle Street. He was aware of the potential for trouble should the moths escape. And escape they did. Accounts vary on how this happened. Some say the eggs were lifted by a breeze through an open window. Others believe that the caterpillars dispersed from the trees in his yard on which he had been culturing them. Regardless of how they got out, Trouvelot knew enough about the species to surmise that he had a problem on his hands. He contacted entomologists in the area, but nothing was done.

Thirteen years later, Trouvelot had given up entomology and returned to France. He had taken on a new hobby, astronomy. Not much could go wrong there; in fact, he became so successful in this new endeavor that a crater on the moon was named after him.

About this time William Taylor, the man who had bought the house at 27 Myrtle Street, noticed serious caterpillar problems in his yard. In fact, he soon realized that they were feeding in huge numbers throughout the neighborhood. He noted the sound of crunching and the frass falling like rain from the trees. By 1889, Massachusetts realized that the state had a serious outbreak of the Frenchman's imported caterpillars. One year later, a bill was passed appropriating $25,000 to take care of the problem. It was the first time a state law was passed calling for the eradication of an insect. Now the state, with the help of national government agencies, was taking action. This marked the beginning of a war that continues today.

Northport, Long Island, New York, 1979. I'm hiking around a pond with my girlfriend. Once again that "dry rain" appears, spilling frass from above onto our heads, spoiling any amorous plans I may have been hatching. In fact, once she realized what it was that was collecting in our hair, she began getting worked up into a panic. She kept on walking, but the wild look in her eyes was making me a little nervous. I suggested we leave. That was what she needed to hear, and it was all I could do to keep up with her as she raced out of the park.

Many people have similar stories about this insect. It has made such an impact that, unfortunately for all the other species, it is what people think of when they hear the word "moth." (Adult moths are shown in the photo section that follows page 160.)

The Gypsy Moth is in the tussock moth, or Lymantriidae, family. Gypsy Moths generally hatch in spring, and the hairy larvae feed voraciously on tree foliage. Although they've been known to feed on hundreds of different kinds of trees, they seem to prefer oaks. They feast at night, then find a shaded spot, often on the ground, to rest during the day. Their pupal stage lasts about two weeks. Once the female emerges, she begins calling in the males with her pheromones. The males, medium-sized, pale brown triangles, fly in frenetic spirals day and night attempting to home in on a female. They rarely land until they find her.

Because the female is flightless, dispersal occurs by the caterpillars. The early-instar caterpillars can "fly" on a light breeze by releasing and hanging onto a long strand of silk. This is called ballooning. (You may recall this method being employed by Charlotte's spiderlings as they left their egg case in E. B. White's *Charlotte's Web*.) Humans also aid in the moths' dispersal when their vehicles, which may have either larvae or egg masses attached, move from one place to another.

The female lays her eggs (up to 1,500 of them) on the surface of anything that *has* a surface, but most often on trees. I have found them on my house, car, rock walls, garbage cans, woodpiles, and once on the sheet I set up to attract moths. She covers the eggs with hair from her own body. This is how they overwinter.

Population levels seem to ebb and flow widely. The moths may not be seen for years, only to reappear in epidemic numbers.

Nineteen eighty-two. I'm out and about in my yard in East Haven, Connecticut, when I notice that the trunk of our apple tree is literally covered with Gypsy Moth caterpillars. I express my concern to Betsy, my new wife (the girlfriend who had braved the rain of frass three years earlier; you don't let a woman like that get away!). We decide that on the next day we'll pick up one of those sticky band things to wrap around the tree. In the early 1980s, you saw these traps everywhere you went. They became part of the suburban landscape. This method of control was designed to trap the caterpillars when they migrated down from the tree to ride out the day.

The next day, I checked the tree. The caterpillars were still there. But something didn't seem right. I looked a little closer. Each and every one of them was dead, stopped in their tracks. Many appeared desiccated, as if they had melted in place. I assumed that some kind of virus or fungus got them. As it turns out, I was right.

In our hundred-year battle with the Gypsy Moth, scientists have employed a variety of tactics, releasing predators, viruses, diseases, and fungi into populations of this ravenous insect. Unfortunately, non-targeted species sometimes get hit just as hard, if not harder, than the Gypsies. One of the most notable examples is the effect that a parasitoid fly, called *Compsilura concinnata,* had on wild silk moths. This insect, brought in from Europe, had been used for decades to battle the Gypsy Moth. The fly lays eggs on the caterpillar, and the eggs emerge as larvae that feed upon their lepidopteran host. Unfortunately, the larvae also take a liking to some of our most beautiful, and harmless, silk moths. For years, light pollution, DDT, and loss of habitat were blamed for the dramatic decrease in the number of silk moths, but recent studies now point in the direction of this little fly, which is now a naturalized U.S. citizen. *Compsilura* hasn't been released in about a decade, but as they say, it does no good to close the barn door once the cow has gotten out.

There is also a fungus, *Entomophaga maimaiga,* from Asia that is decimating populations of Gypsy Moths. The larvae eat the fungus and *melt.* The fungus was introduced from the Orient in the early 1900s, then disappeared. It was rediscovered about ten years ago in the corpses of the caterpillars that had ingested it and died. *Bacillus thuringiensis,* better known as Bt, is another control measure. This bacteria, which occurs in nature, kills the larvae. It is now used to control a number of insect pests.

Mice and shrews consider Gypsy Moth pupae, and in some cases late-instar larvae, a delicacy. The caterpillars are not of much interest to most birds because the caterpillars' hairs irritate the birds' throat and stomach lining. However, black-billed and yellow-billed cuckoos don't seem to mind. They seek out these caterpillars and those of tent caterpillar moths.

Despite our war on this insect, and the formation of agencies such as the National Gypsy Moth Management Board, the moth is still spreading. Since its introduction in Medford in 1869, exactly one hundred years prior to my introduction to the insect, it has been chewing away steadily, expanding its range throughout the Northeast. It has made it down to North Carolina and west to Ohio and Michigan. There is little doubt it will keep on going, defoliating millions of acres of trees along the way.

And guess what? There's a new Gypsy Moth in town. The Asian Gypsy first appeared in the Pacific Northwest in 1991. Apparently caterpillars were observed ballooning to land from a Russian grain ship. Three years later another population was established in North Carolina. These came from a munitions ship from Germany.

And guess what else? Female Asian Gypsy Moths can fly!

Year 2000. Killingworth, Connecticut. Two Gypsy Moth caterpillars are seen in my yard on two separate occasions. Not a single adult came to my light sheet. All quiet on the eastern front, so far. Betsy is happy.

Some moth pests are native to North America and became pests only with the advent of agriculture. We create huge monocultures of food crops in an abundance previously unavailable to the insects that take

advantage of this. Their numbers grow, making them more and more efficient at destroying what we provide. Barrels of money are thrown at the
problem of eradication. Countless hours are spent by countless scientists
seeking a solution. We make some inroads. Then we lose ground as the
moths evolve their own inroads. Sometimes we hurt ourselves in the
battle. Take, for example, the war against the Codling Moth. This moth
appeared in California in 1872, spreading rapidly and wreaking havoc
on the apple and pear industry. Then in 1893, the perfect formula was
devised to solve the problem. It called for two compounds called Bor-
deaux mixture and Paris green. Sounds like the birth of a new "minty"
wine; it was actually a mixture containing arsenic and copper, among
other things. This is what was being sprayed on the fruit. For seven years,
fruit was shipped out and eaten—deliciously free of that blasted little
caterpillar but dangerously unfree of toxins. Then a shipment of pears to
Boston was found to have arsenic residue in an amount that could be
"injurious to public health." The amount of arsenic in the mixture was
reduced, but for many years after, apples and pears appeared with
amounts of arsenic still considered too high for human consumption.

In the meantime, the Codling Moth discovered our walnut orchards.

A while back, I came across an article with the heading "Moths'
Penises Could Help Feed India." Oh, I'm readin' this one, I thought. It
seemed there's a problem in India with a couple of species of Heliothine
(Noctuidae family) moths. They're responsible for about six hundred
million dollars in food crop damage and are resistant to pesticides.
Problem one is that there are forty-two species of Heliothines, with only
two causing trouble. If they could be distinguished from the harmful
moths, pesticide spraying could be greatly reduced and the beneficial
pollinators could be allowed to thrive. But, problem two, the only way
to distinguish the different species is to, well, ask the male moths to
drop their pants for a look-see. Unfortunately, the genitalia of the male
Heliothine moth are not only very small but retracted. Enter the
"phalloblaster." This tiny moth-penis inflator invented in Australia will
"blow up" a moth's penis, allowing it to be identified under a micro-
scope. For a cost of two million dollars, this technology could be India's.
At the time of this writing, researchers were still working on it.

Okay, enough on the troublemakers. In at least one respect, moths—
one species in particular—have a place in history that has elevated them

to an almost revered state. The species I speak of is the only living moth no longer found in the wild: a large, flightless creature called *Bombyx mori,* or Silkworm Moth. To look at its entrance into our culture, we have to go back six thousand years in China. Much has been written on the history of sericulture, or silkmaking, and I will only touch upon it here. Although historical evidence shows that there was activity in the silkworm trade between 3000 and 2500 B.C., fossil cocoons in Stone Age sites show that the cultivation of this caterpillar began before 4700 B.C.

Of the many stories on the origin of the use of silk as a textile fiber, my favorite is contained in the ancient Chinese manuscript *Wai-Ki.* The story takes place in about 2640 B.C. when the third emperor of China, Huang-Ti, gave his fourteen-year-old wife, Empress Hsi-Ling-Shih, a mission. Mulberry trees on the palace grounds were being damaged by silkworms. They'd eat the leaves, pupate, and emerge, leaving behind intriguing cocoons. He instructed Hsi-Ling-Shih to find some use for the threads that held the cocoons together.

I guess being a young empress in those days left one with a lot of idle time, and Hsi-Ling-Shih focused her attention on a silkworm caterpillar. She watched it every day as it grew and grew until it finally stopped eating, encased itself in silk, and, apparently, died.

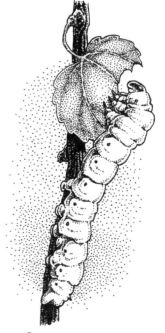

The empress, believing that the cocoon held the spirit of an ancestor, brought the cocoon inside. To her great surprise, a beautiful moth emerged and flew off, freeing the imprisoned spirit. She then brought the cocoon into the palace to show it to some of the ladies of the court. In doing so, she accidentally dropped it in a bowl of hot water that was to be used for washing. When she fished the cocoon out of the water, it began to unwind, and the empress was able to separate a long, continuous strand of silk.

Well, that made one happy emperor, because it didn't take long to figure out how to weave the silk into fabric. Soon his royal garden was filled with mulberry

SILKWORM FEEDING
ON MULBERRY

trees, which in turn were crawling with silkworms. The *Wai-Ki* includes a nice touch to this story. Apparently the length of silk that was fished out of the bowl of hot water was woven into the emperor's royal robe, which was passed down through the generations.

For two thousand years the secret of silk remained locked within the borders of China. Two thousand years! For two whole millenniums nary a loose lip sank the ship—that ship being the silk caravan that carried this prized textile to a silk-hungry world. You would think that someone would have slipped up.

Around A.D. 300, Japan, then India, managed to penetrate China's monopoly, although the secret remained in Asia until around A.D. 550. It was at this time that two Nestorian monks arrived in China, sent by the Roman emperor Justinian I to learn how to make the shiny fabric. At the risk of their lives, they hid the seeds of a mulberry tree and some eggs of a silkworm in their hollow walking staffs and fled the country. They returned to Byzantium, where the secret was revealed.

To this day, silk is produced in much the same way as it has been over the millenniums. In China, where the cocoons are dropped into huge vats of hot water to loosen the silk, the pupae within become cooked. They are then eaten by the workers or sold as a delicacy.

Another moth that has garnered popular attention these days is the Long-tongued Hawk Moth. This Sphingid has evolved alongside what has become a rare (listed by the federal government as "threatened") plant in the western tallgrass prairies, the western prairie orchid. The plant grows to four feet tall, and its pale flowers have the distinction of bearing the longest spur of all the prairie orchids. This spur makes pollination impossible by any insect lacking an equally long tongue. Enter our probosciscally gifted hawk moth. The flower releases its fragrance in the evening to attract this moth, whose proboscis makes it all the way down to the nectar source. While the moth is feeding, pollen is brushed onto its eyes by two specialized pollen-bearing structures. These structures have evolved to match perfectly with the spacing and placement of the moth's eyes. The dusted moth then spreads the pollen to other plants.

Both the plant and moth are suffering from habitat fragmentation and loss. Much of the western tallgrass prairie has been turned into farms, which form barriers for the hawk moths and limit their access to their food source. In addition, moths are being killed off by pesticides, which are targeted at other insects but don't stop there. This is having an adverse effect on the genetic diversity of what have become isolated islands of orchids. If the orchids go, so do the moths. Conversely, if the moths disappear, the orchids will follow.

Therefore, something monumental is occurring with regard to the world of moths. People are creating corridors for them. Moth corridors! What a wonderful breakthrough in the world of Lepidoptera. Humans have come to value the lowly moth enough to work it into their conservation plans. Moths in general are responsible for pollinating nearly 80 percent of our flora, so one hopes that this can serve as a wake-up call to other conservationists as to the necessity of moths in the natural world.

Until now, our look into the relationship between moths and people has focused on the cinema, agricultural pests and saviors, and makers of nice sheets. But there is another connection we have with these creatures, a connection more in the realm of the supernatural. In medieval times, creatures known as sylphs fluttered in the fields of air. The word *sylph* is derived from the Greek word *silphe*, which means moth or butterfly. Only the chaste were permitted to enjoy intimate pleasures with these creatures, which themselves were what had become of the . . . oh, far opposite of the chaste?

In European folklore, moths were regarded as witches. Not a big stretch. Witches are creatures of the night. Moths are creatures of the night. Witches can transform themselves into different creatures. Moths can transform themselves into different creatures (metamorphosis). Witches fly. Moths fly. Witches have long noses. Moths have long noses. There is even a moth in America called the Black Witch. It's a great big, dark Noctuidae with eyespots covering its wings. These are tropical moths, but on occasion they fly as far north as Canada, well beyond their natural habitat. It's a fruitless migration, because their offspring cannot survive much past Florida.

Moths were sometimes considered restless spirits, or ghosts. White moths were believed to host spirits of the dead. Not a far stretch if you consider the depiction of ghosts throughout history: pale, ethereal beings unhindered by gravity. Killing a white moth would be tampering with the workings of the world of the hereafter. This was something that our ancestors took great care to avoid, because it would bring upon them a myriad of undesirable results.

There is a very primitive family of moths called the ghost moths. In a *Smithsonian* magazine article by Richard Conniff, lepidopterist David Wagner is quoted as saying that the scientific name of this family, Hepialidae, means "shivering nightmare." It's easy to get back to the source of this one. This family of moths, found throughout the world, carries on its mating dance at dusk. Individuals swarm in great numbers and hover in the foreground of the setting sun. Dusk has always held mystical qualities in many cultures. It's a time of transition. Add to that a swarm of gyrating creatures dancing in the air, and to that again a seasonal regularity, and you have what could be considered a phenomenon. A phenomenon—take a solar eclipse, for example—because of its repetition through the ages, has time to evolve all kinds of meanings, especially if it's bizarre enough. The dance of the ghost moth fits that bill. I remember reading somewhere that ghost moths can whistle through their proboscises. If this is true, it sure couldn't have hurt the growth of this piece of folklore.

Whereas white moths were souls on the move, black moths were omens of death. If one flew into your home, it foretold that a death would occur under that roof. This had to have happened enough times for it to take on significance in folklore. People died far more unexpectedly of a variety of things hundreds of years ago, and there must have been enough coincidences for this belief to have taken hold. Of course, the Death's Head Sphinx, the species raised by the serial killer in the film *The Silence of the Lambs*, has also been believed to be a portent of death. This large Euro-African sphinx moth feeds on bee honey by piercing the honeycombs with its powerful tongue. It has upon its thorax an image that has given the moth its attributed malefic character—the visage of a human skull. What makes this story even juicier is that this large, dark, hovering skull emerges from an underground cell where the previous form (the larva) had burrowed after growing fat on the deadly nightshade plant. Even the moth's scientific name is foreboding, *Acherontia atropos*. The genus *Acherontia* comes from the Greek Acheron, which is known as the River of Pain in the underworld. Atropos was one of the three Fates, and her job was to cut the thread of life when it was time for a person to die. So, according to its Latin nomenclature, this moth is the Death Bringer from Hell's River of Pain. Not exactly greeting-card material.

A less dramatic omen in those times held that when a moth, any moth, flew into your house, you were in for a bout of bad luck. Our ancestors didn't have screens back then; many didn't even have windows. Moths get into our homes even *with* modern-day screens and windows. And how many days or hours go by without our attributing some occurrence to bad luck? Why not blame it on the moths that just happen to be there?

But moths weren't always assigned negative roles in our spiritual world.

In 1974, Carlos Castaneda wrote the fourth book in his series on the teachings of Don Juan. This series started out as research on the psychotropic drugs used by the Yaqui Indians of Mexico. It ended up with an account of this anthropologist's apprenticeship under Don Juan, a sorcerer, warrior, and man of knowledge. I read this book, and the others, in college and at the time was beyond intrigued by the possibilities of the "separate reality" and "way of the warrior" of which he wrote. For some reason, the only book I still own from that series is the fourth book, *Tales of Power*. The pages have turned a dull yellow-amber, the same color as the large moth on the cover. The moth is surrounded by a glowing gold aura. In the words of teacher Don Juan, "The moths carry a dust on their wings. . . . A dark gold dust. That dust is the dust of knowledge." Although no mention of the moth species is made in the book, the cover illustration appears to be a Saturniid in the genus *Automeris*. As silk moths go, these are generally medium-sized insects with the characteristic eyespot on each hind wing. Apparently there are four species of *Automeris* in Mexico, the caterpillars of which have stinging spines.

Moths, to the Yaqui sorcerer, were "intimate friends and helpers from time immemorial." For the sorcerer, moths *were* knowledge. In *Tales of Power*, Castaneda wrote of his experience in the desert chaparral with his teacher, Don Juan. The young Castaneda, said his teacher, had "an appointment with a moth."

As Castaneda sat in the desert, back to back with Don Juan, the moth appeared and lunged at him, causing Castaneda to flee. Don Juan insisted that he keep the appointment, and they set out again later that night with a lantern. A "sputtering" noise was heard from the bushes, which Don Juan attributed to the moth. He pointed out that something special was happening, partially illustrated by the fact that no other moths were flying around what should have been a busy lantern. The lantern was there to attract one particular moth, the one that would bring the knowledge. The sputtering continued, described by Castaneda as "rich and deep; some [sounds] were produced in a low key, some in a high one. They had a rhythm and a specific duration; some long . . . some short . . . like the staccato sound of a machine gun." At that point Don Juan announced, "Moths are the heralds, or the guardian of eternity."

Castaneda then had a series of visions, which, as happened often, terminated in him screaming and having to be brought "back to earth" by Don Juan.

As for the sputtering sound, some moths can make a noise that is audible to humans. These include members of the Arctiidae, Ctenucidae, Noctuidae, and Pyralidae families. I have found no mention of this ability in the Saturniidae. A tiger moth called *Arctia caja* makes a pulsing sound by contracting a muscle in its thorax, forcing a striated band inward. Some wax moths, such as *Achroia grisella,* rub a "striker" from their wings over their upper thorax, producing a sound. The moth in Castaneda's experience was originally mistaken for a bird, so it couldn't have been one of the smaller moths mentioned above. Could that sputtering have come from the fast moving wings of a large hawk moth? If so, the cover artist picked the wrong moth. Or was it a silk moth, silent in our reality and noisy in Castaneda's "separate reality"? If you have read any of these books, you know that Don Juan would tell me that I'm thinking about it too much and none of those details matter. Then he would say or do something to make me start screaming.

The Teachings of Don Juan series is nonfiction. There is a book within the realm of fiction in which a moth, or moths, holds a strong supporting role. It is the children's classic *A Girl of the Limberlost,* by Gene Stratton-Porter. This story, written in 1909, has been a must-read for every entomologist, because it describes what may well have been scenes from their own early encounters with insects.

A poor young girl, eager to pay her own way through school, collects moths and sells them to the "Bird Lady," who is writing a book on moths. Not only does young Elnora Comstock pay her own way—her experience eventually lands her a job as a natural history teacher.

Throughout the story, Elnora has sought the one quarry that was missing from her collection, the Yellow Emperor Moth. Her mother, who had been unsupportive of Elnora's efforts throughout the story, has a change of heart toward the end and, upon learning that her daughter needs to find this moth, sets out with a lantern into the night to find it herself. Having no luck, she starts back for the house, then sees something from the corner of her eye:

> "Here comes a big one!" she cried. The moth appeared different from the others. On it came, dropping lower and darting back and forth. As it swept near her, she saw that it was yellow. It was a Yellow Emperor.
> Mrs. Comstock held up the lantern and watched its course. Then a second appeared in pursuit of the first. They came straight toward Mrs. Comstock. She ripped off part of her apron and held it out. The moth struck full against it and clung. And then the second moth followed the first. . . . And she sobbed for pure joy.

Find me a naturalist, amateur, or professional, who *hasn't* experienced the heady excitement of going out and actually finding what he or she set out to find. It's what keeps us going out there. Many entomologists think back with great fondness to their early insect collections. Most of them see the collections as the first step on the path that brought them to where they are today. Kids like to collect things. Moths and butterflies, because of their beauty, accessibility, and harmlessness, were often the objects of their desire, and continue to be as these young entomologists grow into adults.

Moths have been collected for reasons other than their beauty, however. Whereas in Mexico the moth was a creature of great wisdom to the Yaquis, just a bit north of them, moths were, and still are, a delicacy. The Pomo Indians of the American West know well the two-year life cycle of the Pandora Moth. When the larvae reach full size, the Indians start a smoky fire beneath their host tree (a yellow or Jeffrey pine). The caterpillars then fall to the ground, where they are collected, partially roasted, and later used in a stew. Sometimes a trench is dug around the host tree to intercept the caterpillars as they search for their pupation sites. The pupae also are roasted, dried, and stored for winter rations. Although the Pandora Moth is the main quarry, a number of other species are eaten.

In the Far West, tribes including Don Juan's Yaqui use empty cocoons for rattles. These have mostly been left behind by the Polyphemus Moth and Ceanothus Silk Moth. The rattles are used as musical instruments and in ritualistic ceremonies. They are filled with sand or pebbles and either tied together on a stick or worn around the ankles. When I first learned of this, it just so happened that I had an empty Polyphemus cocoon, vacated by an adult I had just photographed. I filled the cocoon with sand and gave it a shake. It had a nice, high-pitched sound. I wish I had more of them.

I began this chapter with a personal account of moths, and I will end with one. Mothra was my first remembered encounter with the moth world; my second occurred shortly thereafter, although I did not at the time recognize it as a contact with moths. My Aunt Ann, who played a large role in fostering my interest in nature, also encouraged me to explore a less noble side of myself. She always gave me some interesting novelty item when I visited her. We're talking joy buzzers, fly in the ice cube, whoopee cushions, X-ray glasses, and, yes, Mexican jumping beans.

The directions on the packet of beans explained that they were "magical." There was no mention of what was inside them, but I was instructed to hold them in my hand and the warmth of my palm would make them jump. From all of the cartoons I had seen about Mexican jumping beans, I expected them to bounce all over the room. I remember one cartoon where the hapless character swallowed a bag of them and was bouncing uncontrollably all over the place. The cardboard flap on the back of the package warned not to eat the beans. Were they kidding? There was no *way* I would eat them! The warning was probably to keep young children from emulating the cartoon character Speedy Gonzales. Jumping beans to him were like spinach to Popeye. They gave him his incredible speed when all seemed lost.

Anyway, my jumping beans never did more than flinch. They did feel kind of weird, though. And, I guess, magical in a way. What, I wondered, made these things move? I had to find out. Using a small ball peen hammer that my grandfather kept in the basement, I broke one open. There among the woodlike shards of the shattered bean was a small white worm. A larva, actually. So this was the source of the "magic"! When the worm wiggled, the bean moved. But how did the jumping-bean company get it in there? And how did it stay alive within this pebble-sized sarcophagus? And what should I do with this worm now? I remember finding it disturbing and somewhat cruel that the purveyors of jumping beans would encase these poor worms within these tiny coffins. I released

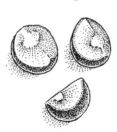

MEXICAN
JUMPING BEANS

the worm outside, along with the others after liberating them from their beans, and therefore unknowingly sealed their doom.

At some point I learned that the worms were *supposed* to be in the beans. And somehow I found myself in possession of another batch of jumping beans. These worms I left undisturbed within their shells. When the novelty wore off, I dumped the beans in my top dresser drawer and forgot about them. Years later, I came across them again and noticed that there were little holes in the ends. And the beans were empty. There was a moment of concern over where the contents could have ended up, but by that time I was growing so many different kinds of insects in my room that I just added them to the long list of creatures that had successfully found their independence.

The missing worms were the larvae of a moth that goes through its larval and pupal stages within the seed capsules of the Mexican bean shrub *(Sebastiana pavoniana)*. The seed capsules are the "beans." The locals call the plant Yerba de la Flecha, which means Plant of the Arrow. This ancient name comes from a time when the sap of the plant was used to poison the tips of arrows.

The moth, a little blue Tortricid called *Lapeyresia saltitans,* lays an egg in the flower of this plant. A seed capsule develops around the egg and falls to the ground. Soon the caterpillar hatches within. As it grows, it feeds on the inner layer of the seed until it is ready to pupate. But just before it pupates, and while it still has mandibles, it chews a little exit hole in the seed, then closes it. When the moth emerges from the pupa, it squeezes out the hole and seeks a new bean shrub.

So why do jumping beans jump? One possible explanation is that they are "designed" to move to a cooler spot when it gets too warm. These are *Mexican* jumping beans, remember, and the hot sun could bake them within their shells. The ability to move, limited though it may be, could help them roll into the shade. This could explain why the warmth of your hand gets them going. It could also be a way for the larvae to spread out, thereby increasing the chance of a successful emergence for part of the population if for some reason the other part was in an unfavorable spot.

Mexican jumping beans have been with us as little novelties for more than fifty years. This moth is part of the history of many a grown child, a small part that we probably haven't thought about for a long time. For some reason, I don't see these beans around much anymore. Perhaps a flinching bean is hard pressed to compete with video games.

꩜ 7 ꩜
The Moth People's
Moths

I'M fascinated by origins. There is a certain energy in the beginnings of things. A spark. A bolt of lightning cracking open a closed door. And a *discovery* is one of the most exciting beginnings there is. To find something that has never before been seen or described has to be the ultimate thrill for the discoverer.

So how do discoverers mark the occasion? How do they take that moment of discovery and keep it alive in perpetuity? And how do they get other people to look at what they've found? They name it. They call it something that they hope will mean something to all those who follow. But first and foremost, the name has to mean something to the discoverer. That's the big reward in our world culture. Finders—well, not keepers, but namers. If you discover something previously undescribed by science, you get to call it what you wish—to a certain extent. There are some guidelines to follow if you want others to use that name as well. This is your one and only shot, too. Once you name it, you can't change your mind, unless that discovery is reclassified further down the line, in which case someone else renames your discovery. So you have to be careful at the outset.

The Swedish naturalist Carolus Linnaeus (1707–78) put some limitations on the naming of flora and fauna. While attending university in Holland, he became frustrated with the confusion of the naming system within the botanical world. In 1735 he published *Systema naturae*. This groundbreaking system of naming things is still, with some changes, in use today. It is called binomial nomenclature.

Basically, everything under this system has two names: the genus name and the species name. They're most often in Latin, the closest to a universal language we have. Many call Latin a dead language, but that is far from true. Every living thing on this planet bears a Latin or latinized name. Whereas common (also known as "vulgar") names can be different throughout different regions, the scientific name remains the same. Take Great Britain's Camberwell Beauties. In the United States we know them as Mourning Cloaks. In Canada they go by several names: Yellow Edge, Willow Butterfly, and Yellow-bordered Butterfly. In Spain they're Antiopa. However, we all know them by their scientific name, *Nymphalis antiopa*. This name, by the way, was given to this butterfly by Linneas himself. *Nymphalis* refers to the group known as the brush-footed butterflies. And *antiopa* is a latinized form of Antiope, sister to the queen of the Amazons. I have a book on the Lepidoptera of the world that is written in Italian. I don't understand Italian. Some of the species in the United States are covered, and their scientific names are the same as they appear in my local guides. I could use this Italian guide to identify butterflies and moths in my own backyard. The same goes for the French and Spanish guides I own. This system works.

When discoverers of new species go to name them, they first have to figure out what family each one is in. If it's a family of diverse groups, or subsets, it may fall into a particular subfamily. That subfamily is broken down some more into the genus—another subset containing species that share a particular quality. The genus becomes the first part of each species' name. Let's say I discover a new moth in my backyard. Because this is my fantasy, let's say also that I have the scientific training and experience to be the one to decide that it is in fact a new species. I determine that this hypothetical moth is some kind of tiger moth in the family Arctiidae. Further study leads me to conclude that this moth shares traits, such as spots running down the abdomen and the presence of a pair of simple eyes, with others in the subfamily Arctiinae. Could it be? Yes! Eureka! I've managed to narrow the genus down to *Apantesis*. So the name is going to be *Apantesis . . . Apantesis johnii.* No, *Apantesis him-melmani.* (Latinized names are usually in italics.) *Apantesis himmelmani.* Nice sound to it; kind of rolls off the tongue. Wait a minute. I can almost hear the grumbling of lepidopterists upon reading of this new find: "He named it after HIMSELF? What a prima donna!"

They're right. You're not supposed to do that. I could name it after what it ate, if I knew. Or for where it was found, in which case it would be called *Apantesis huntersridgeroadsis,* the "sis" signifying place. Nah. I could name it after a characteristic of its physical nature. Maybe. I could name it after my mother, *Apantesis paulinea,* or my wife, *Apantesis elizabethea.* I might even name it after my favorite cartoon character, *Apantesis homeri.* These are good possibilities.

I really would like to give it a patronym, meaning named after a person. But at the same time I should be careful. What if I name it after someone and the moth turns out to be an apocalyptic pest? I have visions of torch-bearing villagers surrounding the honoree's home, taunting him or her to come out. But that's unlikely; if it were a pest, we'd probably have run into it already.

What I think I'd actually do is what many entomologists have done when faced with this question. I would honor another scientist, one who has distinguished him- or herself in the field. One who has contributed to my knowledge in the sciences. I shall name this moth *Apantesis krameri,* after Mr. Kramer, my eighth-grade science teacher.

I do wonder about the names behind some of the moths I find. Who are these people? What did they contribute to my pastime?

Sometimes, nothing. A good number of these moths bear the names of beings that have had very little to do with the advancement of our knowledge of insects. In fact, they may never have walked this Earth. Early-nineteenth-century entomologist Pieter Cramer named one of his finds after the son of Poseidon, an enormous Cyclops from Greek mythology named Polyphemus. *Antheraea polyphemus,* or the Polyphemus Moth, is a large silk moth with a big window, or clear eyespot, on each of its hind wings. Could that have played a part in its naming?

Another example of a character of Greek mythology being used in a moth's name is *Automeris io,* or the Io Moth. This insect, named by European entomologist Johann Fabricius, is the namesake of the daughter of the river god Inachus. The Io Moth is a medium-sized silk moth, yellow to pale brown, with a big eyespot on each of its hind wings. The inner margin of the hind wings is washed in raspberry pink. A very attractive creature.

Zeus had what was known in those times as an aching in his loins for Io, but he also had what was known in those times as a jealous wife. Her name was Hera. In typical Greek mythological fashion, he turned Io into a cow to disguise her, but Hera was onto him and had the cow guarded by Argus, a hundred-eyed monster. Zeus's son came to the rescue by killing Argus, but Hera, still roiling, sent a gadfly to pester Io the cow to the ends of the Earth. Io finally escaped by swimming across the Ionian Sea (giving it its name), then she changed back into her old self again.

Interesting story. I wonder what, if anything, it has to do with the moth? The Io Moth looks nothing like a cow. To the best of my knowledge, an Io Moth is not plagued by gadflies. It doesn't swim. Perhaps its appearance made Fabricius think of a Greek goddess—that I can see. Or here's another, and more likely, possibility: Could the moth have been named for Io, the fifth moon of Jupiter? Galileo had discovered this moon two hundred years before Fabricius discovered the moth. Moths and moons. Moons and moths. They go well together. *Actias luna*, the Luna Moth, was named for Earth's moon, and I could never picture the moth being named otherwise.

The previous two references came from Greek mythology. Roman mythology also lends a name from its rich cast of characters to one of my favorite catocala, or underwing, moths. The Ilia Underwing, *Catocala ilia,* is a large creature with cryptic coloring above and striking red-and-black underwings. It is one of the more common catocalas that come to my sugar bait, and one of the easiest to recognize due to its size and the big white spot on each of its forewings. This moth, too, was named by Pieter Cramer, after a vestal virgin in the Romulus and Remus saga. Ilia was made a priestess by her brother Amulius once he took the throne from their father. This was to ensure that she wouldn't bear any heirs to succeed him. The plan didn't work out very well; Ilia met up with Mars, of god-of-war fame, and bore him two sons, Romulus and Remus. Big name to live up to for an insect.

Catocala ilia also has a common name, The Wife. Sometimes it's called The Betrothed. Underwings are among the more interestingly named of the moths: Sweetheart, Tiny Bride, Dejected, Widow, Betrothed, and, my favorite, Inconsolable. I get a picture in my head of the entomologist pioneers who named these creatures, lonely men spending their evening hours by themselves in the autumn woods pining for non-chitinous companionship. Those early moth men were a breed unto themselves. Theodore D. Sargent wrote of the naming of these moths in his book *Legion of the Night*. In his opening paragraph of the chapter "Of Men and Names," he wrote:

> What great sadness could account for the Inconsolable Underwing (*insolobilis*), the Dejected Underwing (*dejecta*), and the Tearful Underwing (*lachrymosa*)? Might these not be cheered by the company of the Darling Underwing (*cara*), the Sweetheart (*amatrix*), or the Bride (*neogama*)? Better to avoid, perhaps, the Penitent Underwing (*piatrix*) and the Old Maid (*coelebs*). But surely the Serene (*serena*) and Sleepy (*concumbens*) Underwings would make quiet companions.

Sargent went on to tell of raging debates among nineteenth-century entomologists. This was a time when, in his words, "The tendency was to attach a name to every apparently new specimen that came to hand, hoping that time would prove the name worthy of species rank." In this flurry of activity, species were sometimes described and named by two people at once.

I got a taste of those frenzied times upon reading excerpts from a publication called *Papilio*. Within this collection of papers published by the New York Entomological Society in the late nineteenth century, I read firsthand the criticisms, both personal and professional in nature, in what I call the Catocala Wars. It got pretty ugly. Augustus Grote, who had published a number of papers describing new catocala species, became incensed when Ferdinand Heinrich Herman Strecker published his own descriptions of a number of the same species using his own names, as one might expect a man with four names might do. The way it works is the first person to publish the description gets to name it. Grote, and many others to this day, believed that Strecker cheated by postdating his manuscript. Grote wrote: "With regard to the species re-described by Mr. Strecker under the date of 'August,' whereas the publication was not received until November 12, I have shown that Mr. Strecker placed a false date, and have exposed his motive for doing so. . . ."

Could you almost feel Mr. Strecker's shoulders tightening upon reading that deliberately crafted word *re-described*? Words were powerful in those days, and used deliberately. Reading through these exchanges, I could almost hear the angry pens scraping loudly across the paper. A far more dramatic sound than the heavy tapping of a keyboard that we'd hear today.

In that same piece, Grote took on G. D. Hulst, who published his own paper on catocala. Hulst, like Strecker, disagreed with Grote's nomenclature and made a great number of changes. Grote had less regard for Hulst than he did for Strecker and made no effort to hide it. In fact, Grote basically accused Hulst of being nothing more than a mouthpiece for Strecker: "In a somewhat lengthy preamble, in which I find nothing original which is at the same time important, Mr. Hulst likens the present knowledge of the species of Catocala to a diseased infancy. In this Mr. Hulst confounds the state of his own mind on the subject with that of others. . . ."

At one point Grote questioned Hulst, who was actually the Reverend Hulst, about his reason for changing the name of one of his underwing moths, *Anna,* to *Amestris.* Grote wondered aloud at the reverend's preference of a "strange woman's" (read "loose woman's") name to that of a prophetess and said it was "singular in taste for a clergyman."

Hulst responded in a later issue, citing all the species that he and Strecker disagreed on to disarm the empty "mouthpiece" accusation. He also, while recognizing the confusion of who published first, sided with Strecker on his beating Grote to the punch.

The scientific community watched these exchanges with mixed reactions. Some did not appreciate the way in which they began to take on more personal tones. A note from the publication committee of *Papilio* followed Hulst's rebuttal: "It is a subject of great regret to us that anything like personalities should have crept into the columns of 'Papilio,' but Mr. Grote's article having been printed during the absence of the editor from this city, it appeared to be only 'fair play' to allow Mr. Hulst the opportunity of reply. As far as this journal is concerned, the matter will end here, and no further personal remarks will again be permitted in its pages."

Aw, nuts. Fortunately, the Internet came around years later to revive this passionate forum.

Scholars now generally agree that although Grote may have had his names in manuscript first, Strecker beat him to the actual publication. But the jury is still out on Strecker's methods of beating Grote to the punch. The names we use for these debated moths today are Strecker's. So, in the end, he won.

I think of Mr. Grote every spring. Here in Connecticut, his namesake, the Grote's Sallow, or *Copevaleria grotei,* appears at my lights and beer bait in early March. It's not much of a moth with regard to size or beauty. It's a drab, dark gray with mottled white orbicular and reniform spots, making it virtually invisible when it rests on damp bark. What makes it special to me is that it's usually the first owlet moth to make itself known in the new year. Its arrival marks the official kickoff of the moth season.

The moth was named by Herbert K. Morrison, a contemporary of Grote's. Remember, the nineteenth century was the time in history when there was a great amount of activity in the discovering and naming of species. Grote was in the thick of it. His full name was Augustus Radcliffe Grote. I've seen a number of pictures of the man. He was somewhat slight in stature and had a walrusy face partially buried under one of those great big nineteenth-century mustaches. He's been described as a nervous, sometimes volatile fellow with, aside from his entomological pursuits, gifts for composing poetry and opera and playing the organ. He was also a philosopher and theologian and considered a fascinating

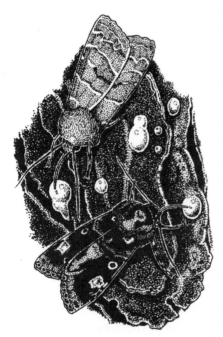

GROTE'S SALLOW (BOTTOM) AND
MORRISON'S SALLOW (TOP)
SIPPING BEER BAIT

dinner guest. He and Morrison were card-carrying members of the mutual admiration society, evidenced by Grote's naming of an owlet in the same family *Eupsilia morrisoni,* or Morrison's Sallow. This moth is not nearly as common in my yard as the Grote's Sallow, but when it does appear it's usually in March and is a result of its compelling thirst for my beer-sugar bait. Although both of these entomologists have long ago passed on, it does my heart good to see their namesakes side by side, having a beer on a cool spring night.

Augustus Grote was born in Liverpool, England, in 1841. When he was seven years old, he moved with his family to a farm on Staten Island, New York, and his insatiable interest in moths developed shortly thereafter.

In those days there were far more meadows and forests to wander, and young Augustus would be up by dawn to see what moths were resting after a night's flight. In his early teens, his collecting trips centered around Brooklyn, New York. This was at a time when the Brooklyn Bridge was still in its planning stages, and Walt Whitman's newly printed *Leaves of Grass* could be found in a Brooklyn bookshop. However, little else could be found in bookshops to supplement the interest of a budding entomologist. It was a great challenge to students of lepidoptera in those times to identify what they found, because there was not much in the way of moth collections or books. But Grote carried on and eventually became an entomologist.

When he was in his thirties, Grote, after studying the cotton worm in Alabama, tried to get appointed to a newly established body called the U.S. Entomological Commission. He did not succeed, and believed that his failure was the result of fellow entomologist Professor Charles Valentine Riley's interference. Why? I don't know, but Grote had a new enemy, and Riley became the target of many of Grote's vehement criticisms. We have already seen how capable Mr. Grote was in this capacity. What is puzzling is that in 1882, about a decade after what Grote considered a snubbing from Riley, the professor named a pinion moth after Grote, *Lithophane grotei,* or Grote's Pinion. Guess they made up.

Grote also had problems with entomologist Harrison Dyar over the classification of the Saturniidae. Dyar seemed to want to take the larval characters into account, whereas Grote thought the wing venation should be used to separate them. Dyar had a reputation for attacking his peers in print. (One of his enemies, John B. Smith, is discussed later in the chapter.) Although Grote, as evidenced earlier, was not shy about getting down and dirty, he was sometimes the target of personal attacks on his expertise. In the 1899 *Journal of the New York Entomological Society,* he wrote, "Dr. Dyar charges me with entertaining more beliefs than I am conscious of possessing."

In the following years, Grote traveled quite a bit, ranging from the southern United States to Buffalo, New York. He wrote for a number of journals and published the *Synonymical Catalgue of North American Sphingidae with Notes and Descriptions* and the *List of the Lepidoptera of North America.* He also was one of the founders of the New York Entomological Club. In 1884 he moved to Germany, where he spent the last twenty years of his life. His wish had been to return to North America, but he could not find a secure position that suited him.

Although Augustus Radcliffe Grote was responsible for naming about a thousand species of moths, mostly Noctuidae, the true testimony to his craft was the number of species named *for* him, among them *Hemileuca grotei, Ulophora grotei,* and a south Floridian Sphingidae moth, *Cautethia grotei,* or Grote's Sphinx.

I sometimes come across another early-season sallow, this one named *by* Augustus Grote; the Comstock's Sallow, or *Feralia comstocki.* This wonderful black and tennis-ball-green moth shows up at my lights in April. The outer edges of its wings are checkered with black spots, and the moth blends in well with lichen-encrusted conifers. This moth, one of the most attractive of the sallows, is named for John Henry Comstock.

Comstock was born in Wisconsin in 1849 and was orphaned that same year when his father died of cholera while heading west for the gold rush in a covered wagon. The cholera epidemic was reaching its apex in those days, and it took the people a while to figure out the importance of clean drinking water. Comstock's mother became ill shortly after, and Comstock eventually was taken in by a sailor and his wife in Oswego, New York. Young John, who later went by the name Henry, was a tenacious boy who tried to enlist in the Union army when he was fourteen. He was turned down. He spent the remaining early years of his life as a cook aboard sailing vessels on the Great Lakes. He was a small man whose body remained in almost constant motion. He also stuttered. At one point, an uncle attempted to correct his stuttering by beating it out of him. Not surprisingly, it didn't work.

It was a book that twenty-one-year-old Comstock found in a Buffalo bookstore that sparked the interest in insects that would become his vocation. *Report on the Insects Injurious to Vegetation* was chock-full of information and beautiful engravings, and Comstock bought it for ten dollars, which almost bankrupted him. But he had to have it. He cherished the book and studied it from cover to cover. He scrawled a note on the book's flyleaf: "I purchased this book for ten dollars in Buffalo, N.Y., July 2, 1870. I think it was the first Entomological work I ever saw. Before seeing it I had never given Entomology a serious

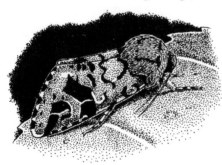

COMSTOCK'S SALLOW

thought; from the time that I bought it I felt that I should like to make the study of insects my life work."

An odd note to write in one's own book, but it gives you a sense of what it meant to him.

Comstock eventually became an assistant professor of entomology at Cornell. Soon after, President Garfield appointed him chief entomologist of the U.S. Department of Agriculture. This was only nine years after Comstock had come across that book in Buffalo. This says something about the passion the man had for insects and is a strong endorsement of the book that inspired him.

Like Grote, Comstock spent time in the South studying the cotton worm. This moth was a major problem for cotton growers. Not only did it have a voracious appetite for the foliage of cotton plants, it could produce up to six generations per year, making it difficult to control. Like Grote, Comstock had an unpleasant relationship with a Riley, but in this case it was William Riley. Riley didn't get along with the commissioner in Comstock's department and refused to share with Comstock any of the data he had collected on the cotton worm over the years. Their relationship could not have improved when Comstock was booted out by the new president, Chester Arthur, after Garfield's assassination, to be replaced by—you guessed it—Riley.

Comstock met his future wife while he was teaching at Cornell. The first time her name, Anna Botsford, crossed his lips was probably while taking class attendance; she was one of his freshman students. The two worked together on many projects; she was a talented wood engraver. I am fortunate to own the Comstocks' *Manual for the Study of Insects*, published in 1894. Were it not so valuable to me, I'd have her engravings cut out of the book and framed to hang on my walls. Anna, a well-trained naturalist in her own right, is referred to in the preface as the "Junior Author" and is credited with some of the text. One side note on Anna: In 1898 she was appointed to the position of assistant professor in Cornell's natural science department. But the board of directors, being made up of nineteenth-century men, knocked her down to "lecturer." Fifteen years later, that nonsense was overcome and she was reinstated as assistant professor; six years after that, she received a full professorship.

One aspect of their book that appealed to me right away was Comstock's breaking up the Latin names into syllables to aid in pronunciation. Although there is often more than one way to pronounce a scientific name, I have an uncanny ability to choose the one not generally used. But the *Manual*'s great success can be attributed to the invitingness of the writing. For example, to describe the family of sphinx, or hawk, moths, he writes: "Of all the beautiful arrayed Lepidoptera, some of the Hawk-moths are the most truly elegant. There is a high-bred tailor-made air about their clear-cut wings, their closely fitted scales, and their quiet but exquisite colors. The harmony of the combined hues of olive and tan, ochre and brown, black and yellow, and grays of every conceivable shade, with touches here and there of rose color, is a perpetual joy to the artistic eye."

And here's the part I really like: "They seldom have vivid colors except touches of yellow or pink on the abdomen or hind wings, as if their fastidious taste allowed petticoats only of brilliant colors always to be worn beneath quiet-toned overdresses."

The Comstocks' book did so well that John started his own publishing business, Comstock Publishing Company. He and Anna went on to create several popular guides on natural history. John worked into his eighties, until he suffered a brain hemorrhage; he died five years later. I would like to have met him, but I'll have to settle for his lepidopteran ambassador.

Earlier on I mentioned the book that inspired Comstock, *Report on the Insects Injurious to Vegetation*. It was written by one of the most revered entomologists of all time, Thaddeus William Harris. I have come across his namesake in two different incarnations: as the Harris' Checkerspot butterfly and as the strikingly handsome dagger moth named by Francis Walker: *Harrisimemna trisignata*, or Harris' Three-spot.

Without having to look it up, I was able to identify the Harris' Three-spot after coming upon it in the field for the first time. I had seen its picture in field guides and it stuck in my mind as something I really wanted to see. It's a medium-sized moth with a wingspan about the width of a quarter. Three large, rusty red dots, each like the eye

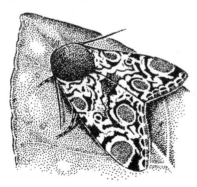

HARRIS' THREE-SPOT

of Jupiter, jump out at you from the three corners of its triangular forewings. I've found this moth only twice, one of those times while leading
a moth trip for the Dennison Pequosepos Nature Center in Mystic, Connecticut. It was the hit of the evening.

So who was this Harris, who made an entomologist out of a galley
cook and whose namesake nearly drew applause from a crowd of newly
initiated moth lovers? He must have been something to have his schol-
arly visage on the cover of the *Journal of Economic Entomology* for
thirty-six years.

Thaddeus Harris was immersed in natural history from the start. His
mother raised silkworms to make her own silk, and his father wrote *The
Natural History of the Bible,* an inspired account of every animal mentioned in the Bible. Thaddeus was born in Dorchester, Massachusetts,
nineteen years after the signing of the Declaration of Independence. As
an adult, he suffered from frequent, severe headaches and often over-
worked himself to exhaustion. He was tall and thin and in a way resembled a clean-shaven Abe Lincoln. He is best known for his passion and
enthusiasm for insects. Although he was trained as a physician, he didn't
enjoy medicine and after eleven years left to take on the job of librarian
at Harvard University. While at Harvard he prepared and studied his im-
mense collection of insects. This was a tremendous challenge in the early
nineteenth century, because so few had paved the way for him, but he
was aided by his keen knowledge of the biology of the insects he studied.
Many entomologists concern themselves with a particular part of an insect's life cycle, usually the part that holds the most interest for them or,
in the case of an economic entomologist, as Harris was, the part responsible for the insect's most obvious, or negative, contact with humans. But
Harris wanted to know everything about the entire life cycle and spent
countless hours rearing his subjects.

Harris was kept busy with the duties of maintaining the library, researching the names of the insects in his collection, and lecturing on
natural history. He also had twelve children, which shows his great interest in the human life cycle as well. He didn't get out into the field as
often as he would have liked, but when he did he was in his element. In
the book *American Entomologists* (Mallis, 1971), T. W. Higginson, a student of Harris's, said: "He had the quick step, the roving eye and the
prompt fingers of a born naturalist; he could convert his umbrella into a
net, and his hat into a collecting box; he prolonged his quest into the

night with a lantern, and into November by searching beneath the bark of trees. Every great discovery was an occasion for enthusiasm. . . ."

In 1841, as Augustus Grote was viewing the world through a newborn's eyes and eight-year-old John Comstock was getting to know his new surroundings upon the death of his mother, Harris published his *Report on the Insects Injurious to Vegetation*. This was a landmark publication that carried information that farmers, gardeners, and anyone who wanted to know more about insect pests thirsted for. I should note that the edition with the beautiful pictures that so inspired Comstock was never seen by Harris. The pictures were added after his death.

In his sixty-one years, Harris became well known in and out of the entomological community. One of his buddies was Henry David Thoreau. Harris, who was a couple of decades older than the writer, had a lot of respect for his knowledge of natural history. At times he would ask Thoreau to collect specimens for him. Harris was quoted as saying, "If Emerson had not spoiled him, Thoreau would have made a good naturalist." Between Harris and Thoreau, Massachusetts was put on the map as a hotbed of natural history discovery and appreciation.

About thirty years after Harris's death in 1856, Grote stated that he "ran the first furrow, and his successors have but widened the field of practical and economic entomology." Grote's respect for his predecessor was shown when he named a parsnip-loving borer moth after him, *Papaipema harrisii*.

Grote, Grote, Grote . . . We continue to come across his name trailing after the genus of some moth he described. I forgot to mention earlier, not only do discoverers get to name their discovery, their name—usually in parentheses—gets tagged onto the scientific name for all eternity. Grote's name follows yet another of my favorite moths, a tiny lichen-feeding insect called *Cisthene packardii*, or Packard's Lichen Moth.

The Packard's Lichen Moth is about as long as a pushpin and a bit wider than a cardboard match. When I first came across one, I thought it was some kind of leafhopper. For such a diminutive creature, the pattern on its wings begs to be noticed. The patterns and colors on insects' wings and bodies have evolved to help them live

PACKARD'S LICHEN MOTH

in their environment. Although I can't see how the toothbrush-shaped yellow-pink line on its forewings has helped this tiny lichen moth survive in its element, I'm sure that in some way it has.

Alpheus Spring Packard, Jr., was born in Maine in 1839 and was a contemporary of Grote's. A modest man with an interest in the arts, he was described by his friend Theodore Cockerell as having an "unassuming and quiet disposition" but a "tremendous spirit when roused to just anger." Packard was tall and thin with a bearded profile resembling that of a Smith Brother of cough-drop renown.

Packard's interest in natural history began with a fascination for seashells, but by his mid-teens his mind was open to many other facets of natural history. Then T. W. Harris and his famous book *Report on the Insects Injurious to Vegetation* struck once again. It got young Alpheus thinking about bugs. He entered college in 1857 and graduated with an M.D., but he spent a great deal of time studying entomology and geology. After his graduation he went to Harvard to study entomology under the great Louis Agassiz. Packard hoped to someday become the curator of the school's museum. He was virtually broke, but Agassiz paid his tuition, as he did for a number of his interns. This arrangement ended when the museum came up with a new policy regarding the insect collections of Agassiz's assistants: They were to become the sole property of the museum. Insect collections can be very valuable and personal items to the people who put them together. This was the case with Packard, so he left Harvard.

Then his career took a brief but interesting side road. He volunteered for a stint as a surgeon in the army. He was trained as a medical doctor, but, like Harris, he spent more time chasing invertebrates than he did healing people. (Bear in mind that in those days army surgeons did a lot of their healing with saws.) Packard's time as an army surgeon (1864 to 1865) marked the end of his medical career. He preferred to travel around this country and Europe, studying this and that, publishing his findings, then moving on to the next project. At one point he teamed up with our friend C. V. Riley when Riley was appointed to the U.S. Entomological Commission, but they did not spend much time working together. Packard's mission was mainly to study locusts in another part of the country. From all I can gather, they got along well.

Packard was what you could call a well-rounded natural scientist. In addition to his published papers and monographs on silkworms,

Geometrids, and Colorado moths, he described mollusks, spiders, bry-
ozoans, and cave fauna. His books, though, were mostly about insects. I
own one of them: *Our Common Insects,* published in 1873. I bought it
because of its subtitle: *A Popular Account of the Insects of our Fields,
Forests, Gardens and Houses.* I was curious about what people were
finding in their homes 130 years ago. The book is really a hodgepodge of
essays, most reprinted from *American Naturalist* magazine; it's a fairly dry
but informative read. In his preface, Packard wrote: "The introduction
was written expressly for this book, as well as Chapter XIII, 'Hints on
the Ancestry of Insects.' The scientific reader may be drawn with greater
interest to this chapter than to any other portion of the book . . ."

What a ringing endorsement for the rest of the book! That would be
like me saying in the introduction to this book, "Don't bother with anything but Chapter Seven. The rest of the chapters are just there to keep
the book from bending."

By the way, as it turns out, people in those times had the same problems with earwigs, carpenter bees, clothes moths, silverfish, fleas, and
ticks that we still have. The louse problem seems to have abated, though.

Packard also wrote another book that I've come across, *Entomology
for Beginners,* published in 1888. It covers everything one could possibly
want to know about insects, from descriptions of insect families to chapters with titles such as "Cutting and mounting microscopic sections of
insects and mounting them whole." In his preface he talks with pride
about one of his most satisfying accomplishments, the moving of the
Hymenoptera order (including ants and wasps) to "crown the summit of
the tree of insect life." This bumped the beetles from that esteemed
position and was, entomologically speaking, a really big deal.

Toward the end of his life, Packard became more and more interested
in evolution, specifically with regard to one of its earliest proponents,
Jean Baptiste Lamarck. Lamarck had published his theories more than
fifty years before Darwin's *On the Origin of Species* appeared in 1859.
Packard had been fascinated by Lamarck since he was a child; the last
book Packard wrote before his death in 1905 was entitled *Lamarck, the
Founder of Evolution.*

A few years back, while on a walk with friend and fellow lepidopterist
Andy Brand at West Rock Ridge in New Haven, we came upon a caterpillar on a grapevine. That was the one and only time I have seen this

particular insect at this stage, but I remember it vividly. From the size and shape (about two and a half inches long), we presumed it to be a sphinx moth. The green saddles it had running all the way up its back assured us that we'd have no trouble looking it up when we got back home to our books. Sure enough, I did find it in a number of my reference guides.

I talked to Andy a couple of days later. "Did you get the caterpillar we saw the other day?" I asked.

"Yeah, it looks like an Abbot's Sphinx."

"That's what I got," I said.

I returned to the spot shortly after, but all I found were the leaves it had been feeding on. It had probably gone into pupation.

In 1821, William Swainson painted this moth for a three-volume collection entitled *Zoological Illustrations*. He chose to name it after one of the first truly American naturalists, John Abbot. Swainson, for whom a hawk, a warbler, and a thrush are named, was a successful nature artist and naturalist who at one point was a friend of John J. Audubon. They had even talked about working together, until they had a falling-out over access to some bird skins. Over the years Swainson had been buying the artwork of John Abbot and chose to honor him with the naming of this sphinx moth.

Prior to Abbot, most of the big-name entomologists resided in Europe and had their insects shipped to them from overseas, where the identification took place. Abbot, born in England in 1751, had a great love of fine art and insects. He was an ardent collector, and when he began to create his own artwork it was no surprise that most of his models had six segmented legs. He soon craved more new finds to collect and paint. Mark Catesby, who had traveled all over America in the early 1700s to collect information on flora and fauna, had published *Natural History of Carolina, Florida and the Bahama Islands* upon his return to Europe. In addition to a variety of mammals, birds, and fish, Catesby had illustrated twenty-seven insects, including the Cecropia Moth and Luna Moth. The book,

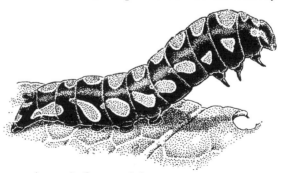

ABBOT'S SPHINX MOTH CATERPILLAR

published in 1731, was given as a gift to Abbot, who was greatly inspired by Catesby's finds. Abbot sold his insect cabinets, collections, and drawings to buy a ticket on a ship to the colonies.

Abbot touched down in Jamestown, Virginia, in 1773. That same year, a few hundred miles north, a group of colonists dressed as Mohawks were tossing crates of tea into Boston Harbor. The ripples of that action would reach Abbot shortly, but there were more pressing concerns in his new part of the world. In 1948 entomologist Charles L. Remington discovered some of Abbot's journals and shared the notes of Abbot's arrival in the colonies in one of the earliest issues of the *Lepidopterists' News*. Abbot wrote: "Soon after my arrival ... it became very sickly in the neighbourhood, with fevers & fluxes ...; in one family 22 died in 2 years white & black leaving only a little Girl heir to the Estate."

Although Abbot escaped the sickness for two years, when he finally came down with, and recovered from, "the Ague and fever," there were other problems. He was still dependent upon English entomologists when it came to pinning names on his finds. Although Abbot was not considered a scientist, he was conscientious and meticulous with the collections he sent back to Europe. It was important to him to have his collections seen by scientists with the hope that they would tell him what he had, and perhaps tell him that what he had was new to science.

I can only imagine how devastating it was for him when twice he lost his entire collection—the first one on a ship that sank on its way to England and the second one when another ship sank even before it left port. The closest I have come to that happening to me was when my computer crashed and I lost a year's worth of my data. Because I am not a collector, I rely on my photographs and notes to keep track of how much fun I'm having. The year of missing records just happened to coincide with the year I got lazy with my photography. I called on some of my most creative vocabulary to get me through the ordeal. But I hadn't traveled to a new continent to find these things, and I am sure that none of my losses were new to science. Knowing this, I can't help but wonder how much my "creative vocabulary" paled next to Mr. Abbot's. I do know that he was devastated and seriously contemplated giving it all up and returning to England.

After serving as a private in the Revolutionary War (on the winning side), Abbot moved to Georgia and ran a plantation. He continued his pursuits as a naturalist and artist, producing thousands of watercolor paintings of birds and insects. He made quite a name for himself and was known by Thomas Jefferson, who had referred him to ornithologist Alexander Wilson as an expert on Georgia birds. Wilson, for whom a warbler and a plover are named, hired Abbot to collect specimens, paying forty-five dollars a bird.

I've seen some of Abbot's paintings and am impressed with his technical skill and attention to detail. He seemed to have a gift for depicting the Lepidoptera. A few years ago, Lawrence Gall, an entomologist at the Peabody Museum of Natural History in New Haven, Connecticut, was researching early entomologists and underwing moths and came upon some paintings Abbot did of these moths. The paintings were so accurate that the moths could be positively identified down to the species. Dr. Gall soon realized that he was looking at paintings of species that were supposedly "first described" in the late twentieth century! It appeared, though, that for two hundred years Abbot "owned" these moths.

Unfortunately, much of Abbot's work was carelessly destroyed by children who were playing in his room after he died. That loss seems to me to be far greater than his sunken collections.

Some of Abbot's artwork did survive, including a self-portrait that appeared in Remington's "Notes on My Life" article in the *Lepidopterists' News*. Apparently it is the only known portrait of this artist, and he looks to me like a cross between Rowan Atkinson (of Mr. Bean fame) and Prince Charles. Abbot's heavily lidded eyes make him look a bit sleepy, but there is an almost childlike smile beneath his ample nose. He has the look of a man who is pleased with what he does, not in an egocentric way but in a satisfied and quiet way. This may seem like a lot to pull from a self-portrait, but what makes his natural history art so appealing is his ability to capture the essence of the creature. Why not assume he did this with his own image?

I was going to end this chapter with an account of one more entomologist, but a moth I found last night begs to be added. It's a Geometrid that I come across often; the one I'm looking at as I write this is the first of the season. It's only about an inch and a quarter from wing tip to wing tip; at rest its shape suggests a flattened pyramid. The upper half of its forewings is a rich, almost purplish brown. The lower half is a mottled tan. The trailing edges of the wings are tattered; they're supposed to be, because the overall shape and color of this moth give it the appearance of a dead leaf.

HÜBNER'S PERO

The moth's name? *Pero hubneraria,* or Hübner's Pero. It was named by a busy mid-nineteenth-century entomologist, Achille Guenée, for German entomologist Jacob Hübner, who was considered the first of the world's great lepidopterists. He was born in Augsburg, Germany, in 1761. Augsburg is the birthplace of Leopold Mozart (Wolfgang's dad) and two words: *diesel,* as in the engine, named after Augsburg native Rudolf Diesel, and *Messerschmitt,* as in the airplane designed by local man Willi Messerschmitt. The Augsburg Confession, the basic statement of faith of the Lutheran Church, was drawn up here during the Protestant Revolution. Although Hübner may not have had the worldwide recognition of these people and events, he is well recognized within the circles of entomologists. There is not much information on his childhood, but it is known that he had an interest in art and often sketched his findings. Early on, he was producing copperplate illustrations of Lepidoptera; by the time he was twenty-four, he'd completed his first work on moths, containing descriptions and illustrations of previously undiscovered species.

Hübner is best known for the controversial publication *Tentamen,* which appeared in 1805. This small pamphlet created some big waves. It suggested a different way to classify butterflies and moths. Hübner added the categories of suborder, family, and genus to the Lepidoptera he described. The subtitle of this pamphlet read, "An attempt to fix, arrange, and name the individual races of Lepidoptera to experts for examination and the expression of an opinion." This "attempt" was more than realized; his revised classifications stirred up a myriad of reactions, including praise, confusion, and great debate. Although it was never published officially, it was passed along through his friends in the lepidopterist community.

Hübner went on to publish what he himself considered his most important work, a collection of a systematic and bibliographical catalog of the world's Lepidoptera. He included hundreds of new names and more of his divisions into families and genera. And he did this from his home base in Germany. Although many moths named by him are found in the United States, they were shipped to him to be identified and described. Scientists in those days had their important positions in Europe and could not gallivant in the New World. Hübner died in 1826 in the city where he was born. Nearly two centuries later, his Napoleonic face comes to mind when I see the moth named for him.

That brings me to the last of the great moth men in this chapter, John Bernard Smith. About nine hundred species of moths, mostly owlet moths, were named by him. At least one of them was named *for* him and lands in my backyard every September. *Xestia smithii,* or Smith's Dart, is not the most spectacular moth I've come across. Actually, it's quite drab. I use a slide of the Smith's Dart when I do presentations on moths to illustrate the typical dart moth. The fuzzy buffalo back, the tentlike position of the wings, the two field marks—orbicular and reniform spots—present on many of that group are easy to point out on this moth, because there is not much else to distract the eye.

Pieter Snellon gave the moth its name in 1896. It was to honor his contemporary, John Bernard Smith. If ever there were one person I'd like to be out in the field with, it would be J. B. Smith. He was a jovial, beer-loving German who liked to go out with his friends to hoist a few and talk bugs. In 1886, while working as an entomological curator at the U.S. National Museum, one of his duties involved the eradication of the insects that plagued the precious hops crops. You want a jovial, beer-loving German for that kind of job.

In 1858, Alfred Russell Wallace, bedridden with malaria in Indonesia, wrote his paper on the survival of the fittest. It is quite possible he "scooped" Charles Darwin on that theory, but it is clear that Darwin is the one we associate with the theory of natural selection. That same year, Abraham Lincoln and Stephen Douglas were going at it in their famous debate in Illinois. Meanwhile, in New York City, Mrs. Smith gave birth to her son, John Bernard. John's father, a cabinetmaker, made John his first insect boxes, which he soon filled with his collections of moths. Despite his passion for insects, John became a lawyer, but that career was short lived, and as soon as he quit the law he got a job as special agent with the U.S. Department of Agriculture. Over the years that followed, Smith held a number of positions as an entomologist and gained a reputation as

SMITH'S DART

a tireless researcher. He eventually became president of the American Association of Economic Entomologists and of the Entomological Society of America. One of his greatest achievements was his work in battling mosquitoes in New Jersey. He and his staff initiated today's practice of ditching to drain mosquito breeding swamps. Although there is sometimes controversy over this method, Smith was the guy who brought New Jersey citizens welcome relief from those piercing proboscises and the malaria that followed.

In *American Entomologists* we get a taste of a different kind of entomological warfare or, more accurately, the entomologist warfare of the time. Remember Dyar, the guy who went to battle with Grote over the Saturniid issue? Well, he and Smith also were famous enemies:

> Although Smith was good-natured, he was stubborn and somewhat opinionated. Thus when he and the sarcastic H. G. Dyar locked horns on a number of occasions the reverberations were felt throughout the entomological world. Such journals as the *Entomological News* record a few encounters between the two behemoths. In fact, according to several of their contemporaries, the feud reached the stage where Dyar named an insect *corpulentis* in honor of the rotund Smith, and Smith reciprocated the honor by naming one *dyaria!*

This account may have been apocryphal, but it's a fun tale.

John Smith died in 1926, leaving behind tomes of research on the world of insects. He described and gave names to so many species of moths that he must have begun to run out of things to call them. Could that explain why a moth he found in 1893 was given the name *Lithophane innominata,* or the Nameless Pinion?

The battles over names still occur with as much fervor as they did more than a hundred years ago. Scientists are not fighting so much over new species as over insects that have been discovered and already named. Many of the disagreements revolve around trying to standardize the common names. Most of the species in question are butterflies. I just sit on the sidelines and let our modern behemoths fight it out. When the chips fall, I'll still call the moths what I've always called them, with their new name in verbal parentheses. I'd like the species I dream of adding to that list to be a tiny, tiny moth, so small that nobody would care what I called it. Which would be just as well, because—forget Mr. Kramer—I'd use all numbers and consonants!

8

Modern Moth-ers

AS an amateur lepidopterist, I rely on the discoveries and descriptions made by real scientists to further my relatively modest pursuits. I read their books and papers, peruse their articles and e-mail messages, and sometimes have the opportunity to join them afield. I am often as interested in their person and methods as in the quarry we seek. As do many with a strong interest in natural history, I find the act of learning to be greatly fulfilling. Granted, I only retain a fraction of what I'd like to, but that just allows me the opportunity to learn it again.

One of my favorite TV programs is A & E's *Biography*. There is something compelling about discovering the backgrounds of people who are at the top of their game. Sometimes I've never even heard of the featured person, but it doesn't matter. People are interesting. When I have the chance to learn more about the people whose work I admire, it's all the better.

Over the years I have been fortunate to have met some of these accomplished people within the field of Lepidoptera. In June of 2000, I was given the chance to meet a whole bunch of them in the same place. I received a message from David Wagner inviting me to Tennessee; more specifically, the Great Smoky Mountains. The letter read, in part:

Dear Mr. Himmelman,

I would like to formally invite you to participate in a moth survey in the Great Smoky Mountains National Park this July. This survey is being conducted as a part of the All Taxon Biological Inventory (ATBI) that has been proposed for the park.

We ask for your participation in a week-long survey in the fourth week of July, that will draw Lepidopterists from across North America (both Canada and the U.S.) to the Park. The week's pinnacle event will be a 24-hour "bioblitz" where we will capture as many species of Lepidoptera as possible. We hope to draw national attention to the GSMNP ATBI and provide the Park with abundant occurrence data.

Sincerely,
Dr. David L. Wagner
Associate Professor
Ecology & Evolutionary Biology
University of Connecticut

When I read "survey ... that will draw Lepidopterists from across North America," I was in! What a great opportunity to meet some of the big kahunas of the moth world, and see how they work. I was also excited about sampling some of the amphibian life, as I had heard that the Great Smoky Mountains had more salamander diversity than any other place in North America.

I did have two concerns, though. One, I doubted my ability to contribute much to this endeavor. My familiarity with moth names beyond the common vernacular is limited. Because my focus through the years has generally fallen within the confines of an interpretive naturalist—that is, I glean information from the scientists and feed it to the public in a more digestible form—common names have suited me fine. I know all too well the eye-glazing effect Latin names can have on the average person, myself included. However, most scientists don't *know* the common names. Many disdain them.

When I mentioned this concern to David, he assured me that I would be able to help in other ways: setting up traps, running errands, shining shoes ... My other concern was that this was going to be a major collecting trip. I had never killed a moth in my life—well, not on purpose. Any time you get behind the wheel of a car on a warm evening, you're making orphans of their caterpillars. How would I handle this? I have no problem with scientists killing insects, and I understand the necessity of it. I wish there were a better way, but at this point there isn't. As for my own pursuits, there has never been a reason or desire to take the life of my quarry. I would no sooner shoot a bird out of a tree for a closer look than snap up a moth in a killing jar. But soon I would be surrounded by thousands of freshly killed moth specimens. In all honesty, I was curious about what my reaction would be when the time came.

With the windows rolled up and the air conditioner blasting full tilt in my rented Dodge Caravan, I couldn't feel how hot it was outside. The built-in car thermometer tipped me off; it read ninety-eight degrees. Tennessee in July is hot. I hate the heat—HATE it! But for some reason, I tend to find myself in places where heat prevails. A month earlier, I had spent a week and a half in the Venezuelan Llanos, a season and place where only an Orinocan Goose stood a chance of sporting a goose bump. But life abounds where it is warm and humid—bird life, amphibian and reptile life, insect life. Usually enough to balance the discomfort.

I had picked up the van at the Knoxville airport. It was way more than I needed for just me, my suitcase, and moth-watching gear, but the price was right. Heat and all, I was glad to be there. As I raced down Route 321 on July 24 and watched the Great Smoky Mountains loom before me, my excitement grew, overriding any apprehensions. I could not get there fast enough.

With a bit of searching, I found the house at the Cades Cove campground where I would be spending the next three nights. The actual event was to begin at 3 P.M. on July 25 and end at the same time the next day. I wanted to arrive a day early to get to know the place a little and to meet some of the people. To my great relief, the temperature was in the comfortable mid-eighties in the mountains. When I walked into the house, two of the lepidopterists who had arrived a day before were busily sorting through a pile of dead moths on the kitchen table. Strewn across the countertops were boxes of deceased moths, along with pinning equipment, books, and killing jars. I made a mental note to watch what glass I reached for should I need a drink.

Marc Epstein of the Smithsonian Institution and Mike Poque of the U.S. Department of Agriculture (USDA) had set out their traps the previous night to add specimens to the collections of their respective organizations. While Mike worked on the larger Noctuids, Marc was painstakingly pinning and spreading moths about the size of the largest letter in this sentence. When moths are spread, their fore- and hind wings are pinned perpendicular to the body. This allows for close inspection of the hind wings, often a valuable clue to the moths' identification. The challenge of doing this kind of work is made greater by the tendency of the dead moths' wings to snap back to their original position. As Marc talked, I watched him repeatedly battle this problem with a particular moth. He'd push up the wing with a pin and it would snap right back down against its body. He showed no evidence of frustration. Had I been in his seat, someone walking into the room would have seen an empty table before me, the box of specimens having long since been sent flying through the window.

Their conversation reminded me of two people speaking while immersed in a good TV show. It was somewhat stilted, as if part of their attention was directed elsewhere. I call this "speaking from the top of the brain." It's something that naturalists do in the field. One of the great assets of nature study is that it's often as much a social endeavor as a scientific one. We enjoy one another's company in the field, but at the same time we understand the need to concentrate on finding what we are looking for. There's an understanding that you may be ignored or interrupted in the middle of a sentence if something of interest comes into view. We sometimes have to remind ourselves while talking to those not in our little fraternity that it can be considered odd to reach over that person's shoulder in the middle of a conversation to flip a leaf to check for caterpillars, or to have your eyes repeatedly darting up to the sky to find the source of passing shadows.

I left Mike and Marc to their work and poked around the grounds. The Smokies are crowded in summer. As it turned out, we were there at the peak of the tourist season. An estimated one and a half million people pass through in July. Despite this, I was able to find some spots to myself. It's a big place.

David Wagner was at another end of the park about ninety minutes away. He had also arrived earlier to get a feel for the place and coordinate the event. This was his baby. I knew David mostly through e-mail correspondence, although we had seen each other briefly a couple of times at Connecticut Butterfly Association meetings. I once had the opportunity to be out in the field with him when I joined him and his University of Connecticut students one fall evening on a Connecticut mountain to collect some moths.

At dusk, after a long and bumpy ride up a mountain road, I pulled up to the research building where David was working. He was standing alone in front of the building, apparently mulling over where to put up the moth sheets. I stepped out of the car and we shook hands. He had a friendly but distracted smile. He looked up at the sky. "Not looking too good," he said. The wind was blowing—not ideal for setting up sheets—and it felt as though it was going to rain. "We'll set up anyway and see what happens," he said.

My impression of David up to that point had been that he was an intense man, very focused, no nonsense, serious. He was about my age—in his forties, of average height and healthy build with a neatly trimmed mustache and closely cropped blond hair slowly heading north up the temples. But as the night wore on, I learned that Professor Wagner could be quite easygoing. He seemed relaxed and at home in the company of his graduate students. He was obviously happy to be where he was. And he had a sense of humor. He laughed at our jokes. But I still had the impression that his mind was always racing.

His students were busily sorting through insects they had gathered earlier in the day. They were supposed to be collecting representatives of a certain number of families. The students worked by lamplight, there being no electricity in the building. David strolled among them, casually peering over their shoulders and answering questions by asking new ones. He then joined me outdoors as I searched flower heads for nectaring moths. We talked about a variety of things, from katydid calls to the frustrations of publication. He enjoys being out in the field, especially with his close friend and fellow entomologist Mike Thomas. Both of them have been studying dragonflies intently over the last few years and have become two of the leading authorities in Connecticut.

There was not much activity among the flowers, but a few moths were beginning to arrive at the moth sheet. I was surprised that David knew many of them by their common name. I tried not to bombard him with questions, but he didn't seem to mind. I asked him what he liked to do when he wasn't immersed in insects. "Volleyball. And playing with my kids. Anything that doesn't involve routine. I hate routine. I don't want to leave a legacy that my yard was well kept." That yard, though, was special to him and was his favorite mothing location. A few years ago, he discovered a new moth species in his yard, making that little microcosm all the more special.

David became interested in insects as a child and attributes that interest to his moving so often. "It was hard to make long-term friends because we were always on the move," he said. The little critters filled that niche. By his late teens, he had amassed a collection of ten thousand butterfly specimens. This probably contributes to his view of amateurs in science. Says Wagner, "Even a fourth or fifth grader can make useful contributions to entomology."

With a young lifetime filled with a fascination for insects, David went to college to study . . . fungus. Specifically, mycorrhizal fungi. Not surprising. If every kid with a fascination for insects became an entomologist, we'd have nearly as many entomologists as insect species. It wasn't until his last year at Colorado State that his professor, Howard Evans, an expert on sand wasps, steered him back to insects. Professor Evans suggested a "fascinating" group of insects for his promising student to wrap his life around—click beetles. But click beetles didn't do it for David. He felt that there wasn't enough room for discovery in that area, at least compared to the group he ultimately chose as his focus: moths. There weren't a lot of people in this field, and the moths, specifically tiny micromoths and the larger ghost moths, were not studied to the extent of other insects. And there are so many moths. And he liked them. He thought they were beautiful.

Over the years, David's interests became more refined. He now prefers to focus on what he calls the "ugly ducklings" of the Lepidoptera, the caterpillars. In fact, when I first walked into the cabin, Wagner had showed me with contained effervescence the contents of each vial from a pile sitting on the counter. They contained caterpillars of a variety of moth species that he had hoped to rear and photograph. Later, as we sat in front of the massive stone fireplace of the research station, David's voice rose with excitement as he compared a caterpillar to a "phoenix rising out of a flame. They symbolize a second chance. . . . Every one is a little Christmas present."

I have his book in front of me as I sit at my computer. It's called *The Caterpillars of the Eastern Forests*. This has been my bible for caterpillar identification. Like David, I get a genuine thrill from taking in a caterpillar, feeding and housing it, watching it change, then releasing this "phoenix" back into the wild. It's even more exciting when I have no idea what the caterpillar will turn into.

I also have in front of me a draft of Dr. Wagner's checklist of the moths of Connecticut. At this point, it contains more than 2,300 species. Since the most findable moths have been found, the best chance I have of adding to that list is to discover a new micromoth, which are usually overlooked. One of those tiny ones that would have driven me to throw the collection out the window in the Smokies.

Back to the Smokies. The morning of the twenty-sixth was about as frenetic as could be expected. Buckets of moths were being dumped onto tables to be sorted and identified. The smell of various killing agents lingered in the room. The doors were left open. Smoking was not allowed. Wagner coordinated the teams of entomologists based upon their area of expertise. He was the picture of calm amid the surrounding frenzy. He seemed to be enjoying himself. I could almost picture him striding through the room like Robert Duvall, wearing dark aviator glasses and a colonel's hat, saying, "Ah, I love the smell of cyanide in the morning." Against one wall was a line of backs bent over microscopes. These were the backs of the micromoth specialists. The macro guys were busy pushing the larger specimens into ever-growing piles.

I sat down at one of the tables to help sort a large pile. My job was to group the moths by families, then, if possible, into species. Here at once was the point source of my two apprehensions. One, my ignorance would be revealed to all, and two, I had to deal with all these corpses. To my surprise, the latter didn't bother me. I even found myself enjoying the opportunity to inspect the insects close up without worrying about harming them. They were already dead, and would have been whether I was there or

David Wagner (left) and Brian Scholtens (right) sorting moths at the "Blitz" in the Smokies

not. It was no different from looking at a collection, which I do enjoy when I have the opportunity. And as far as the whole ignorance thing went, I saw that a *lot* of people had questions. Besides, all I really had to do was put the like moths together in piles. Four of us sat in a circle around the moths on the table and began sorting. It reminded me of when I was a kid doing a jigsaw puzzle with my family. I'd be concentrating on my area and would occasionally have to reach across to put a piece in my brother's section, or he in mine. Then I realized something: Hey, I know that moth! And I know that one, too. And that one! Don't know that one, or that one. But I know *this* one. . . . I recognized the names of a whole bunch of the moths I was coming across. I even knew the names of a few that the others did not.

However, as I had feared, I knew them by *different* names. There was hardly a person in the room who knew the common names of moths. They had no need to. It is virtually useless in their profession, and these were professionals. The uninterested looks arising from my knowledge of the common names eventually closed my mouth. But I was happy. I was genuinely happy! Rarely does a summer night go by when I am not looking at the moths in my area, and it was paying off. I blame the fact that I did not know their scientific names on a man named Charles Covell, Jr., although he would most likely admonish me for not trying to learn them.

In 1984, Charles Covell, Jr., published the book *A Field Guide to the Moths of Eastern North America*. It was part of the Peterson Field Guide Series and was one of three easy-to-obtain guides on moths in North America. Covell wrote the book at the suggestion of Dr. Charles Remington of the Peabody Museum of Natural History in New Haven, Connecticut. There was already a Peterson Field Guide to butterflies, which had been an inspiration to Covell, and he thought that a companion book on moths was in order. The other two moth books out there were *The Moth Book*, by W. J. Holland, and *Butterflies and Moths*, by Mitchell and Zim. Holland's book, containing 1,600 species of moths, was first published in 1901. It had since been reprinted several times by Dover Publications. Although it covers about three hundred more moths than Covell's book, the plates are more difficult to decipher and the names are outdated and are all in Latin. Mitchell and Zim's book is nicely done within the Little Golden Guide format, but it covers a tiny fraction of the information in the other two. Covell's book was the best one for laypeople interested in identifying what they were seeing.

Charles was born in Washington, D.C., in the winter of 1935. He still recalls the time in Tidewater, Virginia, when his mother took him in her arms to see swallowtails gathering on a blooming cherry tree. Apparently it didn't have the effect she expected, because it scared the bejeezus out of him. He obviously overcame his fear of butterflies and was an ardent collector by the time he was fourteen. He was now scaring the bejeezus out of swallowtails.

Like Wagner, Covell went in an early direction that had nothing to do with insects. He taught English at Norfolk Academy in Virginia. Then in 1959, while in the U.S. Army Reserve, he had the occasion to drive his car to Fort Knox, Kentucky, for summer camp. Along the way he was surveying Virginia for butterflies and wanted to find the way to a place called Poverty Hollow near Blacksburg. He sought a special butterfly there, the Northern Metalmark. This diminutive butterfly looks as though someone had detailed its wings with a soldering iron, adorning them with beads of liquid metal. I've seen two of them in my lifetime and can attest that they are worthy of a pilgrimage. Covell visited Virginia Polytechnic Institute to ask a biology professor how to get to Poverty Hollow. He was sent to Dr. James M. Grayson, head of the newly formed entomology department. Charles left with more than directions. Dr. Grayson had asked about his collecting interests, which were quite ambitious. Covell had contributed to the Smithsonian collection as a senior in high school and had been going strong ever since. The professor convinced him that he should change his professional focus to entomology.

I can't help but wonder whether, if not for his search for those metalmarks, I would have had the benefit of his book many years later. There is no doubt that without *that* book, you would not be reading this one.

Covell's specific interest in moths came later at the suggestion of Dr. John G. Franclemont of Cornell University, who suggested the Geometridae, specifically their subfamily Sterrhinae, or waves, as a group needing a lot of investigation. Covell's treatment of the waves is found on plate 46 in his field guide. One of the Sterrhinae, the Large Lace-border, is a common resident in my yard. It's a pale, butterfly-like moth with a broken dark pattern along the edges of the wings. It sits flat, with its wings spread against the surface of its resting place. Of this insect Covell wrote, "This moth and other white waves resemble washed-out bird droppings when they rest with their wings outstretched on broad leaves of low forest plants." I can see this, but to me the moth better resembles what the common name suggests, a lace doily. Its scientific name, *Scopula limboundata,* because of my own ignorance of Latin, tells me little about this creature. The only picture the Latin name conjures in my mind is a little white moth doing the limbo.

Flipping through the pages of Covell's book, I come across names such as "The Scribbler," "Nondescript Dagger Moth," "Slippery Dart," "The Slowpoke," and one of my favorites, "The Festive Midget." These common names were assigned for a number of reasons based upon a description of the moth often reflected in the original scientific name. Most of the common names in Covell's book come from *Common Names of Insects and Related Organisms* by D. W. S. Sutherland. Covell, for the purpose of making this a field guide for the general public, coined a few names of his own. In most cases he simply de-latinized them. How do you de-latinize a moth name? Take the Slippery Dart, whose Latin name is *Euagrotis lubricans.* Darts fall into a group of triangular, fuzzy-backed Noctuids. Within the group called darts is the genus *Euagrotis,* which, for some very specific reason, is where the Slippery Dart fits. *Lubricans,* the species name, refers to an earlier description of the individual moth as slippery, so the translation didn't have to venture very far from the original Latin name. The same goes for the Festive Midget, *Elaphria festivoides,* a small moth within a group of moths called elaphria, or midgets. The descriptive name "Festive" is a de-latinized form of *festivoides.*

When a moth is named after a person, the moniker is called a patronym, and the de-latinization is often simply a matter of removing the "i" (for a male) or "ae" (for a female) at the end of the species name and placing the name before the common name for the genus. For example, *Lithophane baileyi* becomes Bailey's Pinion, pinion being the common name for a group in the genus *Lithophane,* and Bailey being the person honored.

It is my understanding that Covell himself rarely uses these common names. In fact, Covell wrote in his book, "Although common names are emphasized in Field Guides, one should try to learn and use the Latin name, since it is the 'official' name recognized by scientists worldwide." A friend told me a story about a mycologist preparing a field guide to the mushrooms of North America. He got several of his mycologist friends together, opened a few bottles of wine, and flashed slides of various mushrooms on a screen. The mycologists called out common names and the best ones stuck. I imagine that as the bottles emptied, the names got more interesting.

These days, Covell's favorite place to collect moths is any neotropical area not already sampled. He shares the wish of many of us to be the first to find something new. What is it about seeing something no one else has seen before, or doing something no one has done before, that makes it so appealing? There has to be adrenaline involved, because to be the first, you have to put yourself out on the edge. Discovery is a rush!

One interesting note about Charles Covell involves his passion for the game of soccer. He told me, "I have been keenly interested in soccer since high school junior days, and played for forty-seven years. Now I enjoy watching games and collecting the stamps and related philately concerned with soccer." I wonder how many soccer players have a keen interest in moths. I doubt it's reciprocal.

Because many moth common names are rooted in scientific names, with effort I was sometimes able to communicate with the lepidopterists at the gathering in the Smokies. And vice versa. Some of the names are similar in both English and Latin forms. One of my housemates, Dale Schweitzer, was particularly adept at figuring out what I was talking about and did have some familiarity with the common names. He seemed to enjoy the challenge of trying to understand the moths I attempted to describe as I found them.

Schweitzer—who had caught a ride to this event with lepidopterist James Adams, another well-known moth man—arrived the night after I did. The car engine hadn't cooled before Schweitzer set out to paint sugar on trees. I told him what had been suggested to me the night before: that we refrain from painting the trees because of all the bears in the park. Think of the ingredients in moth bait: sugar, beer, sweet stuff. No self-respecting bruin would pass up the chance to lap this ambrosia off the bark, and if there were moths in it, all the better. This information seemed to pique Schweitzer's interest. "Really?" he said. "I've never seen a bear." The fact that someone had been killed in a bear attack a month before, and right at our camp, didn't seem a concern. Concluding that I could probably outrun the lepidopterist should it come down to that, I decided to join him.

Schweitzer is past his fifth decade. He has a somewhat stocky build and a face covered by a healthy beard that preceded his mane in turning white.

It gives him the look of a learned professor. He is not shy with his knowledge, or taciturn, and I probably learned more from him than anyone else during those three days. He, too, is a night owl, and we made a couple of rounds that night checking the bait. It turned up very little, mothwise or bearwise. I have to say that I was a little disappointed on both counts.

The light that our group had set up outside the house became the focal point of the evening gathering. We talked a lot about moths. Oh man, did we talk about moths! When a bunch of lepidopterists get together, they talk shop—shop being moths, with the occasional butterfly story thrown in. Day and night, breakfast, lunch, and dinner, in the car, on the trail, side by side at the urinals, it was moths, moths, moths. I guess the need to talk builds up over time, there being too few people among the general public who care to listen to this topic. When you find yourself around people who *do* care, the moths spill out in a seemingly inexhaustible flurry. I sometimes found my attention drifting in and out, picking up again only when I recognized a person or species they were talking about. My knowledge of moths did increase, although mostly subliminally, because much of the talk was Latin to me. Not the least of what I learned was how important it is for people of like interests to hook up now and then to purge their built-up enthusiasms. I should mention that immediately following this bioblitz was the Lepidopterists' Society conference, so for many, this was just the warm-up.

Marc and Mike generally turned in early, leaving Dale, James, Paul Goldstein, and me to man the ramparts. Paul, a lepidopterist with the Field Museum in Chicago, is one of the most frenetic men I've ever come across. He'd been coming and going full tilt since he arrived, swearing about the "bear jams" slowing him down. A bear jam, I learned, is the backup of tourist cars wherever a bear is spotted. You're stuck there until the bear moves on. Although bear jams didn't bother me, because I got to see bears, the "deer jams" were annoying. Deer are like squirrels where I live, and although they're majestic and all that, I would have taken a pass on sitting in traffic to see one. Earlier, I had offered to help Paul set a moth trap, not knowing it would be a two-mile run up the side of a mountain. Run, because we were racing the dark and neither of us knew where we were going. When we got to the top, we realized that a road ran to within just a few feet of the summit.

This house mothing was a casual affair and had nothing to do with the bioblitz. It's just something we do wherever we go. For me, it was an opportunity to take pictures of live moths, because most of the ones I came across during the actual event were postmortem.

On the last evening, Mike and Marc had called it a night. James had turned in shortly after, leaving Dale, Paul, and me. We sat outdoors by the moth light, drinking beer and chain-smoking cigarettes bummed off of Paul. Neither Dale nor I usually smoke, although we both had in the past. Don't know what came over us. And we talked moths. And we talked moth people. There was a whole lot of talk of Papaipemas, which meant nothing to me. Finally, after about an hour of hearing that name, I asked what it referred to. Dale thought a moment, wrestling with an English translation. "Borer moths," he said. I should have asked sooner. I knew that group and could have cared a whole lot more about what they had been talking about.

It was clear to me that Dale was in his element. The work was just about done, and he seemed about as relaxed as a man can get, to the point where he had forgone the lawn chair for the ground. Having lived in Connecticut at one point in his life, he was interested in what I was still finding there. I think we did pretty well in making ourselves understood.

Everybody there knew Dale Schweitzer. I had heard of him years before, because he had built quite a reputation as a lepidopterist in my parts. He had lived in Connecticut for eight years, six of them spent doing research and curating insects at the Peabody Museum of Natural History. Schweitzer now resides in New Jersey, where he works for The Nature Conservancy as a research zoologist. One of his main focuses revolves around conservation. He is an ardent crusader with the message that in order to protect a species you must protect its environment. It makes a lot of sense to me. Too often, fistfuls of dollars are thrown at a species in peril while ignoring the fact that without giving it a foothold, we are wasting our time.

Schweitzer grew up in Philadelphia, where his interests as a child centered around butterflies. Over time, though, he found that access to good butterfly-collecting areas was limited, and he felt that moths offered more potential. They also had a longer season. With moths, he could keep busy from March through November. Butterflies are more fair-weather friends. Once he was able to drive, he could wander farther in his pursuits, and he found that the Pine Barrens in New Jersey were worth the hour-and-a-half trip. For me the Pine Barrens will always conjure up John McPhee's book of the same name, which painted the area as an odd little enclave of backwoods people and pristine nature. Schweitzer found it far more interesting than "depleted" southeastern Pennsylvania. He ultimately discovered a new moth in the Pine Barrens, a small, grass-eating species he named *Spartiniphaga carterae*. "*Carterae*" was in honor of Annie Carter, who worked with him in the barrens. She died shortly before her namesake was added to the ranks.

Schweitzer has two other Noctuids flying about with names he pinned on them. I thought that this had to be something exciting for him, but he seems to shrug it off. "Writing up original descriptions is tedious and boring," he said. "Not only that, but to do it right, you have to dissect the genitalia and then find someone to illustrate it for you. It's not easy." He added, "There are a lot of people out there sitting on new species because of the time it takes to write them up."

Schweitzer said the process of finding moths is more rewarding than naming them. He particularly likes baiting. His three favorite groups— the underwings, zales, and "winter moths," the latter sometimes known as the sallows—are best lured that way. "The good thing about using bait is that it's easy," he said. "You can have an established trail and just touch it up before dark. When you're done, you're done. No equipment to set up or take down, and you don't have to empty a trap in the morning." His favorite area is about fifteen minutes from his home. His own yard has too much light pollution.

Schweitzer also likes to rear caterpillars and at one point was an avid cocoon hunter. His mention of this flicked on a light in my head. About ten years ago, a friend told me about a man who could identify skippers on the wing and spot a Promethea Moth cocoon hanging from a branch while driving sixty miles an hour down the interstate. It had just dawned on me what that man's name was. Dale Schweitzer. I was speaking to the man! At the time, the story seemed like just an urban legend, a Bunyanesque tale meant to fill young lepidopterists with awe. I mentioned this to Schweitzer, who said, "Yeah, that was me, but my eyes aren't as good as they used to be. I can still do it, though. It's easiest to spot them by looking through the driver's window from the passenger side, especially if the shrubbery is close to the road." He then explained something about "rapid adjustment of focus" and the difficulty of spotting "objects coming closer from a distance."

Doesn't matter. As far as I'm concerned, the legend lives on.

Schweitzer was one of the early inspirations for local lepidopterist

Dr. Lawrence Gall. They hooked up at the Peabody Museum and spent time studying the Catocalas. When they had first met, Gall was a promising high-school student. Schweitzer speaks of him now as a respected colleague.

I once stopped in at Gall's office in the Peabody Museum, where he is now involved in managing the collection and categorizing the electronic database. His office is one of the neatest and most organized I have come across; it's the antithesis of my own, where I hesitate to put something down lest it disappear forever. But he is a categorizer, and it should be no surprise that this is reflected in his environment.

Gall was kind enough to spend his lunch break with me to answer my questions about his career. I had run into him from time to time over the years and had on occasion called him with moth-related questions. We took a short drive from the museum to Long Wharf Park in New Haven, Connecticut. We figured we could watch the migrating butterflies as we talked and ate. Leaning against the giant marble V of the park's Vietnam War Memorial, we did just that.

Dr. Gall is a soft-spoken man in his mid-forties. His black hair is kept neat and short, as is his mustache. He has a thin, athletic frame that suggests he is a runner, although I never asked him if he was. He does play tennis and volleyball, and at one point played semipro soccer. It had occurred to me that we have Wagner, a volleyball player; Covell, a soccer nut; and Gall, who has an interest in both as well as tennis. Could there be a correlation building between lepidopterists and games with nets?

Gall's eyes were alert behind his wire-frame glasses, almost birdlike, and on that day were on autopilot, set to pick out passing butterflies. It was a sunny, warm afternoon and we were treated to the occasional Painted Lady, Mourning Cloak, and Orange Sulphur sailing over the grass. Gall likes warm afternoons. No, he likes *sweltering* afternoons. His favorite place to collect is in Tennessee, preferably on days when the temperature is ninety-five degrees. I had learned what those Tennessee days felt like, and my mind stretched for an explanation. I was already aware that his favorite group of moths was the catocalas, or underwings. He is known throughout the entomological circles as one of the leading authorities on this group. Schweitzer credited him with being the guy who finally sorted out the "taxonomical mess" the catocala group had been in for well over a century. Gall knows these insects inside and out. He knows their biology, their habits, and their history. These are the insects that were the subject of great debate by the nineteenth-century megaliths of science with regard to who named what first and who cheated whom when. The catocalas are a big and boldly colored group of moths, but to Gall their equally colorful history adds to their allure. They are also one of the top five diverse genera in all of the families of moths. Diversity is important to scientists. Keeps them busy. "And," says Gall about the catocalas, "they're fun to collect."

So, what did sweltering afternoons have to do with collecting nocturnal moths? To the best of my knowledge, the best way to find catocalas is to paint the trees on a muggy evening. Following that, a good light burning through the night brings them in. I asked Lawrence Gall why one would go hunting for moths during the day when they could most easily be found at night. He answered with the question, "Did you ever go tree whipping?"

"Um, no," I answered, suddenly feeling a little uncomfortable.

"You've never gone tree whipping? Oh, you really have to try it!"

"Tree whipping?"

"It's also called tree tapping," he said. I was starting to get the picture, or so I thought.

"Oh, like tapping a tree for maple syrup," I suggested. "The moths come to the sap."

"Noooo," said Gall, "You get a baseball bat and smack the tree. This makes the moths fly to another tree. Then you watch where they land, sneak up on them, and grab 'em." He demonstrated using his tuna fish sandwich as the moth jar.

He explained that because the underwing moths are virtually invisible as they rest on the bark of a tree, the best way to find them is to scare them into flight. They quickly land on another tree and close their wings again, making them blend in. They are also very aware of their surroundings, so you have to be quiet as you approach. Tree whipping works only on very hot days, though, because heat makes them active. Gall considers this method of collecting "sporting" because the moths are given more of a chance to escape. He also says it can be somewhat difficult to explain to passersby. "One time on West Rock Ridge, there I was, shirtless and walking around banging a baseball bat on the trees. Five kids saw me and got so scared they ran out of the park."

Moth watching can be dangerous, too. Gall has been shot at in Colorado by men thinking he was a cattle rustler, swarmed by hundreds of tiny ticks after twisting his ankle in a hole, and stopped by the police on many occasions. "You learn to talk your way out of these things," he says.

Gall is the list owner of the world's most active, and immediate, forum on butterflies and moths. About four hundred people subscribe to this e-mail discussion group, which includes some of the top entomologists in the world. A gardener whose gladiolas are being eaten by caterpillars can post a question about it and get a barrage of answers. A butterfly watcher in Ireland can compare notes with a colleague in South America. Valuable information is exchanged and disputed. It sometimes gets heated and ugly. The most "lively" discussions usually involve conservation, the use of common names, and collectors versus anti-collectors. Whenever I see someone new post a message on one of these topics, I grab the arms of my chair and wait for the ride. There are strong opinions and personalities out there. Although many call for peace and civility when the exchanges reach crescendos of personal attacks and bitter diatribes, I silently hope for more. This is better than any "reality TV." During these raging battles, I watch the peacemakers try to distract folks from that sore topic and attempt to guide the conversation toward a more productive and scientific discussion. A few bite, but these attempts prove futile, because such battles must die a natural death. The debates never really die, though. Every once in a while the topic will rear its head again. It doesn't take much to get the snowball rolling. And when it gets tiresome, as we are often reminded on the list, "there is always the delete button."

This forum began in 1994, and once Gall took it over, it became an important entity in the world of Lepidoptera. He is content to let participants police themselves, although at times he contacts individuals who try to sell stuff or get way off the topic. He sees this medium as a modern version of the letters that would have been exchanged prior to this technology. I see him as the host of a big party for people who like to talk about butterflies and moths.

One of the names I occasionally come across at the bottom of a message in this forum is Gary Anweiler. I see the names of these people, read their thoughts and opinions, and have no idea who they are and what they look like. I got to meet Gary in the tiny town of Steveville in Alberta, Canada. Steveville was once a small hamlet at a ferry crossing of the Red

Deer River. It was named after, well, some guy named Steve. The
Steveville campground, where we would be staying, is all that's left to
keep the name alive.

I had been up to visit a friend, John Acorn, to do a little of what
he called "good ol' Alberta mothin'." I had first met John a couple of
years earlier in McAllen, Texas, where I was giving a talk on moths and
he was giving one on beetles. There are some people you feel you've always knosn, and he turned out to be one of them. We've kept in touch
ever since.

Before I get back to Gary, I need to digress a moment about John. He
had come to Connecticut one spring for a visit and to speak to our butterfly association on Alberta Lepidoptera. I had a little gathering of nature types in my yard and had set up the light to see what moths would
come in. It was Luna Moth season, and John doesn't get those where he
lives. We were all sitting around exchanging parasite stories, sipping
single malt scotch, occasionally getting up to check the sheet for moths.
A few things showed up—no Lunas, but other nice critters. Then John
said in his cowboylike drawl, "Ya know, I wonder if it'd be possible to
identify the moths from here using a scope." He was referring to the tele-
scopes that birders use. I looked at him as the thought registered and
said, "I'll be right back." I brought out my scope and set it up. We were
about fifty feet from the light, and, I'll be damned, we *could* identify
them with the scope! Well, most of the bigger ones, anyway. Ol' Mr.
Acorn had succeeded in removing the need to leave the table, where the
scotch was, and walk the whole fifty feet over to the sheet. Just a little
insight into how the man's brain works.

John and I made the four-hour drive from Edmonton to where we
met up with Gary and his common-law wife, Judy, at the Steveville
campground. It's a small place nestled among a copse of cottonwood
trees. We were in the badlands of Alberta, a place where the dinosaurs
had roamed and westerns were filmed. Richardson's ground squirrels
stood with craned necks along the highway; prairie rattlesnakes made
you look where you leapt; and mosquitoes were king.

It was dusk as we pulled into the campground. Before we were even
out of the car, Judy popped her head out of the screen door of their
camper, shouting, "Quick, get in!" SLAM—the door was shut again.
Once John and I had stepped out of the car, we saw and heard what she
was talking about. We were immediately engulfed by swarming hordes

of mosquitoes as we made a dash for the aluminum sanctuary. "Close the door!" shouted Judy as we squeezed into the camper. Squeezed was the word; there were already three others taking refuge: Chris Schmidt, "Physics" Dave, and Gary, all charter members of their loosely formed group, the Alberta Lepidopterists Guild, or ALG. John attempted to add "and et cetera" to the name, turning the acronym into ALGAE, but the idea was pooh-poohed by the rest. A host of others were to join us later that evening. Were we all going to pile into this thing? It was very humid, and rain was on the way. I was offered a warm beer, and accepted.

As the evening wore on, the mosquitoes died down to the point where we could go out in sorties to set up the equipment. I had doused every inch of exposed skin with DEET and virtually soaked my hat in the stuff, but they were still biting. When it comes to mosquitoes, I tend to get stubborn. They're freakin' bugs, for crying out loud! I'm *Homo sapiens*. I eat bugs for dinner! Which, actually, I was.

There was to be a variety of light sheets set up, supplemented by baited trees. Our holy grail was the catocala. I joined Gary as we waded through the tall grass to paint some trees around the perimeter. I could not stop thinking about the rattlesnake that John and I had seen just up the road a few hours ago, but I didn't say anything because Gary appeared unconcerned. The mosquitoes didn't seem to bother him. He was focused on preparing for a night of "good ol' Alberta mothin'."

Gary is a self-described old hippie in his mid-fifties with gray hair and a rugged build, which, since giving up smoking, he admits is getting "puffy." An ample mustache rides beneath his nose. His needs are simple. He does not own a suit; almost everything he wears is denim. He's never spent more than thirty dollars on shoes and owns no more than two pair: one good, one "mothy." He and Judy travel around Alberta in their camper, a twenty-one-foot 1980 Class C motor home that has become a virtual laboratory on wheels. It has a refrigerator, which Judy sees as a plus, and a freezer filled with dead moths. ("Frozen moths keep good!" says Gary.) He has little interest in venturing much farther, because he feels there are lifetimes of fauna to discover close at hand. And Alberta's got a lot of room to stretch. His favorite mothing spots are down in the arid grasslands at the southern end of the province. Judy's interest in Lepidoptera pales in comparison to her companion's, but they enjoy their time together. While he's chasing the leps, she contents herself with setting out a lawn chair or a hammock and reading a book.

Gary is a self-taught lepidopterist who has, well, gotten a little carried away. He has taken his vocation to the level of genitalia dissection. There's one in every group. "I do a fair amount of this and, strangely enough, I really enjoy it," says Gary. "Inflating a moth vesica [bladder] must be a bit like glassblowing. The whole process is delicate..., finicky, and you need a very steady hand. It is like visiting another world where all these interesting bits of information reside, often the bits you need to identify a moth that can't be identified in other ways. It's a kind of alchemy, a place where only the initiated venture to learn these secrets. Strange stuff.... Not really that challenging, I don't think, but one of those things that sounds intimidating [yet] is quite simple once you get past all the mystique."

Unlike most of the professors who do this for a living because they have to, Gary has a totally unrelated job—something to do with building maintenance—and basically does mothing for himself. Of course, he has an ulterior motive: discovering and describing a new species. And he has done this, several times.

Whereas his lepidopteran pursuits throughout most of his years have been solo ventures, he has recently fallen in with what he describes as "a group of comparatively young [twenty- and thirty-year-old] guys who love moth collecting, drinking beer beside a moth sheet, and just being out there looking for new bugs." These were the folks I was hooking up with that night.

Throughout the night, people arrived to set up tents and look at the moths that were gathering, none of them catocalas. A campfire was built, and the smoky ring brought a brief respite from the mosquitoes. At one point I passed by the fire to pick up on a conversation that Physics Dave was having with one of the children among us. Dave was describing the principles of making a Ping-Pong ball bomb by filling it with match heads. The kid hung on every word, his mind seeming to absorb every step and detail. "And then you throw it against a wall, and it bursts into flames!" exclaimed Physics Dave, bringing the boy to giddy laughter. It was clear that, to him, Physics Dave was a god.

I turned in after midnight but earlier than I had expected. The travel was just catching up with me. Those who stayed up were rewarded with a catocala. I don't remember what kind, and don't care, because I missed it anyway. We woke the next morning to pouring rain. My tent seemed to serve more as a vessel for holding water than repelling it. And my left eyelid itched. The previous night I had noticed a blackfly inside the tent and was too tired to go after it. Guess I should have.

We all photographed a Poplar Sphinx moth that had arrived in the night. Gary had spared it for the photographers. This whole outing felt like his show, though I am sure he would deny it. While the others were knowledgeable, Gary seemed to have the greatest amount of energy and enthusiasm. He was the most focused on finding moths. He calls himself "unambitious," but I believe that's a relative term, and it surely does not apply to his "hobby." I'm not saying he didn't have a good time. In his own words, all he asks for in life is "a warm summer night with a sheet, a mercury vapor light, a six-pack, some mosquito repellent, and my buddies Dave and Chris. Lots of stars. Some night birds. And every now and then a REALLY GOOD moth."

John and I said our good-byes, crammed our wet stuff into the rear of his car, and headed back to Edmonton. Later that night, we sat in his delightfully mosquito-free yard sipping McAllen scotch. In all, I think it was a good outing. I agree with Gary: At times the moth sheets are just backdrops for a night spent with good people.

The ALG (Alberta Lepidopterists Guild) gang in front of the mothmobile in Alberta's Badlands. Gary Anweiler (with mustache) in back; John Acorn in mosquito/rain gear

Twenty-four hours later, I was back in my studio doing sketches for a story I was working on. I had the use of only one eye; my left one was completely swelled shut. Damn blackfly.

I'd been hoping to see some of the ALG folks at the gathering in the Smokies. They would have enjoyed it, although it would have been a long trip for Gary's aging mothmobile. As it turned out, the Smokies event was a huge success. Seven hundred and six species were identified. Of those, 301 were new to the park and 25 were new to science. That just boggles my mind. In one twenty-four-hour period, twenty people finding twenty-five species new to science is a testament to how much is out there we don't know about. Wagner had told me on that mountain in Connecticut, "The opportunity for discovering a new moth is still very high. That's why I like going to the tropics, where I feel like I'm the first person to see these things."

Although the bioblitz in the Smokies, and Wagner's own backyard discovery, prove that you don't have to leave the country to be the first person to see a new moth, the tropics do offer a wider range of discovery. That's the draw that has brought scientists of all disciplines down there over the last two centuries. It is what brought a fellow Killingworth resident, Annette Aiello, to Panama. She went, didn't come back, and doesn't plan to.

The town of Killingworth rests on the geological feature known as the Killingworth Dome. The earliest European settlers chose paths around the dome's hills and rocks, but over time the inconvenience was overcome, and it is now a rural town of about six thousand people. We have one cop, no supermarkets, and a post office in our convenience store. It is the kind of place where a person with an odd vocation can stand out. I'm the "bug person" in town, probably the only one. But I wasn't always.

For years I had been asked if I knew the bug lady. People told me she didn't live here anymore; she was somewhere in the Panamanian jungles studying insects. Nope, never heard of her. Then one summer afternoon I came home to find she had left a message on my answering machine. She was in town visiting her parents and wanted to know if we could get together to talk moths. Apparently someone had told her about the other bug person in town. I was thrilled, and she agreed to put together some slides of the caterpillars she had been studying over the years in Panama.

I picked up Annette at her parents' house the next evening. I got a brief history of the town as we drove; needless to say, much had changed. She was an active woman who had recently entered her sixth decade, although she could easily pass for a decade younger. The jungle had been kind to her. Not until I turned on the moth light in my yard (much later; it was still light) did she reveal that she hadn't looked for insects in her hometown in forty years. She went from flower to flower in my meadow, finding caterpillars and putting names on their families and the flowers they fed on. She drew comparisons to the species she had grown accustomed to in Central America and talked about what it had been like in this town when I was just a little larva myself. It was a thrill to host this reunion. This is where she grew up and now she was home again, communing with the plants and insects that had formed her early interests.

Earlier in the evening, I had found a Brown-hooded Owlet caterpillar on a plant in my yard and brought it (still on the plant) indoors to rear. I had left it on the kitchen table with the jar open, figuring it would stick around on its plant long enough for me to show it off. It didn't. It was out of the jar and could have been anywhere in the room. After a thorough search, I couldn't find it. I figured it was a lost cause. But I could see that it was bothering Annette. Her life revolved around finding these little creatures, and it was she who turned it up, instinctively knowing where to look.

We were soon joined by friends Gary and Carol Lemmon, who I knew would be interested in seeing Annette's slides. They were impressed. Later we went out to inspect the moth sheet. It was a slow night, and Annette admitted she had far more interest in the caterpillars than what they turned into. So did Carol, so they had a lot to talk about. In fact, Carol sent Annette home with her own copy of Wagner's caterpillar book.

Annette has a diverse and ambitious background. She works as a staff scientist for the Smithsonian Tropical Research Institute and is an accomplished photographer and lecturer. Her subject titles range from "Caterpillar shelters on plants: We're still at the 'Oh my' stage" to "Behavior of Daddy-long-legs in Panama." Her field research has brought her to Florida, the Dominican Republic, Jamaica, Mexico, Costa Rica, Colombia, Ecuador, and Panama. She now lives with her husband in the little Panamanian town of Arraija'n and works in the nearby Tupper Laboratories, a Smithsonian headquarters built with donations by the founders of the giant "burping" container company. Emanating from her office are the sounds of classical music. She loves music and at one time

(continued on p. 160)

A New Moth in North America

NOCTUA PRONUBA

On June 13, 1996, while blacklighting for moths in my yard, I came across a moth that wasn't in any of my field guides. This surprised me, because this moth had some notable features that would usually cause a species to be included in a reference book. The forewings were a dull brown-gray and had black dashes near the tip, so at first glance this moth appeared relatively drab colored. However, its hind wings were deep yellow with a single black subterminal band. This arrangement suggests a catocala (underwing) moth, a genus that is fairly cryptic in appearance when its wings are folded but which can have bright orange, yellow, or red as the base color for the hind wings. However, two characteristics ruled out this genus for the moth I found that evening.

First, the shape was wrong. When at rest, this moth had a long, rectangular contour, unlike the triangular shape of most catocalas. The second was the single black band on the underwing. Almost all catocalas with a yellowish base on the underwing have one and a half or two bands. No catocala I knew had just one. I was beginning to get excited. Maybe I had a new geographical record for this moth. I took a couple of pictures and figured that at some point I would show the slides to one of several entomologists in the area.

A week passed. I was casually leafing through a copy of *Butterflies and Moths* by David Carter, an Eyewitness Handbook with lots of good photos of Lepidoptera from around the world. As luck would have it, right there on page 253 was my moth! It was a Noctuidae called *Noctua pronuba*, or Large Yellow Underwing. Its listed range was Europe from North Africa to Western Asia. What was it doing here? And were there any other records?

I sent a message with a description of the moth to Larry Gall at the Peabody Museum of Natural History in New Haven, Connecticut. He told me that he had seen the same species for the first time last fall and had seen several more on his porch that summer. One was even flying around inside the car of a friend. According to his best recollection, this species was relatively new to our state. He suggested I contact David Wagner at the University of Connecticut; Anthony Thomas, with the Canadian Forest Service; and/or Donald Lafontaine, from Agriculture Canada. Larry believed that this moth was first introduced to the Western Hemisphere in Canada.

As it turned out, he was correct, and I was able to gather more information by corresponding with these three people.

It seems that *Noctua pronuba* was accidentally introduced into Nova Scotia from Europe in about 1979. It was first recorded in Halifax. Before that it was probably not around much, because it became common within a few years of its first sighting. In other words, if it had been out there before 1979, someone would have known it. It reached Newfoundland and Fredericton, New Brunswick, in 1984, and Maine in 1985. By 1996, it was in Maryland. Its spread had been well documented, and a number of papers had been published reporting an ever-increasing area of occurrence.

In the United Kingdom, this is a common, sometimes abundant moth. In recent years I have heard reports of moth collectors being deluged by many hundreds of them at their lights. Given this moth's great numbers "across the pond," one has to wonder what took them so long to get here.

In Connecticut they were first recorded in 1993 by John Trouern-Trend. They had been seen in good numbers by several people in the state since then. I had missed it by three years! In the big scheme of things, though, that's not very long.

I got a call from a friend the June following my discovery of this moth. He had found some pupae in his yard a few towns over and didn't know what they would turn into. When I saw him a week later, he told me the moths had emerged, and added, "I can't find them in any of the books."

(continued)

He then described *Noctua pronuba*, which I just happened to have with me. I had included some live specimens for a moth exhibit I had put together for the Connecticut Butterfly Association.

Since then, this moth has become very common in my area. It appears in my yard from June through September, flying into the lights like a drunken bomber. I actually hear them crashing into the light sheet. It's not uncommon to find a pair mating right on the sheet. The females can lay up to 450 eggs at a time, and the caterpillars sometimes hibernate through the winter, not pupating until the following spring.

Noctua pronuba feeds on dock, dandelion, and a variety of grasses. According to Carter's book, this moth is considered a mild pest of garden flowers and vegetables in Europe. Given its rapid spread, I wonder if we will regret the arrival of this newcomer. I can't help but wonder if I was among the first to view the moth equivalent of European starlings or purple loosestrife. It is not a given that their feeding habits will cause them to fall into such disfavor, but they are worth keeping an eye on.

A few years after finding this moth, I did a cover illustration of it for *The Lepidoptera Journal*, a scientific publication put out by The Lepidopterists' Society. For months after the illustration appeared, I heard from people grateful that I had solved a mystery for them. They too had seen this moth and could not find it in any reference guide. Like me, they could not understand how a moth so bold in appearance and attitude could have been omitted from books covering their area. There is nothing more satisfying than a mystery solved.

For now, I still enjoy seeing these big clumsy moths coming to my lights. They are attractive. I just hope they behave themselves.

studied piano at Juilliard, although she says she hasn't played in years. She loves it in Panama and has no plans to leave. "I could never live where I grew up," she says. "It's so culturally sterile. In Panama I interact daily with different cultures, languages, and classes. There's a richness there. It's awake, alert, alive." She adds, "And I'm sick of winter."

She lives on the edge of the Panama Canal area, and a good number of her subjects are found right outside her door. Those subjects are mostly caterpillars. She went to Panama as a botanist after spending time in the West Indies, where she had discovered five new genera and two new species of plants. Her interest in insects came about at the lights set

Tortricidae

*Choristoneura
fractivittana*

Slug Caterpillar Moths *(Limacodidae)*

Skiff Moth
*(Prolimacodes
badia)*

Spiny Oak-slug Moth
(Euclea delphinii)

Smaller Parasa
(Parasa chloris)

Ermine Moths *(Yponomeutidae)*

Ailanthus Webworm Moth *(Atteva punctella)*

Bagworm Moths *(Psychidae)*

Ghost Moths *(Hepialidae)*

Common Bagworm Moth case
(Psyche casta)

Silver-spotted Ghost Moth
(Sthenopis argenteomaculatus)

The Infamous Gypsy Moth

Gypsy Moth female on pupa

Gypsy Moth male

Some Day-Flying Moths

Yellow-collared Scape Moth
(Cisseps fulvicollis)

Virginia Ctenucha
(Ctenucha virginica)

More Day-Flying Moths

Black-and-yellow Lichen Moth
(Lycomorpha pholus)

Celery Looper Moth
(Anagrapha falcifera)

Snowberry Clearwing
(Hemaris diffinis)

Hummingbird Clearwing
(Hemaris thysbe)

Anania funebris glomeralis

Nessus Sphinx
(Amphion floridensis)

Eight-spotted Forester
(Alypia octomaculata)

Grape Leaffolder Moth
(Desmia funeralis)

More Day-Flying Moths

Delicate Cycnia
(Cycnia tenera)

White-striped Black
(Trichodezia albovittata)

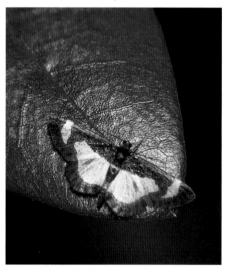

Common Spring Moth
(Heliomata cycladata)

Primrose Moth
(Schinia florida)

Some Cryptic Moths

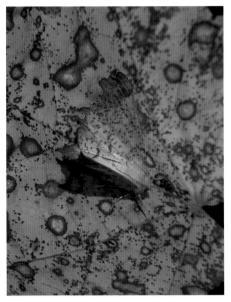

Maple Spanworm Moth
(Ennomos magnaria)

Georgian Prominent
(Hyperaeschra georgica)

Black-blotched Schizura
(Schizura leptinoides)

Canadian Melanolophia
(Melanolophia canadaria)

More Cryptic Moths

Bold-based Zale
(*Zale lunifera*)

Lobelia Dagger Moth
(*Acronicta lobeliae*)

White-ribboned Carpet,
bird-dropping mimic
(*Mesoleuca ruficillata*)

Antaeotricha schlaegeri,
bird-dropping mimic

up by the entomologists at night. She now spends much of her time rearing caterpillars. She loves them. There is an enthusiasm in her voice not unlike Wagner's when talking about this subject. "Do you know what it's like?" she asks, describing the finding of a caterpillar or larva of a fly or wasp. "There's no way of knowing what it's going to be. You watch and study it for days or weeks, and you have no idea of what it is you're watching. Well, you have *some* idea, but you just can't be sure. Then it pupates. I can't sleep at night when it [the pupa] turns dark [the signal that the moth will emerge]. I have to be there when it comes out." Annette, who enjoys mystery books and movies, likens her career to that genre. "What interests me is the process of using evidence to solve a mystery. It fits: Caterpillars, pupae, and larva food plants are evidence. Systematics is mystery solving. I have often thought that if forced to choose another profession, I'd select epidemiology or forensic entomology."

One of Annette's biggest challenges in her work, though, comes when she has to kill her subjects. She does so with great displeasure and only when killing is absolutely necessary. She told me that at one point she even had a hard time pressing flowers. "When a creature seems so alert and intelligent, I can't kill it. I get so attached to the caterpillars because I've spent so much time watching and getting to know them. It's so much easier to do [kill] it immediately after they emerge as an adult. I haven't had the chance to grow attached to it yet."

To get a sense of the work that Annette does in the tropics, I looked through some of the papers she published over the years. In addition to discovering new plants in the West Indies, she found a new day-flying prominent moth for Panama and a new beetle and has described the life histories of a great number of insects. One paper that caught my interest was on something called the "Bathroom Moth," found on Barro Colorado Island in Panama. The paper, entitled "Life History and Behavior of the Case-bearer, *Phereoeca allutella* (Lepidoptera: Tineidae)," was published in *Psyche,* a journal of the Cambridge Entomological Club. Case-bearer moths are better known as clothes moths. They are scavengers that feed on dead insects and animal hair. They're the guys that chew holes in your wool sweaters. The larvae spend their lives in silk-lined "cases" of their own creation that are covered with sand and other small particles, such as insect droppings; they use what's available. I suppose this is not much unlike the practice of the aquatic caddisfly larvae, a favorite bait of fishermen.

Annette studied thirty-four of these tropical members of the clothes moth family in her bathroom. She'd put a drop of white correction fluid (Liquid Paper) on each of their cases and give each a number using a triple-0 technical pen. For about two and a half weeks she measured the distance the larvae would travel, which wasn't very far; they averaged 42.4 centimeters. The process made me think of a frog race, where the competitors are put in a circle and the first one to hop out wins. Annette wrote of the cases, "Most stayed within 30–80 cm ranges, with an occasional sudden change from one wall to another. For example, individual '6' was frequently found out on the floor at night, but rested against the wall under the sink by day. After ten days of this pattern, '6' moved into a nearby corner."

I know that "6" has long since passed, but I couldn't help but worry about him. Was he depressed?

At one point, to get a peek at what happens inside the cases, Annette installed "windows." She cut a rectangular hole in one side of the case and covered it with a lightweight piece of plastic held in place by glue. "I observed turning movements, feeding, excretion, molting, and pupation through these windows." She included in this report pictures of the cases with the home improvements. Although case-bearers are not the most resplendent of creatures, Annette has the distinction of being the first to observe their lives in such detail. She had to have grown attached to them, as she says she does with all her subjects. In fact, in a way, they were a part of her: she fed them her own hair.

When I was in the Smokies, I asked the group if they had heard of Annette Aiello. They all looked at me as if I were crazy for asking. Everyone had heard of her. It was with a bit of pride that I mentioned she grew up in my town.

On the last day of my stay in the Smokies, I put aside the moths and butterflies to look for salamanders. Salamanders do something for me. I have spent countless rainy nights in search of them and have managed to find all the species that can be found in my state. There is a primordial quality to salamanders, and on my last afternoon in the Smokies I was in a primordial mood. Because my flight wasn't leaving until evening, I had the whole day to "sala-meander" through the park. I flipped a lot of rocks and logs and managed to turn up four different species, including the indigenous Jordan's salamander. The Jordan's are closely related to the slimy salamander, a lungless species I've found in Connecticut. The Jordan's can exude a sticky, gluelike secretion from their skin, making them distasteful and tough to swallow. I picked one up to move it into a better position to photograph and got my hands covered with this stuff. If you remember making dioramas in elementary school, you may recall creating ground by sprinkling dirt over Elmer's glue. This is similar to what happened to my hands. They were soon black with dirt and wouldn't come clean. I wore this badge of discovery for about a day and a half.

I found another species, the dusky salamander, in many areas of the park. This is a species I find in my own yard. It was interesting to see it in a different locale. It looked familiar, yet it didn't. It's funny how it made me think of my own part of the world.

I'd had enough of the Smokies. I had just returned from Venezuela prior to this trip and had spent little time at home, and I was looking forward to flipping the logs in my own yard and turning on my own moth light to see some familiar faces. My yard is my favorite place to explore. Every creature in it is an extended part of my family. We share the same air, the same land, and the same water. The property taxes are on me. I once wrote an article about the moths in my yard. About a year later I received a handwritten letter from a man named David Ostrander. He had read the article and was inspired to try moth watching in his own yard in Pennsylvania. Here's an excerpt from the letter, dated June 22, 1998: "Sometime ago, I came across your article 'Watching Moths' in the May/June 97 issue of *Bird Watcher's Digest*. I was fascinated by what I read. I now have a sheet hanging in the yard and a bug light with transformer wires cut hanging beside it. I am having fun, experiencing frustration, and losing sleep."

That last line carries the words of a true moth watcher. Since that letter, I've gotten to know David better. We have corresponded a number of times, and we talk on the phone a few times a year. At the end of every season, he sends me some of the pictures he has taken to see if I can help identify them. His pictures are crisp and colorful, not surprising from a man who learned photography on hummingbirds. I'm looking at a picture of David himself now. Over the last three years that we have kept in touch, I never knew what he looked like. Of course that's not important, but sometimes it's nice to put a face with the voice, so I asked him to send a picture. He looks almost exactly as I imagined, with a lean build and an open, friendly face. His eyes smile. He wears glasses, but who in their eighties doesn't? I didn't picture the beard, though—white, ample, and neatly trimmed.

Ostrander was born in Pennsylvania in 1920. His family had little money, but they made do. Young children generally don't dwell on their parents' lack of prosperity, and he was no exception. They had a home to live in. They weren't hungry. He and his brother spent a lot of time exploring the woods, and he remembers with fondness the spring of the great snail hunt. "Didn't know much about them," he said. "We kept them in cans and would let them out once in a while so we could watch them crawl around. They just had a funny way of moving, and it was very interesting to us. Then, eventually, we'd let them go."

Ostrander's interests evolved from mollusks to butterflies by the time he was thirteen. He and his brother had built a modest collection. "I didn't know anything about preserving them, so we just laid them on a piece of cotton and put a piece of glass over it. It worked well enough at the time." He still remembers the year they caught a Zebra Swallowtail, a rare species for northern Pennsylvania.

Eventually, David entered seminary, then became a pastor for the United Brethren of Christ. He also moved on to a new interest, bird photography. A pastor's salary left him little freedom to spend money, but he bought an inexpensive camera and taught himself how to use it. Over the years, through trial and error, he managed to take a number of satisfying pictures of birds on their nests. Then he came across a book on hummingbirds. He was inspired and determined to photograph this group. I have the sense that when David gets a subject in his head, he has to chase it down, whether it be slow-moving snails or whizzing hummingbirds. However, Pennsylvania is not exactly the hummingbird capital of the United States, there being only one kind, and the photo opportunities were limited. But soon that would not matter. A change occurred in his life that opened new opportunities. Elaine, his wife, retired from teaching. They had some retirement money to spend, and Elaine said, "We're going to buy a trailer." Soon they were off to Arizona, which *is* the hummingbird capital of the United States. It was there, while trying to photograph hummingbirds at feeders, that Ostrander said what all photographers have said at many points in their pursuit: "I've got to have better equipment."

Hummingbirds are tough subjects to photograph. But David was still determined. He found an electrical engineer to build him a high-speed electronic flash. "Expensive," he said, "but I'd gotten to the place where there's no turning back." Then he built a frame with two electronic eyes hooked to relay switches. When a bird broke both beams at the same time, it triggered the shot. He says he was able to get "pretty good photos of twelve species of hummingbirds."

He now uses some of his knowledge gleaned in hummingbird photography to shoot moths. To date he has photographed about 180 species in his yard in Pittsfield. Of those, he has been able to identify 140. And he does this for himself. He doesn't sell the photos and has no plans to publish them. The photos are records of his meetings with these creatures who share his yard. They have become a part of his life and, I suppose, Elaine's, as she has supported his flights of fancy through the years. She was there when he was chasing hummingbirds. She was there when he raised peach-faced lovebirds but couldn't find a market for them. She is there now, while he is bringing insects into the house to photograph on their dining room table. David is getting interested in dragonflies. I'm sure Elaine is braced for that, too.

I see myself turning into David. He has taken the trails I have taken— some before me; some, as with the moths, after me. It doesn't matter who walked them first, because we both, with forty years between our ages, are following someone else's footsteps. Yet, we are seeing these things as if no one had ever seen them before. We jump from one passion to the next, like hummingbirds nectaring in a garden of flowers. And we basically do it for the same reason, professional and amateur alike. We are a wildly curious people who need to have our questions answered. We are driven to do things the average person might find a bit odd. Wagner and Aiello are chasing caterpillars, hoping to discover what they will turn into. Schweitzer is checking his baited trees to see what may have stopped in for a drink. Covell is sampling new species in some neotropical jungle, hoping to be surprised by something he finds. Anweiler is having a beer with a couple of friends by a light in the badlands of Alberta. And Gall is whacking a tree with a baseball bat on a hot July afternoon in a park in Tennessee, chasing after the evicted moths with a jar.

We do these things because, in the words of Ostrander, we "just thrill to the wonderful world around us and want to get to know it better."

Ah, the man still has a bit of the preacher in him. Amen, David.

❧ 9 ❧

Growing Moths

MOTHS make lousy pets. If you went to a pet store to buy a certain type of moth, you would most likely be asked what you intended to feed it to. A caged moth spends a good amount of time flying into the walls of whatever is holding it. When it's not battering its delicate wings, it sits there doing nothing. And it doesn't live very long, which is not a desirable quality in a house pet.

That's not to say you can't bring a moth indoors for a short time. I do that often. One of the best times to find moths is at the crack of dawn. After flying throughout the night, they often ride out the daylight hours in a state of torpor. A moth approached on a chilly morning can usually be coaxed onto a finger, where it will hang on and allow you to study it up close. Picking up a moth is similar to picking up a parakeet. You place your index finger in front of its legs and slowly work it under the moth until it steps onto your finger. At the end of each of its six legs are tiny hooks that can latch onto nearly any surface, including glass, with no effort. It's an adaptation that allows moths to rest in trees without being pried loose by the wind. The hooks are so efficient that you have to be careful when lifting a moth from where it is resting. Sometimes the moth is more firmly connected to what it is resting on than its legs are to its body. No need to go into graphic detail about the possible consequences.

Once you have the moth on your fingertip, you can place it anywhere. Some species are far more cooperative than others. I've found that the Lasiocampidae, sphinx moths, and tiger moths are among the easiest to handle. A few years back, my daughter Liz and I found a Virginian Tiger Moth on the light sheet early in the morning while we were waiting for her school bus. This medium-sized insect is white, peppered here and there with small black spots. I picked the moth off the sheet and placed it on Liz's shoulder. With no visible effort, it held on tightly to her T-shirt. Liz went to school

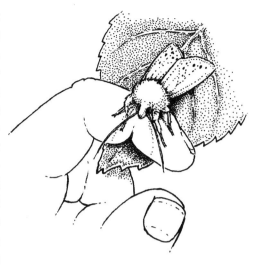

COAXING A MOTH TO YOUR FINGERTIP

with the moth on her shoulder, where it remained all day. It was still there when she got off the bus in the afternoon, although it was missing some furry scales from its thorax; this particular species just begs to have its back stroked, and her friends couldn't resist. We put it on a tree in our yard and wished it well.

The prominents are good perchers, too. Liz recently showed up to a rehearsal with a Georgian Prominent on her shoulder. Unfortunately, between all the attention it received and the warm stage lights, it "snapped out of it" and flew up to the ceiling. During the play I had images of it lurking in the rafters, watching the performers à la Phantom of the Opera.

I sometimes visit schools with a program called "I've Got Moths on My Face." After showing my slides, I ask for a volunteer from the audience to pose for a picture with a live moth on his or her nose. The moth has brought about some interesting facial expressions on the inevitable volunteer. It is a natural impulse to smile when there is a moth hanging from your nose. Perhaps the smile belies the incredulity of this bizarre act, or illustrates the effect of tickling legs on the face. Sometimes, I am sure, the smile is a nervous one.

One thing is for certain, though: When you get up close and personal with these creatures, they are a fascinating eyeful. The fluffy faces and large eyes lend many of them a somewhat teddy bear–like quality. Walt Disney knew the effect this had on people, as is evidenced by his big-headed, large-eyed creations. Perhaps it's a subconscious visual connection to our own big-headed, large-eyed offspring.

One of the more satisfying ways of bringing moths closer to you for examination is to rear them. Not only do you get to see them as you can rarely observe in the wild, another connection is forged between you and this creature for whose life and well-being you have taken some responsibility. You have become, in a way, its foster parent. And like that parent, you feed, house, and clean up after it. You worry about it and second-guess your methods of rearing it. You feel a sense of pride and wish it well when you send it off on its own. And you look forward to seeing its offspring and many continued generations.

People rear moths and butterflies for a number of reasons. For collectors, it is a way to guarantee a clean, undamaged specimen, because the insect has avoided the beatings and scars associated with living in the wild. For the photographer, too, a freshly emerged insect makes for crisp, clear images. Scientists gain the opportunity to study the stages of life as the moth or butterfly goes from egg to caterpillar to pupa to breeding adult. Insect suppliers for catalogs that distribute these insects to schools have breeding down to a science. This saves them a lot of running around with butterfly nets, while at the same time reducing the possibility of viruses and parasites in their stock. Then there are those who wish to re-populate an area with a particular species they care for. Indoor rearing removes a lot of the danger that a wild insect must face, ranging from predation and disease to human landscaping practices. Here is a case where human intervention in the natural world can be a positive act, providing, of course, that the species you are helping actually belongs in that landscape. If you found the insect in your yard, as opposed to importing it from another part of the country or world, you can rest assured that what you are doing is probably harmless.

Carol Lemmon, a friend and entomologist with the state of Connecticut, is having fun with Cynthia Moths. Part of her job is to monitor and wrangle out-of-control insects, which often involves making decisions about what insects are allowed to cross our borders. This can be a tremendous responsibility and requires a great amount of research on the history of each insect and its impact on humans. If an insect species is allowed to go free in an environment in which it did not evolve, it can dominate an area within that habitat, forcing out native species.

Some introduced species are benign inhabitants, however. Cynthia

Moths (shown in the photo insert that follows p. 32) are not a native species. Huge and beautiful, they were brought here from China for their silk about a century and a half ago. Over time, they became naturalized in the Northeast, feeding on another Asian introduction, ailanthus, or Tree of Heaven (the tree in *A Tree Grows in Brooklyn).*

Cynthia Moths, at one time common, have been virtually wiped out in Connecticut. There are several theories on how that happened: over-collecting, pesticides, disease, and parasitism. There's also a good chance they were casualties of biological warfare against the Gypsy Moth. Whatever the reason, the Cynthia Moths are nearly gone, and Carol misses them. She is now working to remedy that by rearing and releasing them back into the wild. When asked about the possible negative effects of releasing nonnative insects in an area, she reasons, "The caterpillars of these moths feed exclusively on a very invasive nonnative tree. Reestablishing the population is one way to help keep that plant in check. Also, they are beautiful insects. Why not have them around if they can only have a positive effect on our landscape?"

Last year, in her hometown of Branford, Connecticut, one of Carol's Cynthia Moths emerged from a cocoon on her porch. The moth flew to the screen and released her pheromones into the air. Nine males responded, suggesting that Branford may someday be viewed as the epi-center for Connecticut's return of the Cynthia Moth.

Another reason for rearing moths and butterflies, probably the most prevalent reason, is appreciated by both children and adults. It is a chance to witness one of nature's miracles. The much-used description of meta-morphosis, "miracle of nature," has become a cliché, but with good reason. There is no better way to describe it. A ten-legged, leaf-snipping, worm-like creature encloses itself in a container and emerges as a six-legged, tube-nosed insect with wings that can impress the most stubborn philis-tine. If that's not a miracle, it's one convincing magic trick! Add a couple of miniature white tigers and a flaming hoop and you could sell tickets.

Teachers in classrooms throughout the world have latched onto the effect that this phenomenon has on children and use it to teach this most curious biological adaptation. They can count on this lesson to win the full attention and cooperation of their students. It's an opportunity for hands-on learning, because the subjects perform their feat—meta-morphosis—before the very eyes of the students.

I remember well the first time I witnessed metamorphosis. As a child growing up in suburbia in the 1960s, I had an early fascination with insects, particularly the Pine Tube Moth caterpillars that lived in a white pine in my backyard. At age eight, I didn't know the name of the caterpillars; in fact, I didn't even know they were moth caterpillars. They were just "bugs." The larvae had made hollow tubes out of pine needles. Just the fact that these bugs had *built* something made them a curiosity. I took one of the tubes off the tree and put it into a coffee can. It became one of the many pet insects I kept in my zoo. Then I forgot about it. The can ended up in the garage and was found the following spring by my father. "I think this is one of your bugs," he said, handing me the can.

I opened the can and was surprised to find that the tube of needles had fallen apart. In the pile was the shriveled skin of a caterpillar. Next to it was an empty pupa, and next to that was a tiny, but obviously dead, moth. My first thought was that the moth had somehow gotten inside the can and starved to death, as did the caterpillar. But then I remembered what I'd learned about metamorphosis from my most treasured book at the time, the *Little Golden Guide to Insects*. I put the pieces together: The "bug" had turned into a pupa, from which emerged the moth. I was for the first time looking at physical proof, material evidence that this metamorphosis thing worked! What followed that season, and the rest of my life, was the desire to see this happen over and over again with as many "bugs" as I could find.

Children today, and their teachers, are no less fascinated by the process and are eager to replicate it. Although the Lepidoptera, most often Painted Lady butterflies or one of the large silk moth species, can be bought from mail-order companies, I have always encouraged teachers to have students find their own subjects. Search for them in the leaves and flowers. Learn how they live and hide and eat in their natural surroundings before trying to replicate their environment indoors. Much can be gained from such a foray; besides, children spend too much time inside school buildings anyway.

Raising Lepidoptera can be a fairly easy endeavor, depending upon the species you choose and the stage at which you begin your involvement. Some stages can be more difficult than others. If you start with the cocoon, or pupa, there is no need to gather food. All you have to do is provide a place for the moth or butterfly to emerge. If you start with the caterpillar, you have more work ahead, because caterpillars are virtual eating machines, and there are diseases, viruses, and parasites to worry about. Naturally, to be in on the whole metamorphosis cycle, you would need to start with the egg. Bringing your subject through all the life stages is more of a challenge but by far the most rewarding.

So, let's say you want to raise a moth starting from an egg. Well, good luck, because finding moth eggs isn't easy! Sure, you may be lucky to find some eggs attached to a leaf or flower, but for most of us the only way to tell what kind of eggs they are is to wait and see what they turn into. There's a good chance that the eggs were squeezed from the abdomen of another kind of insect. The best way to get eggs from a known source is to catch a male and female moth. One of the more reliable methods is to find them at a light or bait. Pluck them from their resting surface and put them in a brown paper lunch bag. It's probably a good idea to hedge your bet by putting several pairs in there in case one of the females has already laid her eggs. This will also increase your chances of getting both sexes if you can't tell the males from the females. Generally, the males are smaller and in some species have more feathery antennae.

Unfortunately, collecting the moths at lights will most often yield males, because they are the wanderers and the ones most likely to get sidetracked to the shining lures. But that's not always the case, and it is not unusual to find eggs laid right on the light sheet or on a nearby tree.

Once the moths are in the bag, bring it indoors and keep it overnight in a dark room. If the moths are going to mate and lay eggs, they will probably do it soon, because they have a relatively short life span and time is a-wastin'. The next morning, you may find eggs—sometimes in clusters, sometimes laid singly—either stuck to the sides of the bag or loose at the bottom. Release the moths, because their work is done, and remove the eggs from the bag. If they are stuck to the side, do NOT try to pry them off. This will damage the shell. Instead, cut the bag around the eggs and leave them attached to the paper. It will be their "crib" during incubation.

With the larger silk moths, you can catch a female and use her to lure males. Make a little screened cage for the female with holes small enough to keep her in but large enough to allow the males to pass their abdomen through to accomplish fertilization. Hang the cage from a tree in the early evening and into the night, when the female will release her pheromones into the breeze. If there are males in the area, they will pick up her scent and home in on the cage, where mating will take place. The female lays her eggs soon after. Make sure that you have provided a piece of paper or a leaf for her to attach them to.

Some people tether their female to an area with a thread. The thread is either put through one of the wings or tied between the thorax and abdomen. The next morning, the eggs are collected and the moth is released. I could never bring myself to do this.

A friend, Cindi Kobak, once had a Promethea Moth cocoon that she kept in her kitchen by the window. One afternoon around 4 P.M., while she was in her living room, she heard something banging on the kitchen screen. When she entered the kitchen, she discovered that the moth was halfway out of the cocoon, but that was not the source of the noise. On the other side of the screen, several male Prometheas were throwing themselves against the barrier that kept them from reaching the emerging female. Apparently, she had begun releasing her pheromones before she had completely exited the cocoon.

Cindi brought the cocoon outside, where one of the lucky males immediately latched onto the female. They mated right there on the cocoon. When finished, the female laid her eggs on cherry branches that Cindi had provided, cherry being the favored food of the larvae. All the eggs eventually hatched, a testimony to how fast they became fertilized.

However you gather your eggs, they will have to be put in some kind of clear container. It should have a lid in case the eggs hatch while you are not watching. A couple of pinholes in the lid is a good idea but is not always necessary. Your concern at this point should be airflow, not the amount of oxygen in the container; there will be plenty. You don't want too much moisture in there; it can cause fungus to grow, although it will not always be visible. Think about how the eggs of these insects have evolved over many thousands of years. They are subjected to freezing, wind, rain, snow, and sun but rarely more than a few of those conditions at the same time. Bear that in mind also if you collect the eggs late in the season, when they are meant to overwinter at that stage. They must be allowed to go through cold temperatures to develop and emerge at the time when their host plants are available. The same goes for the cocoons. Unfortunately, many teachers fail to realize this and end up with a doomed butterfly fluttering around the classroom in the middle of winter. If you have eggs that in nature are meant to overwinter, keep them in an unheated garage or foyer. Make sure they don't bake in the sun or become too dried out; they would normally be exposed to some precipitation. Some people overwinter them in a refrigerator. This works well, but remember that refrigerators dry things out. To avoid drying out the eggs, keep a moist wad of cotton in there with them and replace it when it dries out. Or keep them in the vegetable crisper, which is meant to keep vegetables from drying out and should help solve that problem for your moths, too.

While your eggs are incubating, which could take a couple of weeks, you should be locating food for the caterpillars. This will undoubtedly be a leaf of some kind. Many caterpillars are host specific, meaning they will eat only certain plants. One way to find out what your caterpillars eat is to look for mention of their food source in a book or other reference. This is assuming you know the species you are dealing with. If you don't, you will need to wait until they emerge from their eggs; then you'll have to act fast, because they will be hungry.

Usually, the first thing the caterpillars eat is their own eggshells. This is a quick and easy source of nutrients, and eating them has the added benefit of removing from predators evidence of their being there. After that act, the caterpillars are full-fledged herbivores, and it is necessary to find them their fodder. You will need to collect young, soft leaves to experiment with. It would make sense to start your leaf collection in the area where you found the moths or eggs. Take a number of different leaf species and divvy them up among the young caterpillars. You will most likely have to put the caterpillars on the leaves, preferably the underside, which is more tender. To do this, pick up the caterpillar with the tip of a fine paintbrush by rolling the bristles under the legs until the caterpillar grabs on. It can be difficult, not to mention deadly, for the caterpillar if you pick it up with your fingers. The caterpillars are easily crushed.

You may have to try a few different types of leaves before you find the one that is actively fed upon. You will have to watch closely, because at this stage, called the first instar, the caterpillars' mandibles are tiny and weak and often capable of eating only through a single layer or the down under the leaf. Look for caterpillar droppings, or frass, beneath the leaves. This is the best evidence of their interest in a particular plant.

Many people who want to raise moths and butterflies begin with the caterpillar stage. Caterpillars are wonderfully diverse in appearance and behavior and can be relatively easy to find. Wherever there is foliage, there will be creatures that eat it. Except for beetles, the caterpillars of Lepidoptera are the most numerous leaf munchers.

One of the first clues to finding caterpillars in the wild is chewed-up leaves. Some caterpillars, such as leaf miners, tunnel between the layers. Leafrollers roll up the leaf and feed inside it. Most caterpillars, however, feed on the underside of the leaves and along the edges, which keeps them out of sight of birds and other predators. A general rule of thumb is that if you find a leaf with the edges eaten, it was done by a caterpillar. If the center of the leaf is eaten, it was most likely done by a grazing beetle. But don't count on this; there are many exceptions.

A fun way to find caterpillars is with a beating stick. Your supplies for this endeavor should include a stick and something in which to catch the caterpillars. The caterpillar catcher, called a beating sheet, looks like a square kite. A white bedsheet is often used, because it is the best background color to make the insects stand out. The sheet is held taut by two crossed sticks, with the ends of the sticks attached to one of the four corners of the sheet. You hold the beating sheet by the crossbar underneath the branches as you whack them with the stick. This shakes free all kinds of insects, including caterpillars. Then it's just a matter of sorting through the insects and putting the ones you want in a container.

Another way to find caterpillars is to lay a white bedsheet on the ground and throw handfuls of the surrounding leaf litter onto it. If two people do this, you can each grab two corners of the sheet and shake things up a bit. Let the sheet settle back on the ground and remove the leaves. You should find all kinds of little critters, including caterpillars. A number of owlet species feed on dead leaves; the adults look like what they eat. This is how you find their larvae.

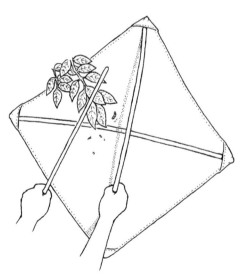

BEATING SHEET

At this point I should include a word of warning: Not all caterpillars are safe to handle. A few have spines whose sting is worse than that of a hornet. In some cases, as with flannel moths, the spines are hidden beneath a soft tuft of hairs. If you brush against the spines with bare skin, they break off and lodge in your skin, causing great discomfort. (You can remove the embedded spines with a piece of duct tape.)

The Limacodidae, or slug

caterpillar moth family's larvae, although fascinating to look at, include species with stinging spines. Nonetheless, I strongly recommend seeking them out. Every fall in Connecticut, several of us go on what we call a slug caterpillar moth caterpillar hunt. Some of these species look like showy little beads; some have what look like multicolored miniature forests of leafless trees growing out of their backs. They are all legless, and move in the manner of slugs, hence their name.

There are also varieties of long-haired, fuzzy caterpillars whose covering can cause itching or mild irritation. It is generally a good idea to avoid touching any spiky or fuzzy caterpillar unless you know that it is harmless. The good news is that everyone's favorite fuzzy caterpillar, the Woolly Bear, is safe to handle.

As with moth eggs, your chief concern with the caterpillar housing should be airflow. Caterpillars will not thrive if their habitat it is too damp or too dry. I find that humidity is a bigger problem to control than dryness. If you see condensation forming on the inside of the container, you will have problems. Suitable containers range from pickle jars to terrariums, all of which should have enough holes in the top to allow air exchange. I like to use small plastic terrariums that are sold in pet stores. The main "box" is clear, like an aquarium, and the lid allows plenty of air to circulate. Take care that the holes in your container are smaller than the caterpillar, because these critters can be quite the escape artists. Another reason to keep the holes small is to keep the parasitizing Hymenoptera out of the container, although this shouldn't be too much of a problem if you're rearing the caterpillars indoors. Some of these wasps and flies can be very small. They reproduce by laying their eggs on or in their hosts. This doesn't kill the caterpillar right away; it's needed to feed the parasite's developing offspring. Some parasites that need more time to develop can induce in the caterpillar a high level of juvenile hormone, putting off the host's pupation and allowing the parasite

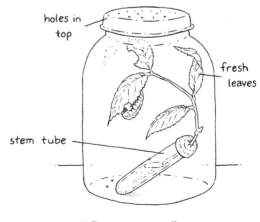

holes in top

fresh leaves

stem tube

"CATERPILLARY"

more time to feed. Sometimes the host is forced into an extra molt. When the parasite is ready to emerge or move on to the next stage of development, the caterpillar dies. Some years I have had more success in raising parasitizing wasps than the moths I had hoped for.

Regardless of the container you use to house the caterpillar, you will have to find it food. If you were fortunate enough to find the caterpillar on the plant on which it was feeding, then you know what to feed it. You will need to keep a fresh supply of those leaves coming. Always pick the cleanest, most tender, uneaten leaves and rinse them in cold water. This will remove potential bacteria, fungi, or virus-containing residue left behind by other insects. It is a good idea to pat them dry with a paper towel to keep mold from growing. To save yourself the trouble of replacing them every day, you can put a small branch of those leaves in water inside the container, but make sure that the caterpillar can't fall into the water; caterpillars can't swim. Little stem tubes used for single-stem cut flowers work well. They look like miniature test tubes and have a plastic cap with a slit for the stem. Ask for them at a flower shop, or look on the Internet under companies that supply flower shops.

Let's say you don't know what kind of leaves your caterpillar feeds on. Here is a fun way to find out: Collect several different kinds of leaves and put one or two of each kind in the bottom of a wide box. Separate the leaves from one another and add the caterpillar. Cover the box and check it every few hours. A little pile of caterpillar droppings, or frass, beneath one of the leaves is a sure sign that the caterpillar was eating that leaf. This method may take a few tries with a number of leaves, and it may take more than a few hours, but it hasn't failed me yet.

Speaking of frass, you will have to remove it from the container every day or two, depending upon how productive the caterpillar is. Some of the larger species have very large frass, which I've found makes good fertilizer for houseplants. It's really just processed plant matter and is odorless. It is not always soundless, though, especially if you're rearing the larger sphinx or silk moths. If you housed them in glass jars and have several jars in one room, you will be treated to a symphony of "tinking" as the frass is expelled and strikes the sides or bottom of the glass. Here's a question to ponder: If you put an infinite number of silk moth caterpillars into an infinite variety of sizes of glass jars, would the frass eventually "tink" the melodies of all of Beethoven's symphonies?

If you are raising a colony of caterpillars, it is a good idea to sepa-

rate them as they grow. Overcrowding and too much moisture are leading causes of unsuccessful rearing, especially with some of the larger
Saturniid caterpillars. If you see them turning dark or spotty, it's probably too late, but they should still be separated immediately. Viruses, bacteria, and fungi are easily spread in moist conditions, causing disastrous
effects, ranging from shriveling up to melting—very disconcerting.

A good way to avoid too much moisture, and having to collect leaves
every day, is to rear the caterpillars outdoors. To keep them in one place,
and to keep out parasites, a rearing sleeve is necessary. This is often just
a lightweight white (to reflect the heat) cotton pillowcase. It is slipped
over the leaves, and the open end is tied tightly around the upper end of
the branch. Because this provides sunlight and allows moisture in and
out, the caterpillars experience temperature variations closer to natural
conditions than they would indoors.

Although trees sporting hanging white bags may not be attractive
from a landscaping perspective, they do make good conversation pieces.
How many people could come close to guessing the purpose of the bags?
It's fun making up less than truthful explanations. I almost had one
neighbor convinced that they were "tree mittens" I had picked up at a
garden supply store to protect trees from the unseasonably chilly spring
weather we'd experienced.

My wife, Betsy, made me a few of these sleeves with the added feature of a small extra opening that could be tied off. This allows me to
empty the frass. I remember looking at my front yard one afternoon,
noting all the bags hanging from the branches of various trees. It occurred to me that whereas
horticulturists cover their
plants to keep bugs out,
I do so to keep them in.
To me, any habitat whose
plants are being chewed by
insects is a healthy habitat
(as long as the insects are
not defoliating certain
trees, and garden plants
are declared off-limits, and
as long as the insects don't
get carried away).

FRASS
OPENING

CATERPILLAR SLEEVE

If you've done your job right, your caterpillar should make it to its last instar. Most lepidopteran caterpillars molt five times, growing larger with each instar. Just before they are ready to molt, they stop eating. At this point they have grown too large within their somewhat inflexible skin. They will then split the skin and crawl out, ready to eat to capacity again. But the time will come when they stop eating completely. This is the signal that they are ready to pupate. Often the caterpillars turn dark. Some "go walkabout." They wander, looking for a place to metamorphose. Depending upon the kind of moth you have, it will either enclose itself within a silken cocoon or leaf or go into the ground as a naked pupa. If you are not sure how it will go through this stage, provide the means for both. Lean a leafy branch of what it has been feeding on against the side of the container. Caterpillars that pupate inside a hanging cocoon will crawl up the branch and use their silk to wrap themselves within the leaves. Caterpillars that will be naked pupae will seek a place on the bottom of the container to shed their last skin, allowing the new skin to harden and encase the changing caterpillars. In this case a layer of dirt or even a few layers of paper towels should be provided to simulate underground conditions. If you are using dirt, make sure there are no spiders or other predatory insects mixed in. You can use new potting soil to play it extra safe.

The easiest way to rear a moth is to start with a pupa, so you don't have to worry about providing leaves to hungry mandibles. Finding a pupa often just requires flipping a few logs or rocks. Or you can dig round the base of a tree; many species do not wander far from where they were feeding. You don't have to dig very deep; pupae are fairly close to the surface, allowing an easier escape when the time comes. Cocoons are best sought in winter, when the leaves are off the trees.

Whichever the case, a stick should be present for the newly emerged moth to climb on. Every moth and butterfly emerges from its pupal stage with wrinkled wings. It needs a place to hang and pump fluid into its wings to stretch, flatten, and fill them out. If there is not enough room for it to do so, the wings will be bent or crumpled and the moth will be unable to fly. Therefore, it is mandatory that there be enough room.

I built myself a "cocoonery" for this stage. It's just a rectangular box screened on three sides to allow the natural elements to wash over the cocoons and pupae. I keep the box hanging on a tree outdoors where it gets some sun and some shade and can catch a breeze. I used basic window screening, which has holes small enough to keep the moth from getting out and other insects from getting in. In addition to parasitic insects, you want to keep out spiders and earwigs, which will also make a meal of your pupa, and mice, which can find their way into anything. I drilled drainage holes in the bottom of the cocoonery and put screening over them as well.

I place the cocoons in there on the sticks they had attached themselves to, or I pin them to the back wall, which is not screened. The naked pupae rest in small, dirt-filled plastic plant boxes. There are a

A custom-built "cocoonery."

few sticks in there for the newly emerged moths to hang from while they dry their wings. Like the pillowcase "tree mittens" on the trees, the cocoonery prompts a lot of questions from our guests.

If you don't want to build a cocoonery, you can use a large jar or terrarium. Just make sure there's enough elbow room for the moth and a stick for it to climb on. Bear in mind that the larger the caterpillar, the larger the moth.

Throughout this process, it is a good idea to write down your observations. How much time elapsed from egg to caterpillar? From caterpillar to pupa? From pupa to adult? What did the caterpillar eat? How did its appearance change with each instar? If you experimented with different host plants, was there a preference? Did the caterpillar eat the edges or the center of the leaf? Did it feed only at night, during the day, or both?

All the information you gain can be used the next time you raise caterpillars and can be shared with others with the same interest. You never know where this knowledge can be useful. I think that one of the most valuable pieces of information is the date the moth emerges from its pupa. This is the part of the life cycle that is most important to me.

There is nothing more exciting than going out to the cocoonery and finding a new moth resting inside, especially if I didn't know what kind it would be. What you do with the moth at that point is up to you. If you have a number of the same species from different populations, you may be able to get eggs from them and start the process all over again. I usu-

Moth Photography

Although I don't consider myself an expert in photography, I have learned a few things over the years about photographing moths. What I once deemed acceptable results ten years ago are "just for the record" today. Our standards change, keeping pace with our abilities. As we learn more about different techniques and improve our equipment, our images continue to improve. Also, new opportunities present themselves unbidden when a particular moth we may have photographed already shows up in an irresistible pose.

Why did I even begin taking pictures of moths? Two reasons. One, my interest in these insects inspired me to keep track of what I saw. It's something we humans do. We collect things we like because we like collecting things we like. Bird photographers savor their finds with photos of birds. Butterfliers photograph butterflies. I once met a woman who hung around airports to take pictures of airplanes. They fascinated her, and getting pictures of different ones became a treasure hunt. That's the essence of it. It's a treasure hunt, the treasure being a new memento of an encounter with an interesting subject.

I am curious about what is living in my area, and my photos are backups to the data I've collected, not just with moths but with many of the creatures that stir my interest. Moths—most adults, and many of the caterpillars—are, simply, beautiful, in either subtle or spectacular ways. Others may not be beautiful at first glance, but are fascinatingly peculiar looking! Photographs allow us to see the tiny details. In addition to moths, I have photos of nearly every frog and salamander in Connecticut, and about half the butterflies, and have begun to document the night Orthoptera. I use these pictures in presentations to clubs and schools. When you have a passion for something, there is no greater joy than spreading the word and enlisting others to join in. Photographs help that along.

ally just photograph the moth and let it go. Sometimes it will sit on the trunk of a tree, waiting for nightfall. Other times, though, it will fly out of my hands, over the lawn, over the trees until it disappears from sight. This is an exceptional and satisfying moment.

When you have reared a creature and come across that same species out in the field, you feel you know it intimately. And to know any creature well is a gift.

A second reason for capturing moths on film is because I like the artistic aspect of it. I am by profession an artist and writer. Photography has become an extension of my art, and creating a good photograph can be as satisfying as making a good painting. I try to be aware of color, shape, shadows, and composition in my photographs and attempt to capture the essence of the creature I'm shooting. Often, out of a roll of thirty-six exposures, I may get just one or two that I'm happy with and ten that are pretty good. The rest get tossed or are saved for reference or records.

I will not spend too many words on the actual equipment you need, because I have not experimented much. I've used the same 35mm Minolta X-370 for about fifteen years. It's a manual camera, which I insist upon. Although I have seen remarkable results with some automatic cameras, I enjoy tinkering with the aperture and shutter speed. It makes me feel as though I have more to do with the process.

Here are some basics for macro photography using a manual camera.

Lenses

Because all but the largest moths are too small for a basic 50mm lens, you will need some way to make the moth appear larger. In the beginning I attached add-on close-up lenses to the end of a 50–200mm zoom. They usually come in sets of three, with each offering a different level of magnification. It would be more accurate to say that the close-up lenses do not so much magnify as allow you to get closer to the subject. It is the equivalent of moving your eye closer to something; it seems bigger as you get closer. The lenses are similar to the various lighting and special-effect filters you can buy: a flat metal ring around a glass disk. They screw onto the very end of the main lens. You can use just one, or combine them to get the desired level of magnification.

(continued)

Attaching a close-up lens to a zoom lens allowed me to keep more distance between me and the subject, which is sometimes an issue with skittish creatures. One of the drawbacks to this method, though, was I would sometimes get a halo of unclarity around the edges.

A few years ago, I switched to a more satisfactory technique: extension tubes. As with the close-up lenses, the tubes often come in sets of three, each with a different level of magnification. The individual tubes are barrel shaped, the deepest one allowing you to get closest. The tubes can be combined; using all three can make the tiniest moths look big. I get sharper pictures with this setup, and it eliminates the halo problem.

The extension tubes are easily attached with a twist between the lens and the body of the camera. After a while, you get a sense of which tube, or combination thereof, you will need for a particular-sized subject. Even then, you find yourself juggling between tubes to find the right one. It can be inconvenient, but the results are worth it. The tubes cost less than a hundred dollars for a set of three.

For the sharpest images, you can use a fixed macro lens. This is a lens made specifically for blowing things up. The drawback in using add-ons and extension tubes is that the main lens is being used under conditions for which it was not designed. If you are a perfectionist, this might bother you.

If you want to make the moth look really large, add a bellows to the close-up lens. A bellows unit, which looks like an accordion, goes between the camera body and the lens. It allows smooth, continuous focus adjustment. Using it, you could fill the frame with a single letter in this sentence.

Flash

When you start using extensions and add-on lenses to achieve super-close-up images, you lose some light. Unless you are shooting in full sun, you'll need to use a flash; sometimes a flash is useful even in full sun. The ideal setup would be a mount with two adjustable flashes to help eliminate some of the heavy shadow that a single flash can produce. Or you could use a handheld flash for more shadow control; even better, use it in conjunction with a mounted flash. Flash rings attached to the end of your lens are also helpful; they provide more even lighting and are handy for picking up detail. Me? I just use the flash mounted on the camera. I have far too much other equipment to carry around in the field.

Natural light, when there is enough available, is preferable. When I suspect there is enough natural light, I try a couple of shots with and without the flash to determine which is best. You can make a note of which shot was which for future reference, but you can usually distinguish the two when you see the photograph.

Film

If you are shooting moths up close, a flash will bathe your subject in light. Therefore, you will need slow to medium-speed film. Film with an ISO rating of 100 seems the most versatile for the variety of light conditions you will encounter. Most people I know use it. It is a compromise between the fine grain of 64, useful in bright situations, and the softer contrast of 200. I wouldn't go past 200.

If your shooting will be fast and furious, buy film in rolls of thirty-six exposures. If your camera will be sitting idle for long periods of time, buy film in rolls of twelve or twenty-four exposures. Images deteriorate on film that sits around a long time before being developed.

Whether to use print or slide film is determined by how you'll be using your photographs. If you want to carry around photographs and show them to your friends, print film is best. If you want to show entire groups what you've been up to, or if the images will be published, slides are best. Bear in mind that although you can turn a print into a slide, it will not be of the same quality as if you had started with a slide. And vice versa.

Camera Settings

Remember this: the smaller the aperture, the greater the depth of field. I try to take most of my pictures with an aperture between f/11 and f/22. This allows me to get more of the moth, and the background, in focus. That is, of course, if you are shooting during the day. At night, you may have to open the aperture, but not too much, because the flash will overpower the surrounding darkness.

Bracket, bracket, bracket. In photography, *bracket* means take several photographs at different settings. I usually shoot both one-half and one full stop over and under the indicated setting. How many pictures I take depends upon how much I care about the photo coming out perfect and how much film I have. Taking just one photo feels like a waste of film. I'd rather save that photo to add to a bracket of shots, even if it's just two.

Here's something that drives me nuts: shooting a roll of film without

(continued)

realizing the shutter speed was on the wrong setting for flash. This results in every slide being half picture, half clear acetate. What makes that even worse is when the half picture looks as though it could have been a good image. If you have a camera that allows this, double-check often. On my camera, the shutter speed has to be set at 60 to use a flash. The problem occurs when I take a picture without the flash, then switch back without resetting the shutter speed.

Naturally, with an automatic camera this wouldn't be a problem.

And now, some tips for photographing moths:

❋ If you are shooting at night, wear an adjustable headlamp so you can illuminate the moth and still have both hands free to focus the camera. You may not always be able to dupe someone into holding a flashlight for you. A piece of red cellophane over the light will make it less disturbing to the moth.

❋ To shoot moths in their natural resting position within a natural setting, check around the perimeter of your light sheet. The moths are often scattered throughout the area. They are most docile in the early morning, while there is still a chill in the air.

❋ When approaching moths in their natural setting during the day, watch your shadow. If it crosses your subject, the bug is out of there!

❋ If your subject is too active, cool it down in the refrigerator for about ten minutes. This will calm the moth without harming it. If you are on the road, put the moth in a container or a net and hold it in front of your car air conditioner. Some people carry a cooler for this purpose.

❋ Sometimes you want to show the underwings. A cooled, or even resting, moth may give you the opportunity to push the forewings open a bit. Use your fingers or a grass stem. Then shoot quickly; the wings won't stay open long.

❋ Once the moth begins to vibrate its wings, it's getting ready to take off. This makes it tough to get the wings in focus. If you place a cupped hand over the moth for a few seconds, it will usually stop vibrating long enough for you to squeeze off a shot.

❋ If you have captured a moth for later identification or photographs, use a container with smooth sides so the scales won't be knocked off as the moth flutters around. The fur on the upper thorax gets worn off easily, giving the moth a shiny bald spot. Put a piece of crumpled napkin or a single unit from a cardboard egg carton in the bottom of a jar for the moth to grab onto.

❋ If possible, avoid putting two moths in the same container. One always gets active before the other, and the fluttering wears the freshness off the wings.

❋ Sometimes it is easier to identify a live moth "in hand" than from your photo. Make a note of the moths you are shooting right after the photo session. You will save yourself a lot of frustration later. Sometimes I do a little sketch of the moth next to its name.

❋ White moths can be tough to shoot. The light of the flash bounces off them and back to your lens, overexposing the photo. Use a higher f-stop. The same goes for moths on a white background.

❋ Sometimes it's fun to show the moth sitting on a fingertip or nose. You should pick up a moth the same way you pick up a parakeet. Slowly move your index finger beneath the "chin," forcing the moth to step onto your finger with its front legs. Once the legs have latched on, slowly pull back. The moth will feel unbalanced and grab on with the other legs. Move slowly and steadily, simulating a branch in the wind.

❋ Don't hold a moth by its wings, especially if you are hoping to get a good photo of it. Your fingerprint will appear as a smudge where the scales have been wiped off.

❋ Vary your angles. Moths are interesting to view head on, from the side, underneath, hanging from a branch, et cetera.

Digital Cameras

I have seen some phenomenal crisp, bright moth images taken with digital cameras. The technology has been improving by leaps and bounds. Because of this, any specific tips I offer here may be outdated in the near future. Much of the advice mentioned above can be applied to digital cameras, except, of course, when it pertains to film. To avoid any graininess, use as high a resolution as possible.

One of the best attributes of shooting with a digital camera is the instant gratification and the ability to e-mail the images to your friends (although you can scan prints and do the same). With a digital camera and decent color printer, you can produce good prints. Bear in mind that not all digital camera models accept a macro lens, but many allow for close focus. The image can be cropped and enlarged on the computer with satisfying results.

✣ 10 ✣

Moths by Day

MY friend Bill is sitting on a bucket in the middle of his meadow. He'd rather be out and about, but his toe is killing him. He has what is referred to as the "disease of kings," also known as gout, which means that his big toe swells into a house of pain, making it difficult to walk.

I've known Bill Yule for a number of years. He's usually the tallest person in a room, with a graying beard and an easygoing nature. He's known within his circle of friends as "the Big Easy." About once a month, he and I get together with several naturalist friends to play poker. When naturalists play poker, the conversation is different from the usual inane topics one would expect to hear at a poker game. Oh, our stories are inane, there's no question, but they are inane stories with a natural-history theme, and Bill always seems able to pull the best ones out of his hat. He was both young enough and old enough to appreciate the 1960s, so he has an edge on the rest of us. As a naturalist, he has an almost obsessive curiosity. When he locks onto some new interest, he bulldogs it, shortly making himself someone you go to for answers on that subject. But at the same time, he exudes contentment while amongst the flora and fauna he is so curious about. He seems to have found the balance between the pursuit of knowledge and the serenity of just being out there.

This latest gout flare-up has dragged on longer than usual. And it's late May, a bad time for a New England naturalist to be out of action. So Bill is in his meadow making the best of it. He has been sculpting this habitat for years, allowing certain grasses to take over, adding native wildflowers, and creating paths for the butterflies to pass through. People driving past his house may shake their head at how this homeowner let his lawn go to pot, but to a naturalist it is a sanctuary. When you wade through this tall jungle of grass, all manner of creatures hop, scurry, and fly at your approach. The thought of Bill in this little haven brings to mind the early *Doonesbury* cartoon strips with Zonker sitting in the middle of a big puddle dubbed Walden Pond. This is Bill's Walden Pond.

Although Bill's specialty has been mycology, or the study of mushrooms, he has always had a keen interest in butterflies. But lately, butterflies have been boring him, so he thought he would try to get to know moths a little better. "I'd already seen the butterflies in my meadows so many times, I was looking for a new challenge. But I've been afraid to begin to learn moth identification because there's about a billion different kinds."

This is a dilemma for a lot of people. There are many moths out there, and many look alike. Yet they *are* out there and are pleasing to look at. Once you become aware of them, they are hard to ignore. A number of moths do fly during the day. It is believed that the prehistoric ancestors of moths were also day fliers, but as more predators, such as birds, evolved to eat them, they began to beat a path to the darkness.

Day-flying moths encompass a wide group of families; in fact, most of the moth families have representatives that have turned their back on the night. When I talk about day-flying moths, I am not referring to the ones that spook upon your approach. Many of the Pyralidae, for example, rest in the grass during the day, and their flight is just a means to get them out of danger. Once they settle down again, they remain virtually inactive until nighttime. Some moths fly both day and night, but a true day-flying moth is one that flies side by side with the butterflies, nectaring on flowers or bait.

On any given day in any meadow or garden, there are likely to be day-flying moths. In some areas, they may outnumber butterflies. This is especially true in alpine zones, where the air is cooler. The moths seem to do better in the cold, having evolved ways to keep warm without sunlight. Because day fliers are at risk of being discovered by avian predators, many appear to look like anything but a moth. Some look like bees or wasps; others resemble beetles. One looks like a little hummingbird.

Some species are unpalatable and advertise this with bright colors and bold patterns. The day fliers can also be swift on the wing and able to perform intricate maneuvers to draw the envy of their nocturnal cousins. In essence, they are equipped with enough attributes to allow a defenseless, nonaggressive creature to survive among the birds long enough to pass on its genes.

Bill is using the day fliers to ease himself into moths. "I jumped into the moth identification fray by playing a mind trick on myself. I'm pretending that the day-flying moths are a group of 'special butterflies,' and it's working!" Butterfly identification is a little less daunting than that for moths. For one, there are fewer of them. Because the day-flying moths are just a fraction of the number of night fliers, you can get to know the few in your area fairly quickly.

One of the common moths that Bill has come across in his meadow is the Yellow-collared Scape Moth. The scape moth is a tidy-looking wasp mimic, black except for a deep orange-red collar on the anterior thorax. According to Bill, it is now an old friend in his yard. He knows these moths well. Well enough to know that they should be called *orange*-collared scape moths; neither of us has seen one with a yellow collar. He also knows them well enough to distinguish them from the other wasp moth in his yard, the Virginia Ctenucha. Both the Yellow-collared Scape Moth and the Virginia Ctenucha (the "C" is not pronounced) are in the Arctiidae family. Within this family is a subfamily of wasp moths called the Ctenuchinae. The two species are similar in appearance, but the Virginia Ctenucha, instead of sporting an orange collar, has an orange head. It is also larger and more wasplike. The body is a beautiful metallic blue, similar to the shiny blue thorax and abdomen of some of the thread-waisted wasps.

I have a patch of mountain mint in my little meadow. The flowers attract a wide variety of wasps; in fact, I never realized how many different kinds of wasps are in my area until I saw them at this plant. Orange and black seem to be the dominant colors among them. Also yellow. These are the colors of the scape moths and the Ctenuchas that feed among them. They are the "sheep in wolves' clothing." The wasps don't seem to mind them, and vice versa. I enjoy watching the feeding frenzy and seeing how the moths fit right in with the wasps. For me, it is moth watching on the edge, because I am always a little nervous in the proximity of large stinging insects. Perhaps I should have gotten over it by now, but while

"The Big Easy" surveying a meadow

I will wade among them in the flowers, I'm not at all relaxed, and I'm constantly aware of any opening in my clothing, especially the leg holes in my shorts. I have this thing about wasps flying up my shorts. What fascinates me about watching these insects is seeing the mimic and the model together, noting their similarities and differences. I wonder how often the birds are fooled. How quickly can they size up a potential meal? Could an extended proboscis of a Ctenucha moth be noticed by a bird, allowing it to see through the ruse? Are the moths better off alone or among the wasps, taking the risk that a sharp-eyed bird will pick up a subtle difference? All I know is that the insect-eating birds in my yard tend to steer clear of the mountain mint patch. I don't blame them.

So, with the Yellow-collared Scape Moth as his old, recognizable friend, and with comfort in his ability to tell it from the Virginia Ctenucha, Bill moved forward in his exploration of moths. He soon learned to distinguish the Snowberry Clearwing from the Common Clearwing at a glance. The Snowberry and Common Clearwings are two of the best-known moths in the hawk moth, or sphinx moth, family. About all they have in common with the two Arctiidae described above is they're all moths. The scape moths and Ctenuchas resemble wasps, or perhaps beetles that resemble wasps. They feed by landing on the flower, usually one with a flat top, and probing for nectar while crisscrossing its surface. (Wasps and beetles lack proboscises and instead feed with chewing mandibles, though they can lap up fluids.) The two clearwings, however, feed on the wing, hovering from flower to flower, dipping for nectar with a long proboscis. The Snowberry Clearwing resembles a bumblebee. The Common Clearwing, also known as the Hummingbird Clearwing, looks and sounds like a tiny hummingbird. Its wings make a soft, sputtering sound and appear as a blur as they carry the moth forward, backward, up, and down in search of nectar. These moths are called clearwings because the center of their wings lacks the scales present in the wings of most Lepidoptera. They do have scales, though; they're rusty brown and run along the borders of the wings, surrounding the "windows."

There is another day-flying, hovering hawk moth—the Nessus Sphinx—that I've had trouble finding. A friend, Andy Brand, told me he comes across them in the nursery where he works; he's been watching the day-flying moths, too. I asked him to grab a Nessus Sphinx for me the next time he found one and I would come out and get it. The moth is similar to the Snowberry Clearwing and the Common Clearwing, except it doesn't have clear wings. The wings and body of the Nessus Sphinx are a rich, red-brown with two bright yellow stripes bisecting the abdomen. I've wanted to see one and photograph it.

I got the call shortly after my request and made the hour-and-a-quarter drive to his nursery. I had brought with me a cooler with some ice in a bag to keep the moth calm for the ride back. I was greeted by Andy when I got to the nursery, and he took me to the barn where the moth was being stored in the refrigerator. The other workers snuck side-long glances as Andy took out the moth and handed it to me. It probably looked like some kind of drug deal. But they had to have known better, because Andy's probably a bigger bug nut than I am.

On the ride home, I had to stop and pick up some mealworms for a children's book that I was doing on that insect. I stayed in the store a little too long, and when I got back to the car I heard the unnerving sound of whirring wings. I looked into the cooler and saw that the ice had melted. The moth was awake and was frantic to get out. I raced home, making the forty-five-minute remainder of the trip in about twenty-five minutes. By the time I pulled into my driveway, the moth had knocked so many scales off its wings that it was in no condition to be photographed. I let it go and remained in a stormy mood for the rest of the morning. Later that afternoon I went out to get the mail. Something caught my eye on a flower to the left of my front door. It was the Nessus Sphinx. "Couldn't relax until I got home, could you," I said. But...hold on a second. I looked more closely at the moth. This one was as fresh as a spring morning and was obviously not the one I had brought home from Andy's! I ran in the house, grabbed my camera, and photographed the living daylights out of it. My stormy mood had lifted. Some may consider the two-and-a-half-hour round-trip to Andy's a waste of time. The way I look at it, I was paying my dues.

It so happens that Andy had another day-flying moth for me a little later in the year. This one was a Black and Yellow Lichen Moth. Like the scape moths and Ctenuchas, this lichen moth is in the family Arctiidae. Whereas the former moths resemble wasps, these look like beetles. In fact, they bear an uncanny resemblance to the carnivorous netwing beetles that share their habitat. They are somewhat beetlelike in flight, too. After seeing this lichen moth in person, I wondered whether I had seen it before but mistook it for the netwings that I find all over the place. I looked at the moths more closely the next time I was afield and was rewarded with the discovery that many of what I may have been calling netwings were in fact lichen moths. I found a good representation of them nectaring on goldenrod flowers in a nearby field in late summer.

The advantages of looking like a stinging insect are obvious, but I wondered how a moth could benefit from looking like a beetle. I suspect that the netwing beetles are distasteful, and advertise this with their bright coloration. This would explain why a moth that shared its habitat as an adult may have evolved to look like it. However, many of the Arctiids are distasteful even when they don't feed on toxic plants. It is generally known that these moths are able to generate toxins on their own. Are the Black and Yellow Lichen Moths among them? If so, they may not be mimicking the beetles but benefiting from what is known as Müllerian mimicry. In this scenario, two species that are both unpalatable and similar in appearance benefit in looking like each other. A bird that tries to eat a distasteful Black and Yellow Lichen Moth will from then on leave them, and the look-alike netwings, alone. After trying a distasteful netwing, a bird will leave them, and the look-alike lichen moths, alone. A similar situation occurs with the Viceroy and Monarch butterflies. It used to be thought that the Viceroy was benefiting in looking like the unpalatable Monarch. This would have formed a relationship known as Batesian mimicry, in which an edible species gets a free ride because it looks like an inedible species. However, studies have shown that the Viceroy may also be distasteful. Therefore, a bird that has tasted either will leave both alone.

Things to ponder whilst among the scaly wings...

Another Arctiid, the Delicate Cycnia (pronounced "sis-nea"), is probably the most "mothy" looking of the group. Delicate is a good adjective for this moth. Its wings are translucent pearly white, and there is a wash of pale yellow on the head and along the leading edge of the forewings. When resting upside down, the moth looks like a small white heart. I find these moths wherever there is dogbane. On sunny days they flutter loosely from the grasses to the flowers, from the flowers to the grasses, apparently needing no more than a short flight to fulfill their needs.

The Cycnias are in the subfamily Arctiinae, meaning they are tiger moths. The clearest identification of a tiger moth is the markings on its abdomen. Most have rows of black dots on a background of yellow, orange, or salmon. In the Cycnia, the abdomen is the same straw color as the edge of the forewings. It is as if these little specters were given just one color to work with and chose to hide most of it beneath their wings.

Back to Bill's meadow. Although it is unfortunate that he has had to limit his activities to this one microhabitat while awaiting relief from his malady, he is lucky to be in a place that hosts one of the more attractive of the day fliers, the Eight-spotted Forester. The forester is overall black, medium sized, with two big oval yellow spots on the forewings and two white spots on the hind wings. Its front and middle legs are wrapped in fuzzy fiery orange socks, perhaps meant to resemble the pollen that would be collected on a wasp's hairy legs. The moth is somewhat wasp-like, but I think more people mistake it for a butterfly than a moth. In fact, I have heard on more than one occasion the suggestion that it be considered an "honorary butterfly." I prefer "ambassador of the moths." People get excited when they come across this insect because they don't recognize it as a moth. Their minds race as they try to figure out what category of butterfly to put it in. Upon learning that it is in fact a moth, they are impressed. I get the sense that the status of moths gets moved up a peg by the forester's membership in this group.

It is hard for me to imagine, both from my occasional observance of this forester moth and its good looks, that it could be considered by some to be a pest. But apparently it is. The forester feeds on plants in the grape family, which include Boston ivy and Virginia creeper. Although Virginia creeper and other plants in the grape family are exceedingly common in my area, I guess there are places where they are not, and therefore considered more valuable. I imagine that if I had a vineyard, I would be less surprised by the moth's potential for trouble. I read a little about this moth in *The Moth Book,* published in 1903. The author, W. J. Holland, disparaged it based upon the "depredations which it commits upon the foliage of Ampelopsis, which is extensively grown in our cities as a decorative vine." He added, "One good thing which can be set down to the English Sparrow is the work which he has been observed by the writer to do in devouring the larvae of this moth from the vines with which his home is covered." The term *Ampelopsis* has been used to describe both Virginia creeper and Boston ivy, although neither belongs in that genus. The former is native to the United States; the latter, despite its name, was brought from Japan. I'm not sure which one Holland was referring to, although I would guess it was Boston ivy, because this plant is the one most often climbing brick buildings in cities. The English sparrow, better known as the house sparrow, was released about fifty years prior to this publication in New York City to rid the city of injurious insects. I would never have thought the Eight-spotted Forester to be one of them.

A moth that I come across far more frequently, and which occurs in good numbers in Yule's meadow, has no common name. This surprises me. Usually moths that are both familiar and attractive have earned themselves a common name. Not only was this moth shortchanged in that area, but its scientific name has three words, making it all the more difficult to remember. It is a little Pyralid called *Anania funebris glomeralis.* Bill and I, tired of stumbling over the name, just call them AFGs. I've also called them pygmy foresters, because they resemble down to the smallest detail an Eight-spotted Forester. They appear to be products of convergent evolution, in which two different habitat-sharing families each produce a species of similar appearance. The shared habitat is often credited with the shaping of their appearance, producing the most successful model for its surroundings. The AFG, with a wingspan that could be contained in the circumference of a quarter, is much smaller than the forester and has a weaker flight. Whereas the larvae of the foresters feed upon grape leaves, AFG larvae prefer goldenrod. The two plants are often growing in the same habitat, as are the moths. It is a rare treat to find the moths side by side on a flower head, looking like father and son on a day out.

A moth somewhat similar to the glomeralis is a Pyralid that I have written about in other sections of this book, the Grape Leaffolder. Both the AFG and the Grape Leaffolder are in the subfamily Pyraustinae, which includes some of the more intricate and boldly patterned moths in that family. Like the AFG, the Grape Leaffolder is mostly black and has two white spots on the forewings. However, it has no yellow on the body, and instead of two spots on the hind wing it has one big one. The Grape Leaffolder burns the candle at both ends: I find it among flowers during the day and at my lights at night.

Grape is a popular plant for a number of day fliers and is the food of choice for the larvae of a species that continues to elude me—the Grapevine Epimenis. Bill tells me he gets these in his meadow, and I have a standing order with him to grab one for me if ever he can. So far, like me, he's been unable to. The Grapevine Epimenis is related to the Eight-spotted Forester but to my eye appears quite different. It looks like a typical broad-winged, thin-bodied butterfly and has a base color of black, a big blotch of white on the forewing, and deep cherry-red hind wings. I have seen one only on two occasions, each time taking me by surprise; I didn't have a camera or net. The first time I came across this moth was while doing a bird-a-thon with friends. We were winding our way through the thickets when a stunning red-winged insect came racing toward us. It went right past our heads and kept going. I was speechless for a few moments, unable to put it in any category of butterfly that I knew. Was it some kind of southern vagrant? Could it have hopped a ship from another continent? It didn't dawn on me that it could be a moth. It was all I could think about for the rest of the day, and I felt a mix of frustration and excitement. When I got home, I pored through all my butterfly books, and then, as a last resort, I checked my moth book. There it was. Again my emotions were split, this time between satisfaction and disappointment. Satisfaction because the mystery was solved. Disappointment because I hadn't discovered a new butterfly for Connecticut.

The second time I saw this creature was while walking along a wetland boardwalk at Chatfield Hollow State Park in Killingworth. Once again it came from out of nowhere, sailing down the path, going past my head, and disappearing around the bend. I turned around and tried to catch up with it, planning to scoop it up with my hat. As I ran, I failed to remember that one of the boards was missing from the boardwalk. My foot went through the opening. I fell, rolled, and grabbed the post of the railing, catching myself just in time to keep from going over the edge and into the swamp. The epimenis kept going, right past two kids.

"You all right?" one of them asked. I stood up, still looking past them to see if I could spot the moth.

"I'm all right," I said.

"Was there a bug chasing you back there?" asked the kid, nervously looking past me.

"No," I said. "I was chasing a bug."

I've walked that boardwalk countless times since, camera hanging from my neck and net in hand. I've yet to see another epimenis.

Another day flier is far rarer than the Grapevine Epimenis and has also succeeded in eluding me after first teasing me with its presence. It is the New England Buck Moth. Buck moths are silk moths, related to the well-known Luna. The New England Buck Moth is about two inches across with translucent black wings crossed by a heavy band of creamy white. Its body is fuzzy and black, and the abdomen is tipped with feathery orange scales, giving it the appearance of flames shooting out from the tail.

I came across two of these moths while walking along another wet-land boardwalk, this time at the Platt Nature Center, where I led the moth walk described in Chapter One. This time it was late August 1994 and I was itching to get out of the house. The nature center's trails are less than ten minutes away from where I live, so I thought I'd go for a hike before it got dark. At the end of the trail is a little boardwalk built by a local Boy Scout years earlier for his Eagle Scout project. As I came to the end of the loop, I noticed two moths aimlessly fluttering along the edge of the swamp. They were a blur of black and white, each trailing those orange "retro-rocket flames." The batmobile came to mind. I knew they were buck moths because I had recently seen a documentary about them. They were an endangered species, and efforts were being made to rear and release them back to their habitat. "Oh, my God!" I shouted to the woods. I had discovered a new locale for an endangered species. My heart picked up in pace, fueled by excitement. What do I do now? Do I try to catch one? Do I hold back so I can memorize the details of their markings and behavior? I decided to do both. I'd walk alongside them and try to pick up every detail I could. If one or both of them flew within reach, I'd make a grab with my bare hands. As soon as I made this decision, the moths disappeared into the swamp. That was the last I saw of them. I raced home and hit the books. It was then I learned that there are two kinds of buck moths in Connecticut. One, the endangered species, is *Hemileuca maia,* or just plain Buck Moth. It feeds on scrub oak, a plant that did not grow in the habitat I just came from. In fact, now that I thought about it, the documentary showed this moth living in the pine barrens in Long Island. In Connecticut, it had been virtually wiped out. The moths I had seen were *Hemileuca lucina,* New England Buck Moth. Although not endangered, it is still a good find. As with my search for the Grapevine Epimenis, countless trips of trying to find this buck moth again have been fruitless.

Along the back of Bill's meadow is a small band of forest. Because of this, he gets another two species of day fliers. Both are geometers: the White-striped Black and the Common Spring Moth. He has watched both of them nectaring on flowers that grow on the forest floor. White-striped Blacks are delicate little moths, black except for a heavy white stripe through the forewings. I first came across them while backpacking along the Green Trail in Vermont. It was mid-June, hot and sunny, and I was laden with everything I would need to survive in the woods for a week and a half. I was also not in the best shape. As I trudged along, I thought of cold beer and air-conditioning. I normally backpack in early spring and late fall to avoid the heat. Because I was joining my son, Jeff, on his annual Boy Scout trip, I had no choice of dates.

Into the third day, I began to notice little black and white moths all along the trail. The farther I went, the more I found. They fluttered weightlessly in the dappled sunlight at the edge of the woods. There was something crisp and refreshing about them. They made me think cool thoughts. The moths were there day after day, and I never tired of seeing them. I credit them with lightening the load I was carrying, in more ways than one.

According to *A Field Guide to the Moths of Eastern North America,* by Charles Covell, their larvae feed on impatiens. Most people are familiar with these annuals as a cultivated plant growing neatly at the borders of our gardens and filling our window boxes. How, one might ask, did a moth that fed upon this plant survive before the advent of gardening? And where were they finding these plants in the Green Mountains of Vermont? My questions were answered when I consulted Joseph Dowhan's *Preliminary Checklist of the Vascular Flora of Connecticut (Growing Without Cultivation)*. I looked up impatiens in the index and discovered that the genus is one I am familiar with. Two wild forms of impatiens grow along our woodland borders, *Impatiens biflora* and *Impatiens pallida*, better known as spotted jewelweed and pale jewelweed, respectively. After discovering this, I learned how to find the White-striped Blacks. I look for patches of jewelweed, a common plant throughout New England. It grows at the edges of moist woods, right along the Green Trail, and on the border of Bill's meadow, where he had described to me finding the nectaring adults.

The Common Spring Moth—like many of the day fliers, it seems— is another black and white moth. It is a delicate and "fluttery" flyer with a wingspan of an inch or so. The first time I came across this moth was at my black light a number of years ago. I usually get one or two a year this way, but, like Bill, I come across most of them during the day as they nectar along the forest floor. A few springs ago I was in Missouri at Ha Ha Tonka State Park in the Ozarks. It was April, early for the Lepidoptera, but some were out and about. Dozens of Falcate Orangetips chased one another up and down the hillsides. Juvenal's Duskywings sunned themselves on money plant, and the occasional Zebra Swallowtail zipped past me. There was one day-flying moth that got my attention, though. I saw it flying at the limit of conjecture over the deep valley of the park. I could barely make it out with my binoculars, but I had a feeling it was a moth. A second moth came into view, soon joined by a third. Then I lost sight of them all. They were so far out on the edge of my vision that when they moved just a bit farther, they appeared to vanish into the air. This went on throughout the day; for some reason, they were always on the opposite side of the valley from where I was. This made me even more curious as to what this insect was. The fact that I thought it was a moth made it more special; whereas all butterflies fly during the day, only a select group of moths show themselves in the sun.

Toward the end of the day, I was on top of a hill overlooking a huge freshwater spring. I was completely alone. The sun was setting and the birds were moving here and there, getting in their last meal and singing their last songs before nightfall. A white-eyed vireo sat in a bush behind me, requesting someone to "get-the-beeer-check." Then, from the bottom of the valley, a little fluttery creature appeared and slowly worked its way up the hill. Another joined it. I began to make out some of the details. It was a moth. It was a black and white moth. It flew closer and closer until finally I saw that it was a moth I knew from back home. The moths I had been seeing throughout the day were Common Spring Moths. The two moths crested the hill and fluttered madly by me at about waist height. The setting sun made the white seem so white and the black seem so black. The moths semed to fly with a purpose, desperate to find what they were looking for or to get to their destination. Where they stopped and where they were going I'll never know.

When I see Common Spring Moths in my area, I think of those two moths in the Ozarks and how at that moment they were the most resplendent creatures in that vast woodland.

Nearly everyone who watches butterflies, and that's probably in the millions by now, has noticed the Celery Looper. More people have probably said, "Oh, it's just a moth," upon coming across this insect than about any other they've encountered. This is because (a) the loopers fly during the day, and (b) they look and fly like skippers. Relatively small, mothlike butterflies, skippers are hard enough to identify at any time, let alone when there are real moths that they can be confused with. The similarities are only superficial, though, and an issue only when the moth is in flight. At rest, there is no question that this looper is a moth. As with many of the Plusiinae, or loopers, the wings are held folded like a pup tent over the body. The moths look hardy and make me think of dry-docked battleships waiting to be commissioned. They often rest with the scales of their thorax raised in the air like battle flags. I've noticed that the scales of many of these moths reflect a metallic gold when photographed, a result of the light refraction of my flash. I can't recall noticing this as much when they are in the field.

One thing that stands out on the Celery Looper is the marking known as the stigma on the center of the forewing. It looks like a little white fish. These loopers are among the last day-flying Lepidoptera on the wing in fall in New England, nectaring on the flowers of mustard, goldenrod, aster, and dandelion well into November. They return in late March and early April, but at this time of year I find them mostly at night when they are attracted to my lights.

The last of the day fliers I want to talk about is technically not a day flier. However, I have found it only during the day, which is the best time to look for it. It is in the genus *Schinia,* or flower moths, a group that tends to ride out the day in the flowers they nectar upon in the evening. This particular species, the Primrose Moth, is my favorite.

The wings of the Primrose Moth are waxy pink and yellow. They are triangular in shape, as are most in the Noctuidae family to which they belong. The moths blend in nicely with one of the host plants of their caterpillars, evening primrose *(Oenothera biennis)*. I used to think that evening primrose was a naturalized plant from Europe, probably because it occurs with other naturalized plants of roadsides and waste places. But the plant is as native as the moth that eats it. During the day, the moths can be found resting head-down in the flowers. Although the plant is relatively common, the moth is not, and finding one is a challenge. I cannot pass an evening primrose without peering into the flower heads. Sometimes a hundred plants may turn up empty before revealing one of these colorful treasures. It's like opening an oyster and finding a pearl. You start off searching with great expectation, but as the hunt wears on you begin to expect less and less from each flower. When you finally do find the object of your search, you are surprised. That's what a search for this moth is: a treasure hunt. If they were in all the flowers or even half of them, it wouldn't be as much fun.

Bill is feeling better now. He's out and about. To his credit, he has not forsaken the creatures that helped him through his difficult time. He has since graduated to the night moths. Rarely a week or two go by without my hearing about a moth he discovered at his lights or flying around while on his travels. Last night he discovered his first Ultronia Underwing and was singing its praises: "Wow! I see why people get hooked on underwings! This beauty has an explosively dramatic red and black underwing that caught me off guard when I touched the dull smoky brown/gray forewings. That 'startle effect' really works."

It's nice to have him aboard. Bill's newfound enthusiasm is just one more reason why I am grateful for the moths that fly by day.

⤳ II ⤳
To Kill, or Not to Kill

I'M not a very patient man.

I wish I were. Life would be so much simpler. I often think I'm in the wrong profession for my emotional makeup. The writing process, from concept to book, can be excruciatingly slow. Not so much the writing itself, but the waiting between the various stages of the publication process, a period over which I have no control. I compensate by keeping busy. Fortunately, I am the master of distraction, that distraction often being the pursuit of some interesting bug in the grass, bird in a tree, or flower in a meadow. But I can keep my mind sidetracked for only so long. Ever have your eyes pop open in the middle of the night? That happens to me a lot, which is why I think I've evolved to extend my distractions into the darker hours. If there is nothing I can do about the waiting, I might as well be doing something, and something I enjoy. But even the pursuit of nature can try my patience. This is driven home to me at the height of the moth season. Trying to find identifying field marks on a moth with wings whirring in its temporary container can take the resolve of Gandhi.

I enjoy learning the names of things, not the least of which include the moths. I think it's because I like them so much. It's like going out to dinner and sampling a good wine, then wishing to know its name. Sure, part of you wants to know so you can order it again in the future. But another part of you just wants to be able to say the name of what brought you pleasure. Seeing a new moth brings me pleasure, and I am left with a driving urge to know what other people call it. I want a name. I don't always get it, but I try. When I'm stumped it's because (a) the moth is too worn to identify, (b) the books I use for reference don't have that particular species, (c) it is necessary to go beyond the outward appearance of the moth, specifically to the genitalia, to find the key to its name, or (d) I've just plain run out of patience.

There are many species you can't pin a name on without looking at the hind wings. There can be subtle differences among species that only a peek at that part of the anatomy can distinguish. When you look at any serious field guide to moths, you see the insect pinned with the hind wings exposed. How convenient. However, many live moths keep their hind wings concealed beneath the forewings when resting. How inconvenient.

A typical night of trying to identify a new moth might go like this. I venture out to the light and scoop up the moth in an empty cassette case. I slip the transparent case into my pocket where it's dark. This usually calms the moth. I bring it indoors and hold the case over the pictures in my various field guides, trying to find a match. The light in the room gets the moth going again. The wings begin to vibrate, slowly at first, then all out as the moth starts buzzing around the case trying to escape. Naturally, this makes the whole moth blurry and impossible to identify. I put the case in the refrigerator. The cool air calms the moth again. A few moments later, it's out of the fridge and I'm back to the books. Turns out it's one of the species where you have to see the hind wings. I open the case and with a straightened paper clip try to pry open the forewings. They snap back again. I pry them open again. They snap back again. Then the wings begin to vibrate once more. The moth is waking up.

At this point, rationalization sets in. What if I give it a little pinch? What if I "accidentally" put it in the freezer? (We've all put the occasional soda or beer can inside the wrong door in our refrigerator.) The moth would freeze to death; then I could study it at my leisure. When I am out with collectors, all they do is scoop up their moth in a jar containing some kind of killing agent. Within seconds the moth is motionless, dead, and fully cooperative.

But I can't do it. I cannot kill the moth. Why? Because I like it. I like moths. I like butterflies. I like birds. I like katydids and crickets. I like dogs. I like cats. For that reason, I cannot kill any of these things, no matter how much they frustrate me. My daughter's ferocious cat, Tillie, is living testimony to this.

I'm not alone. In fact, there are whole factions out there who cannot kill these objects of their interest. At the same time, there are factions who do this without a second thought. Thus begins the collecting debate.

In recent years those who kill insects and those who believe it is a waste of innocent life have been butting heads. The debate is both passionate and polarizing and has mostly revolved around butterflies, which have been elevated by society to a status above all other insects. Most people don't care about moths, but they are slowly working their way into the debate as the butterfly people expand their interests to the "other Lepidoptera." In a way, this debate is fruitless: Those who see no harm in collecting will not be convinced by the opposing faction that it is wrong, and vice versa. It is not unlike the abortion debate or the death penalty. It is conservatives versus liberals. Hunters versus animal rights activists. The pious versus the atheists. Dogs versus cats. No matter how many points are scored on either side, the opposing values of those involved remain unchanged.

Many on the anti-collecting side believe that no collecting should take place at all, even when it is to further our knowledge about the group collected. Many also disdain the practice of catch and release, seeing it as an interruption in the life of a free animal. When I was a kid, I remember reading in a *Ripley's Believe It or Not* paperback that there are shamans in India who value all life so highly that they wear a handkerchief around their mouth so they don't accidentally breathe in and kill any gnats. I imagine they would be anti-collectors.

There are many different levels and purposes for collecting that come into the debate. Probably the least controversial—but still there are detractors—is collecting for the advancement of scientific knowledge. Taxonomists, the people who figure out what insect belongs in what group, make up a large segment of those scientists. For the taxonomists, the only way to sort out individual species, forms, and families is to have many of them side by side—and quite dead—for close inspection. Taxonomy, for many Lepidoptera enthusiasts, is the ultimate expression of their passion for these insects, and they need to have unmoving insects in front of them to accomplish what they do.

When a scientific census of a butterfly or moth population is conducted, large numbers of individuals are killed in a variety of ways, then stored, mounted, and dissected for a variety of reasons. Then there are the amateur collectors, or hobbyists, who work to build their treasure of insects for enjoyment, curiosity, records, and advancement of their own knowledge. There is also a commercial trade in butterflies and moths, both living and dead specimens. I remember while in Tobago coming across day-flying Urania Moths encased in clear acrylic that were being sold as paperweights. It's not difficult to find the insects in a similar form serving as jewelry and wall decorations. For every level and incarnation of the practice, there are levels of tolerance and intolerance to which people ascribe.

A few years back, I visited a man whose passion for collecting cannot be equaled. His name is Bob Muller. Bob's collecting practices have added many specimens to museums and have appeared in a number of books. I had stopped by his house at his invitation to see the collection of butterflies and moths he had been building for more than half a century. Although I had yet to meet him in person, we'd had a number of conversations over the phone, and he was always eager to fill the gaps in my knowledge of the Lepidoptera.

Bob lives in a modest house on the edge of a marsh in Milford, Connecticut. He greeted me at the door with a friendly smile and a cigarette between his fingers. (Occasionally, Bob had sent me packages of cocoons, which I always knew came from him because of the telltale smell of cigarette smoke on the box.) His gray hair was combed back neatly away from his clean-shaven, no-nonsense face. He comes from a family of machinists, and with just a high-school diploma worked his way up to vice president of a reputable manufacturing company. Every spare moment away from work, however, was spent building his collection. He's got a sharp mind with a gift for attention to detail. Possibly a machinist's trait. He has been retired for a number of years, which leaves him more time in the field.

We went down to his basement, where I immediately became aware of the strong smell of naphtha. I've always been fond of that smell. It brings back memories of my grandparents' basement, which was a fun place to play as a child. From where I was standing, though, this looked nothing like my grandparents' basement. This was a museum. It was floor to ceiling birds, mammals, and insects that Bob had hunted, killed, and mounted. The naphtha was to keep the little live critters from eating the dead ones. I remember thinking of my elementary school trip to Sagamore Hill and the trophies that Teddy Roosevelt had amassed to display throughout his estate. The ol' Bull Moose would have felt at home down here.

You have to remember that I don't kill things. Here I was surrounded by the lifeless bodies of thousands of creatures. If they'd had souls, I imagine that Mr. Muller would spend many a sleepless night being haunted by their tiny ghosts. What he had mounted, stuffed, and spread throughout his basement were creatures that I enjoy watching fly, swim, hop, and crawl. And yet . . . and yet, my curiosity overrode what could have been great discomfort. I could actually get close up and see some of these creatures as I had never seen them before. These weren't blurry wings in a clear cassette case, or the silhouetted figure of a duck through a telescope. They were frozen in time. With the butterflies and moths, many individuals from the same species were side by side, and I could see variations that I'd be hard pressed to notice otherwise. And there was a symmetry in the arrangement that I found almost aesthetically pleasing, especially with the Lepidoptera. It was, in a way, a form of art. Of course, this is not the first time I have seen a collection of Lepidoptera. I've been to museums and have seen many other private collections, but what drew me to this one was that these were butterflies and moths of Connecticut. These were *my* insects and therefore all the more interesting.

Bob was able to give me the history behind every creature on display. Although he is eager to use his collections for the advancement of scientific research, he told me that this was not his main drive to collect. He explained:

> Each day I visit my room and look at my collections. The greatest thing that comes to mind are not the specimens I see, but the memories connected to them. I can remember the first *Idalia* I'd ever seen. My Dad was with me and spotted a female on clover in Southbury. I could right now take you to the exact spot, which is now someone's front lawn.
>
> I look at the Giant Swallowtail I caught in 1941 at my old homestead in Stratford. I was in the backyard when I saw it come flying up the driveway. I ran into the house, got my net, came running out the front door heading it off. One swing of the net and it was gone, but not in the net. My dad came out and asked what happened. When I told him, he started looking around the ground. As he reached down behind a bush and picked it up, my body started shaking. He'd found my butterfly. This was and is the only one of that species I have ever collected.

Bob wrote me recently to elaborate on what his collections mean to him. He had just come up from his "museum," and thoughts were racing through his head. As someone who is passionate about his pastime, he was eager to share his reflections and observations:

> I could tell you every day of the events leading up to collecting every duck in my collection and almost every butterfly or moth. I can't believe what came back to me as I looked at each and every specimen: good and bad times, the best of life and the worst, loss of my first wife, who was a great companion, loss of my son at 21, loss of my baby at one week . . . I think to this day he was me and was going to be the collector. My collections are not just bugs in frames or ducks on a base. They're my life.

I suppose that is why many of us collect anything. Yes, there is the treasure hunt aspect of it. We enjoy completing sets of things we find interesting or beautiful. But there are also memories associated with our finds. These are mementos, trophies, reminders of our conquests.

It is not surprising, therefore, that Bob has strong views on the "anti-collectors." To him, these are the people who threaten his pleasure in life, his way of building those memories he expressed. They are a thorn in his side that he did not have to deal with as he was growing up. The anti-collecting movement is a relatively recent event that the old-timers have watched evolve with much chagrin. "Collecting is a major part of finding what is out there," said Bob. "I, for one, have had enough of these do-nothing "Anti" [collecting] NUT CASES! How much land have they protected? How many species of anything have they protected? They're all a bunch of talk and NO ACTION!"

According to Bob, it is not the collectors who are responsible for the decline in species, and some species *are* declining or have already disappeared. He and many others blame loss of habitat: "The anti-collector people should look at things the way they are and put their efforts into saving the habitat that all species require to continue on this planet. Collecting is not going to eliminate them, destruction of the lands will. We should all work together and push for more open space to be protected. This is the key to the future of protecting all that God has put here for us to enjoy."

Okay, now the other end of the spectrum. Jeff Young is a professional photographer I met years ago through my involvement with a local birding group. Whenever I was out chasing some rare bird, there

was Jeff with his bazooka-sized camera firing away at it. To him, the difference between a good bird and a bad one was the light that washed
over it. Any bird that lent itself to a good photograph was a good bird.

In 1994 several of us got together to start a butterfly and moth club.
Jeff, an ardent butterfly photographer and topnotch amateur lepidopterist, joined us. So did his partner in crime, Jeff Fengler. The two
of them were on a mission to photograph every species of butterfly in
Connecticut during mating. Whenever they came upon a conjoined
pair, they'd exclaim, "Leppo-looove" and proceed to take lots of pictures.
Everyone needs a calling in life. Actually, it's a good way to show the
sexual dimorphism in butterflies. There they are, side by side (well, end
to end)—the male usually a little smaller—doing something important.

Young is a tall man with dark gray hair whose appearance and de-
meanor always make me think of actor Tom Bosley. Jeff makes me laugh,
too. Calling his sense of humor dry is like calling the ocean damp. I
remember Jeff at the first organizational meeting of the Connecticut
Butterfly Association: After volunteering for the position of treasurer, Jeff
stood up and took ten dollars out of his wallet, then put it in his side
pocket, declaring himself the first member.

Like Bob Muller, Jeff Young does not hesitate to express his opinions.
Unlike with Bob Muller, though, an insect landing on Jeff's shoulder will
most likely live. In Jeff's words, "Collecting is killing, and it is wrong."

When talking about the pros and cons of collecting, the subject of
field guides often arises. Most of the paintings in the guides to birds and
butterflies are made from dead subjects. Yet the purpose of many guides
is to encourage people to go out and see these creatures in the wild. One
of the most famous field-guide creators was Roger Tory Peterson, who
revolutionized the modern field guide by pointing out characteristics that
could be identified in the field.

Muller uses Peterson and his guides to support his position on
collecting:

> Look back into the early years, and you'll find that the collecting
> efforts of all the past people . . . sparked the interest in everything we
> view today. Roger Tory Peterson field guides were developed by the
> use of collected bird specimens, not by pictures. He had a massive col-
> lection of mounted bird skins to use as a reference in his painting of

field guide pictures. For some unknown reason the nut case "antis" don't see this as being part of our history.

But Young uses the creation of those same field guides to support his opposing view:

Audubon had to shoot the birds for his work. But by the 1920s whole populations of bird species were reduced and driven to near extinction for commercial purposes. Laws were passed to protect them. The late Roger Tory Peterson came out with the first field guide to teach people how to learn the individual species without killing them. Yes, he had to use specimens for his early illustrations. But he also included behavioral characteristics in order for us to make an identification. After the development of quality telephoto lenses and films capable of documentation, Peterson became an accomplished nature photographer to add to his list of talents. Jeffrey Glassberg's *Butterflies Through Binoculars* books do the same for butterflies. If a collector kills and mounts a specimen, only its physical characteristics are still apparent. With the use of photography and especially video, behavior, life cycles, and other aspects used in identification and study can be documented.

I suppose you can't witness "Leppo-looove" with dead specimens.

Muller doesn't give much quarter to the reliability of photography:

The venture by the Connecticut Butterfly Atlas Project to determine what species of butterflies are present in our state is a fantastic undertaking, but could never have been accomplished without the efforts of many people collecting butterfly species. Many people provided pictures, but they were not as positive as the true specimens. There is no way to determine what is out there without collecting.

I know that Muller is not alone in holding this view. Many entomologists will accept only specimens as records when conducting population surveys. They know all too well how easy it is to mistake one insect for another based upon mere observation. This is also true in the birdwatching community; however, it is unthought-of to even consider taking bird specimens when conducting a census. If it is a rare or questionable species, photo documentation is a must, but shooting the bird to prove identification just doesn't happen. In fact, most birds are legally protected from such an action, at least in the United States. We as a society consider the life of a bird more valuable than that of an insect, even when the bird would be sacrificed in the name of science. At the same time, we have placed certain other animals in the "inconsequential" category.

According to David Chesmore, an electronics engineer who works with computer-aided taxonomy in Hull, England,

> Identifying Lepidoptera, especially microlepidoptera, can be difficult and may require dissection for examination of genitalia. It is therefore vital that voucher specimens are collected for correct identification. In addition, the regional and national recorders often will not accept records without seeing voucher specimens. I have personal experience of this with a number of species of macrolepidoptera which were easily identified—even then, the Yorkshire recorder needed to see the actual specimen. Of course, the identification problem becomes harder if the insects are Braconid Hymenoptera or aphids. This leads to an interesting dilemma—most people will happily say that it is OK to kill wasps, bees, aphids, moths even, but NOT butterflies. I was in the unfortunate position of having to resign from the Butterfly Conservation (I was chairman of the Yorkshire branch) because of such ridiculous opinions. At one meeting, I was told that it was wrong to kill butterflies but OK to kill moths!

Young, on the other hand, sees great potential for wasted life in the practice of collecting Lepidoptera for censusing. He and Muller use the same example, the Connecticut Butterfly Atlas Project, to make opposing points:

> An example of waste is the Connecticut Butterfly Atlas now being created. In the late 1980s birders did a study of the breeding birds of CT. The Atlas of Breeding Birds of Connecticut employed a grid system based on the US Geological Survey quadrangle system. One hundred and twenty-one ... quadrangle maps cover the 5,009 square mile area of the state. Each quadrangle was divided into six equal-sized parts, each termed a block. For five years, ornithologists and birders surveyed each block during the breeding season, observing birds, their behavior, and nesting. The study was published in 1994. Seizing upon this idea, entomologists decided to obtain a grant and map the distribution of butterflies in the state.... [I]n order to prove a species exists in each block, a specimen would be taken. This would result in the killing of over 7,000 butterflies.

Fortunately, some board members of the Connecticut Butterfly Association were able to convince them to accept photographic documentation and we were able to keep the death toll down to about 5,000. Many of the species in this study are common and easily recognizable. A sight record should have been sufficient. The project was an excuse to collect. One major participant was responsible for over 1,000 specimens taken. When published, the resulting work will become a map of where collectors can find butterflies, in addition to its limited scientific and historical value.

I sat in on one of the identification sessions for this survey. The records were divided into dead specimens and photographs. As we sorted through the specimens, I saw that even with some of the species in hand, identification was difficult. This was especially true with the Erynnis, or duskywing, species, many of which look the same. These were put aside into a separate group to be worked on in more detail later. Getting a positive identification of a duskywing from a photograph would have been difficult and in some cases impossible.

One might ask, so what? Why do we have to know down to the species what was found where? Well, maybe we don't, but if a survey *is* going to be conducted, the data should be accurate. Such data form the foundation of any conservation effort made on behalf of the species, and those data must be trusted.

At the same time, however, a couple of people contributing to this survey sent in piles of dead butterflies, all the same species, all collected in the same place. Often these were species that could not have been mistaken for anything else. It seemed that this redundancy was unnecessary for our purpose. There was no reason to kill all those butterflies.

I have always been interested in what motivates people. When you get down to that level, you can sometimes reach a place where opposing sides can agree. When you find the root of an action, a motive, you are forced to acknowledge why a person does something. You may not agree with the motive, but there will be little you can do to change his or her subsequent actions. Knowing this saves you a lot of wasted effort in peripheral argument. If you choose to debate, you can get right to the crux of it.

So, let's get to the root of collecting. A large number of contributors to this census were collecting long before they found a scientific outlet for their efforts. They collect for themselves because it is something they enjoy doing. There may be some who argue with me, but I think most will agree. It can be compared to deer hunters donating venison to food pantries. Most don't go out and hunt for the purpose of supplying the food. If that were their sole motivation, they could save a lot of time and money by just buying some steaks and donating them. No. They are out hunting because it's something they like to do. The contribution, albeit admirable, is a bonus to their pastime. The insect collectors enjoy collecting. Being able to contribute to research while practicing an activity they enjoy is icing on the cake.

The root motivation, though, is tough for some people to swallow. It's a motivation that Jeff Young has difficulty understanding:

There is absolutely no justification whatsoever for the personal collecting of any living species. What right do we humans have to do it? Who gave us that right, God, Mother Nature? Like all species, humans originally hunted to survive, and it seems that obsolete behavioral trait still exists in some individuals. In nature, one species on the food chain kills and eats only what it needs to survive, and then stops. Were butterflies and moths ever a food source? I don't think so.

Then there is the human species. Because we have the ability to invent tools like the gun or the net, we think it is all right to go around wasting other creatures. The butterfly or moth a collector kills today is what may have been tomorrow's breakfast for a bird or its young. Thus by wasting a food source for personal pleasure, a collector places a strain on the entire chain. A specimen for the collection here and there may seem to some as a very trivial issue, but it's just the tip of the problem.

As I child, I wielded a butterfly net, but even then I always released what I caught. In fact, catch-and-release seems to be the compromise that takes place with many organizations that run entomological outings. It seems to offend fewer people while allowing close views for identification and the thrill of the hunt. It is fun catching things in nets. I was leading a butterfly trip a couple of years back, catching, passing around, and releasing butterflies without giving much thought to it. Jeff was on the trip, and I learned that this was disturbing him. "There's really no reason to be catching them when you can see them perfectly well where they are," he said. Later he reminded me that a butterfly's sensory organs are in the feet and antennae, and those are the parts that most often get damaged in the net: "Recent studies have shown that animals and other critters do feel pain. Even plants increase the production of defensive chemicals when attacked by disease, parasites, and insects. Are 'Leps' aware of what it is like to be netted, and stuffed into a plastic box? Do they experience stress, pain, and shock?"

I hadn't really thought about that. It was the first time that I, always having advocated leaving things alive in the field, got a polite dressing-down from someone who took the sentiment even further than I did. I had to respect that. And I did. I will still catch and release, but not as indiscriminately as I used to. There is a new interest growing in dragonflies. Many of my close friends are involved in it. My favorite thing about them is trying to catch them. They are a challenge to get in my net. But too many times while swinging the net I have broken a wing or worse, ruining the whole experience. There goes another fun thing from my life.

Some collectors never kill their quarry; they build collections from dead insects they find while out and about. Many butterflies and moths are killed by cars and trucks. I remember watching European starlings and house sparrows picking dead moths from a truck's grille at a truck stop. Considering the distances these vehicles travel, I imagine there could be some interesting specimens there.

That got me thinking. Many who choose not to take the life of butterflies and moths end up doing just that. Any warm summer night that you go for a drive, you are attracting moths to your headlights. Many of those moths die on impact or get knocked down to the road and run over. I remember racing along a Missouri highway and seeing my first Mourning Cloak butterfly of the trip as it collided with my windshield and dropped to the road, where it was then run over by a pickup truck. When you walk through the leaves, you are stepping on resting moths and their pupae or cocoons. Leave on a porch light and you are attracting moths to their doom as they get caught in the webs spun by opportunistic spiders. At best, if there are no spiderwebs, you are drastically interrupting the moths' natural cycles. Mow your lawn and you're beating the daylights out of the little Pyralids that call that monoculture of monocots (grass) their home. Turn on your indoor lights at night and moths get trapped in your screens or in your house, where if they don't batter themselves to death, they starve. Check your windowsills; there's carnage going on there.

And it's not just the moths. We are always killing things. Sometimes we can't help it. With some things, we feel worse than with others. I admit that I am a hypocrite. Although I would not think of killing an insect for personal pleasure—for example, to create a collection—I kill other insects on purpose. Ever since my kids and dogs were stung repeatedly by yellow jackets after stepping on a nest, I've had no qualms about destroying yellow jacket nests I find in the vicinity of my house. These are not the insects that attacked my family. Chances are good that these other yellow jackets would leave us alone if we left them alone, and go about their business filling that predator niche in nature's world of insects. But I don't care. I kill them anyway, and although I don't enjoy the act of killing them, and do feel a twinge of guilt, they are made dead nonetheless.

One of my friends loves yellow jackets. She finds them beautiful and fascinating. So although there are many who would cheer me on as I take out the nests, I know there is at least one person, and I am sure many more, who would rather I didn't.

As a backpacker, I have killed hundreds of beetles. When you are camping, you build a campfire. To fuel that fire, you use dead wood. If you peel back the bark of some of those logs, you find many flat, pale yellow bark beetle larvae. They are just minding their own business, munching away on the dead wood, not bothering or threatening anyone or anything. If they happen to be in a log destined to feed a hungry campfire, well, they're toast. I am aware of this when I throw the log in the fire. Do I feel a little bad about that? I have to say that, when I do think about it—and I don't always—I feel a twinge of guilt. Do I take the time to peel off the bark and put the larvae next to another dead log so they can continue their happy little life? Rarely.

If attached to the bark were the silk-encased pupae of one of my precious Tolype moths, would that log get tossed in the fire? Absolutely not! I have consciously chosen, based on some kind of value system that in *some* ways can be flexible for *some* things, what I will go out of my way to spare. I think many of us do that. Take the gardener who plants extra parsley for the Black Swallowtails but doesn't hesitate to wipe out every Tobacco Hornworm that he or she finds in the garden. In my opinion, the hornworm turns into a much more attractive insect than the swallowtail, but most people don't wait or have no interest in seeing the final result. Hence, Mr. Chesmore's dilemma, which led to his resignation from the Butterfly Conservation in England.

This hypocrisy transcends the insect world. Countless people who abhor hunting eat meat. They don't eat it just to survive; they eat it because they like it. What they probably don't like about hunting, though, is the fact that some people derive pleasure from the act of killing. But what about the slaughterhouse worker who enjoys his job? Is he a bad person in the eyes of a nonhunting omnivore? We make conscious decisions on where we draw the line, and those decisions are not always in keeping with what we believe our values to be.

A relatively new controversy has arisen over the practice of releasing butterflies at weddings. Companies ship live butterflies, most often Monarchs or Painted Ladies, tucked into little envelopes. They arrive in a box, and the envelopes are divvied out among the guests. Instead of throwing rice as the bride and groom emerge from the church, guests open the envelopes and out fly the butterflies, symbolizing all sorts of good things. A similar practice takes place at funerals, except that Mourning Cloaks are used instead of Monarchs and Painted Ladies.

One may wonder what could possibly be wrong with this. How could anyone have anything against releasing a bunch of pretty butterflies? It's an action filled with positive symbolism. Can you imagine the aesthetically pleasing effect of a cloud of fluttering orange wings around the bride and groom? The wedding photos are probably spectacular. But life just ain't that simple. For everything that everyone does, there are people who have a problem with it. For every joke you make, someone is offended. For every donation you give to a charity, there are people out there mad at you for wasting your time with your meaningless cause when their cause should be supported instead. You can't please everyone.

With this butterfly release issue, though, there are legitimate concerns. Some entomologists worry that releasing butterflies shipped from another part of the country could negatively affect the gene pool of the local species. Or the new butterflies could be carrying viruses to which local butterflies have no resistance. The Monarch butterfly is regularly monitored by amateur and professional agencies and individuals that are trying to track the exact migration routes and learn how many of the butterflies that start out actually make it to Mexico. This information could become valuable in conservation efforts, but with thousands of Monarchs being released in areas where they might not otherwise be found, the data could be thrown off. Science has little use for inaccurate or manipulated data, whether that manipulation was done intentionally or not.

The butterfly-release companies deny that these are legitimate problems and give reasons why their business should be of no concern to those worried about these possibilities. They match opposing scientists with their own scientists. I hear both sides, and in the end I don't know what to think of their findings.

However, science aside, there is another aspect to this that some find disturbing: Not all of the butterflies arrive alive. Most do, but not all. And those that do, do not always take flight. How would you like to be the person who opens up your envelope only to have your butterfly drop to the ground? For some reason, that's the one that gets noticed, and the person who tried to release it can't help but feel bad for the butterfly. And it may not be dead. If there is too much of a chill in the air, or if it's too cloudy and the butterflies were not given time to warm their flight muscles, they plummet. Not the kind of symbolism the newlyweds may want for their new life together.

There is also the matter of the condition of the butterflies prior to release. Some people may find it upsetting that the wings are folded back and the butterflies are confined in skinny little envelopes, unable to move from the time they are packed until the time they are released.

Lastly, there is the matter of dignity. Butterflies are often viewed as symbols of freedom, flying high and free. Butterflies living in the wild stir a variety of feelings within us. Some find their use as a party favor demeaning to the creature.

Personally, I detest the practice, mostly for the last two reasons. Yet I am once again being hypocritical. Don't I enclose moths in a confining container, where they most obviously would rather not be? I even chill them in a refrigerator for a while to calm them down. They can't be too crazy about that either. I try to justify it by saying, Well, it's just for half an hour, just a brief inconvenience in their life before they go free, all safe and unharmed. I also tell myself that there is no other way, aside from killing them, of learning to identify one from another out in the field. I need to see them in the light and up close. And I catch only the ones I've never seen before. As the years go by, the law of diminishing returns will dictate that fewer and fewer new moths will be left for me to puzzle over. Rationalization can be a wonderful thing.

But even if I didn't catch them, don't I disturb their natural patterns merely by turning on my light to attract them, just as the Monarchs' natural pattern is being disturbed by releases? I do all these things, yet I have once again drawn my line of tolerance.

That said, I suppose I can live with that line. I can live with it because I have chosen to learn, and to educate people about moths and butterflies using the most reliable way that causes the least disturbance. Many people who have had their eyes opened to moths' beauty, or more often to their mere presence, have vowed to stop killing them. I see that as a good thing in the big picture. With butterfly releases, the insects are reduced to baubles and are being used for a different motive, one that I find less noble: profit. I suppose that is my way of rationalizing the difference between what I do and what purveyors of butterflies do. Do the individual insects directly affected on both sides care what our motives are? No. But what are we going to do?

Although butterfly releases are a fairly new enterprise, the commercial trade in butterflies and moths—and many other insects, especially beetles—has been going on for centuries. These are mostly dead insects that are sold or traded to individuals and museums that are building up their collections. Remember the film *Papillon*? Dustin Hoffman and Steve McQueen were running around Devil's Island catching Blue Morphos for a trader who paid good money for them. This is a practice that happens all over the planet; the insects are collected and traded like stamps in a stamp collection.

In some places the collecting has helped support small villages. Doug Yanega, an entomologist with the University of California's Entomology Research Museum, told me of a situation where the *prohibition* of collecting actually led to a population's demise:

> There was a village in a valley in Santa Catarina state in Brazil where, some decades ago, the locals collected Morpho butterflies for sale, year after year. That was their livelihood. When Brazil clamped down on wildlife export, they shut down this enterprise. Within a few years, the locals, having no other viable option, deforested the area, and that particular Morpho has not been seen since.

Yanega has no problem with people collecting and sees no reason for restrictions on individual collectors, but he does see a need to regulate commercial trade because, in effect, the seller profits from what is taken from someone else's land. He points out that in most commercial ventures in the Lepidoptera trade, the profits don't make it to the locals who live off that land. So what happens? The locals find a way to survive that is not always beneficial to the surrounding fauna.

Although I will never be comfortable with the thought of living creatures being killed and traded to fill someone's personal collection, I have to admit that in some cases, as in the one above, it becomes the lesser of the evils.

Earlier, I mentioned catching bugs as a kid. In the old field guides, there were almost always directions and encouragement for building an insect collection. You don't see that as much today. Perhaps this is why collectors feel that their way of life is being threatened. A whole generation of people who don't see the value in collecting, or are appalled by the practice of killing insects, has a great potential to put limits on it. We have seen this in hunting and, to some extent, the collecting of insects of any kind in federal and state parks. For most collecting, a permit is needed on all but private land. Many collectors who as children had free reign are extremely frustrated by this. But the rationale is that over the years too many people have come to view the killing of wildlife as a bad thing. And these are the "The People's Parks." If a person with a net has become a disturbing image to other park users, people with nets will be forbidden.

The protection of species is also at stake. Parks, being for the most part natural areas, harbor rare species. Rare species are important to us, and collecting too many of a rare species can put a strain on that population. Even some of the most ardent collectors know this to be true and advocate a ban on collecting the species in peril. From the park ranger's perspective, sometimes it is easier to say "No collecting at all" than to allow people to selectively choose what they will take. There's less management that way for the already overburdened and understaffed park officials.

The one thing I've found that collectors and noncollectors share, especially when it comes to the protection of species, is the sense of urgency to protect their habitats. Jean-Michel is the creator of the Museo Entomologico (Entomological Museum) in Nicaragua. According to him, the collecting debate is moot where he lives:

The war between collecting or not collecting is important in Europe and the U.S., but in most tropical countries the war is how to protect really the protected areas. In Nicaragua, the Bosawas biosphere reservation has lost 50 percent (8,000 square kilometers) of its surface, mostly to slash and burn soil preparation for agriculture. I have seen some very nice collecting spots just burned out to seed some corn, beans or rice.

He went on to say that the ground then gets sold for cattle pasture, because it is short-lived in its use for agriculture. As for the habitat of the insects that fill his museum? Gone for good.

Bob Muller and Jeff Young, although on opposite sides of the collecting debate, agree wholeheartedly that the creatures they collect and photograph need a place to live. And those places are disappearing year after year. Both men work at making their yards, their "microhabitats," suitable for the Lepidoptera that are displaced by development. I'm sure they also would agree that it is in their best interest to find a way to work together to preserve the things they hold dear. Perhaps with scientific data in front of them, they may also concede to each other on certain specific points. But there is one area where they and countless others will most likely never see eye to eye. It is the question, "Is it wrong to kill some things when it is not necessary to do so?" Take away the science—and you can do this because, remember, collectors do not always collect for science—and you get down to the core of it: People hunt, collect, photograph, paint, and write about things in nature because they like to. (This is probably also true for many scientists, because many of them do this when they are off work, taking—in effect—a busman's holiday.)

It boils down to the fact that some people put less value on an individual insect's life than do others. And that's what debate will not change. There is something inside each of us that draws these lines, creates these values, protects them, and promotes them. My "hornet line" is in a different place than my hornet-loving friend's "hornet line." My "moth line" is in a different place than Bob Muller's "moth line" but in almost the same place as Jeff Young's. Sure, these lines may move throughout our lives, but that change comes from within.

At this point in my life, I look at each individual moth I come across *as* an individual and am unable to diminish its value by seeing it as a specimen to add to a collection. Although I have an irresistible urge to keep it as a token of my excitement in finding it, I satisfy this desire with photographs and drawings. And, collectively, this book.

It appears that the world's view on the "joy of collecting" is slowly veering toward a preference for a more passive form of this pastime. Who knows why. Scientists are still amassing collections of species of everything that's out there, and we need them to do this. We need to have them learn more about the creatures we care about and to share that information with others. Centuries ago, this may not have been as important, but as we humans continue with our exponential expansion on this finite orb, we will be stressing and depleting many of the creatures we hold dear. The more we know about the biology of a creature, the more we can do to help it. But at the same time, noncollectors have tomes of valuable information to contribute to our knowledge of the fauna, and they should be encouraged to do so. Most of the entomologists I've met over the years agree that knowledge and data need to come from many sources. Laypeople greatly outnumber scientists and can help extend their reach for information.

As for the people who collect for the sheer enjoyment of creating a personal collection of moths or butterflies, I cannot justify stopping them from pursuing their passion when it does no harm to the big picture. Many of these collectors are mindful of the impact they could have on a population and limit their actions to a sampling here and there. Sometimes I'm a little jealous and wish I could move my "line" to allow me to take my interest to that level. I do like looking at collections. I also respect, admire, learn from, and downright like many of the people who enjoy making them. I guess it's like wanting to eat the hamburger without killing the cow. I can't condemn collecting. I can appreciate the efforts of those who do what I would rather not do. I'd rather there was another way. But there isn't.

So I guess I will go on to benefit from the knowledge and collections of those who collect while continuing with my own more passive methods. There's room for both of us. If I were to gain some kind of omnipotent power to change things either way, I think the collectors would have little to worry about. I think I'd let things continue the way they're going. Not so much because the ship seems to be slowly turning my way—because, who knows, it may turn the other direction again—but because I could never live with robbing Bob, and people like him, of their memories.

Glossary

abdomen – third and hind region of an insect's body, containing the reproductive organs

anal claspers – organs located at the tip of the abdomen in the male that are used to hold onto the female during copulation

anal prolegs – hindmost pair of legs located on the abdomen of a caterpillar

antenna, *pl* **antennae** – one of a pair of jointed sensory appendages arising from the head of an insect; in moths, the antennae are feathered, combed, or threadlike

anterior – toward the front

ballooning – dispersal method employed by caterpillars (and spiders) in which a string of silk is released into the breeze, lifting the attached insect and carrying it away

black light – unit that emits ultraviolet light

cell – chamber in the ground where the pupae develop

chitin ('kie-ten) – horny outer covering of insects

chrysalis ('kris-a-lis) – immature butterfly between the stages of larva and adult

cocoon – covering of silk spun by the caterpillar to protect the developing pupa

cocoonase (ca-coon-'aze) – enzyme secreted from the head of an adult moth to melt the strands of silk barring its exit from the cocoon

compound eye – sight organ in adult insects composed of many small eyes, hundreds in moths

corpora allota (cor-'pora al-'lot-a) – gland in a caterpillar that releases a hormone to keep metamorphosis in check

costal ('cos-tal) **margin** – leading edge of the wing, also referred to as the costa

cremaster (crem-'as-ter) – mass of tiny hooks located at the bottom of a pupa

crepuscular (cre-'pus-ku-lar) – active at dawn and dusk

crochets (cro-'shetts) – tiny hooks at the bottom of the prolegs used for attaching to a surface

cryptic coloration/patterning – arrangement of colors and patterns to make the insect blend with the background

diapause ('die-a-paws) – period of arrested development that allows the insect to develop or emerge at the optimum time

diurnal (die-'yern-el) – active during the day

dorsal - situated on the upper side

eclose (ee-'close) – emerge from an egg or a pupa. *n.* eclosion

entomologist (en-to-'mol-a-jist) – person who studies insects

exoskeleton – outer skin of an insect, often composed of chitin

family – classification of a group of animals larger than a genus but smaller than an order

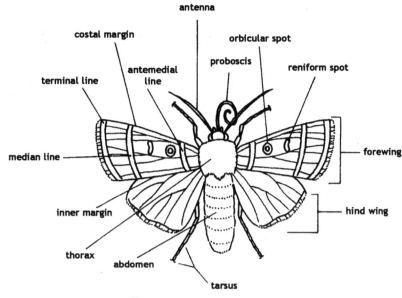

FIELD MARKS OF A MOTH

field mark – a physical attribute (color, pattern, shape) present in insects and animals that is used as an aid in identification

forewings – upper pair of wings on an insect

frenulum ('fren-u-lum) – hook, or hooks, at the base of the leading edge of the hind wing. It connects with the inner margin of the forewings to hold them together in flight

genus ('gee-nus), *pl* **genera** – subdivision of a family, which is then subdivided into species; the genus name precedes the species name

head capsule – head of a caterpillar

hind wings – lower pair of wings on an insect

histosis (hiss-'toe-sis) – act of the breaking down, creating, and rearranging of the organs during pupation

humeral ('hu-mer-al) **angle** – bulge in the base of the leading edge of the hind wings of an insect, used to hold the wings together in flight

Hymenoptera (hie-men-'op-ter-a) – insect order containing bees and wasps; some parasitize the eggs and larvae of Lepidoptera

imaginal (im-'ag-i-nal) **buds** – growth centers located in the caterpillar and pupa

inner margin – trailing edge of the forewings and hind wings

instar – stage(s) between molting in caterpillars

jugum ('jug-um) – thin projection extending from the inner margin of each forewing in primitive moths; it attaches the forewing to the hind wing

labial ('lay-bee-al) **palps** – sensory appendages extending from an insect's lower face

larva ('lar-vah), *pl* **larvae** ('lar-vee) – wormlike stage in the development of an insect; in moths, it is interchangeable with the word *caterpillar*

lateral – situated on the side(s)

Lepidoptera (lep-i-'dop-ter-a) – the order of butterflies and moths

lepidopterist – person who studies butterflies and/or moths

mandible – chewing mouth part in caterpillars and other insects

meconium (mi-'cone-e-um) – waste fluid discharged by a newly emerged adult insect

metamorphosis – change in form that occurs between egg and adult; in Lepidoptera, it incorporates the egg, larva, pupa, and adult

molting – act of shedding the exoskeleton

nocturnal – active at night

ocellus (ah-'cel-lus), *pl* **occelli** – simple eye in the larva and adult used for sensing movement and light from dark; the cluster of occelli found on larvae is called the stemmata

orbicular spot – small, round spot located on the upper forewing of a moth

order – scientific classification of a group larger than a family

oviposit (o-vi-'poz-it) – lay eggs

ovipositor – egg-laying apparatus, often needlelike, in the female of many insects

pheromone ('fer-o-mone) – chemical released by an animal, especially insects, to attract and allow recognition of like species

posterior – toward the rear

proboscis (pro-'bos-kiss), *pl* **proboscises** – strawlike apparatus for taking in liquid nourishment; located on the lower face, it is made up of two separate laterally divided tubes that when "zipped" together form a straw

prolegs – barrel-like appendages located on the abdomen of a caterpillar

pupa, *pl* **pupae** – stage between larva and adult in which metamorphosis takes place

pupation – act of transformation within the pupal stage

reniform ('reen-i-form) **spot** – small, kidney-shaped marking on the upper forewing

species – members of a subdivision in a genus that can breed successfully only with like members

spinneret – organ located by the caterpillar's mouth used for spinning silk

spiracle – one of nine pairs of small openings on a caterpillar's body that act as breathing organs

stemmata – simple eyes, or occelli, found clustered on the sides of a larva's head

tarsus, *pl* **tarsae** – connected segments forming the foot; the last segment carries the claw

thoracic legs – three pairs of legs located on the thorax of a caterpillar

thorax – middle region of an insect's body containing the wings and legs

tympanum ('tim-pay-num) – flat membrane stretched over the hearing organs

ventral – situated on the lower side

Bibliography

HERE are a few books I have consulted that deal specifically with moths:

Brewer, Jo, and Dave Winter. *Butterflies and Moths: A Companion to Your Field Guide*. New York: Prentice Hall Press, 1986.

Carter, David. *Butterflies and Moths*. Eyewitness Handbooks. New York: Dorling Kindersley, Inc., 1992.

Covell, Charles V. Jr. *A Field Guide to the Moths of Eastern North America*. Peterson Field Guide Series. Boston: Houghton Mifflin, 1984.

Dickens, Michael, and Eric Storey. *The World of Moths*. N.Y.: Macmillan, 1973.

Dickerson, Mary C. *Moths and Butterflies*. Boston: Ginn and Company, 1901.

Grehan, J. R., M. Sabourin, and P. M. Hanson. *Maple Feeding Tortricidae of the Northeastern United States: Guide to Identification of Adults*. Vermont: Agricultural Experiment Station, University of Vermont, 1995.

Handfield, Louis. *Le Guide des Papillons du Quebec*. Broucherville, Quebec: Broquet, 1999.

Heitzman, Richard J., and Joan E. Heitzman. *Butterflies and Moths of Missouri*. Missouri: Missouri Department of Conservation, 1987.

Holland, W. J. *The Moth Book: A Popular Guide to a Knowledge of the Moths of North America*. New York: Dover Publications, 1903, 1968.

Ives, W. G. H., and H. R. Wong. *Tree and Shrub Insects of the Prairie Provinces*. Edmonton, Alberta: Northern Forestry Ctre, Canadian Forestry Serv., 1988, 1992.

Kimball, C. P. *The Lepidoptera of Florida: An Annotated Checklist*. Florida: Division of Plant Industry, Florida Department of Agriculture, 1965.

Lutz, Frank E. *Field Book of Insects*. N.Y.: G. P. Putnam's Sons, 1918, rev. 1948.

Mallis, Arnold. *American Entomologists*. N.J.: Rutgers University Press, 1971.

Mitchell, Robert T., and Herbert S. Zim. *Butterflies and Moths: A Guide to the More Common American Species*. New York: Golden Press, 1962, 1987.

Rings, Roy W., et al. *The Owlet Moths of Ohio*. Ohio: College of Biological Sciences, The Ohio State University, 1992.

Rockburne, Eric W. *The Cutworm Moths of Ontario and Quebec*. Ottawa: Research Branch, Canada Department of Agriculture, 1976.

Sargent, Theodore D. *Legion of the Night: The Underwing Moths*. Amherst: University of Massachusetts Press, 1976.

Stanek, Dr. V. J. *The Illustrated Encyclopedia of Butterflies and Moths*. New Jersey: Chartwell Books, Inc., 1977.

Tuskes, Paul M., James P. Tuttle, and Michael M. Collins. *The Wild Silk Moths of North America*. Ithaca and London: Comstock Publishing Associates, 1996.

Wagner, David L., et al. *The Caterpillars of the Eastern Forests*. Morgantown, W. Va.: United States Forest Service, 1997.

Wright, Amy Bartlett. *Caterpillars*. Peterson First Guides. Boston: Houghton Mifflin Company, 1993.

Index

(Numbers in **boldface** refer to color photo pages.)